Reflexive and Reflective Research Approaches
in Applied Linguistics

Research Methods in Applied Linguistics (RMAL)

ISSN 2590-096X

The *Research Methods in Applied Linguistics* (RMAL) series publishes authoritative general guides and in-depth explorations of central research methodology concerns in the entire field of Applied Linguistics. The hallmark of the series is the contribution to stimulating and advancing professional methodological debates in the domain. Books published in the series (both authored and edited volumes) will be key resources for applied linguists (including established researchers and newcomers to the field) and an invaluable source for research methodology courses.

Main directions for the volumes in the series include (but are not limited to): Comprehensive introductions to research methods in Applied Linguistics (authoritative, introductions to domain-non specific methodologies); In-depth explorations of central methodological considerations and developments in specific areas of Applied Linguistics (authoritative treatments of domain-specific methodologies); Critical analyses that develop, expand, or challenge existing and/or novel methodological frameworks; In-depth reflections on central considerations in employing specific methodologies and/or addressing specific questions and problems in Applied Linguistics research; Authoritative accounts that foster improved understandings of the behind the scenes, inside story of the research process in Applied Linguistics.

For an overview of all books published in this series, please see *benjamins.com/catalog/rmal*

Editor

Rosa M. Manchón
University of Murcia

Editorial Board

David Britain
University of Bern

Gloria Corpas Pastor
University of Malaga

Marta González-Lloret
University of Hawai'i

Laura Gurzynski-Weiss
Indiana University Bloomington

Juan Manuel Hernández-Campoy
University of Murcia

Ute Knoch
University of Melbourne

Anthony J. Liddicoat
University of Warwick

Brian Paltridge
University of Sydney

Diane Pecorari
University of Leeds

Luke Plonsky
Northern Arizona University

Li Wei
University College London

Volume 8

Reflexive and Reflective Research Approaches in Applied Linguistics
Edited by Pejman Habibie and Richard D. Sawyer

Reflexive and Reflective Research Approaches in Applied Linguistics

Edited by

Pejman Habibie
Western University

Richard D. Sawyer
Washington State University

John Benjamins Publishing Company
Amsterdam / Philadelphia

The paper used in this publication meets the minimum requirements of the American National Standard for Information Sciences – Permanence of Paper for Printed Library Materials, ANSI z39.48-1984.

DOI 10.1075/rmal.8

Cataloging-in-Publication Data available from Library of Congress:
LCCN 2024058295 (PRINT) / 2024058296 (E-BOOK)

ISBN 978 90 272 1939 8 (HB)
ISBN 978 90 272 1938 1 (PB)
ISBN 978 90 272 4498 7 (E-BOOK)

John Benjamins Publishing Company · https://benjamins.com

Table of contents

List of contributors

Annie R. Allen is an Assistant Professor of Social Work at Facundo Valdez School of Social Work at New Mexico Highlands University. She received her Ph.D. in Curriculum and Instruction from Texas Tech University, and her research concentration is in posthuman philosophy and its implications for social work practice and qualitative methodology.

Wendy A. Bilgen, Ph.D., LISW-S is currently a Professor of Social Work at Cleveland State University. For the past 25 years she has divided her time between teaching, counseling, research, and writing in the U.S. and Turkey, exploring the intricacies of human experiences through an integration of narrative based practices at the intersections of identity, culture, spirituality, and trauma-informed care.

Ana Bocanegra-Valle is a Senior Lecturer and Researcher at the University of Cadiz, Spain. Her main research interests are English for research publication purposes, ESP/EAP discourse and ESP/EAP methodology and education. She is Book Review editor for *ESP Today* and *Spanish Journal of Applied Linguistics (RESLA)*. *Ethnographies of academic writing* (coedited, John Benjamins, 2021) is her latest book.

Xiali Chang, a Ph.D. student at Indiana University Bloomington, specializes in Curriculum Studies and Teacher Education. With a background in Translation (MA) and English Literature (BA), she has spent over a decade as a teacher and teacher educator in China. Her research centers around pre-service teacher education, teachers' professional development, educational reforms and policies, as well as social justice in education.

Jeasik Cho is an Associate Professor of the Department of Curriculum & Instruction at Texas Tech University. He received his doctorate degree from The Ohio State University. He has a new book, *Evaluating Qualitative Research* (2018), and has published many articles in various academic journals. His current research interests include types of compassionate anger and theory of social justice emotions.

Maria Garcia is a Ph.D. student in the Cultural Studies and Social Thought in Education program at Washington State University. She works as a graduate assistant for the Washington State University ROAR program. Her research interests include Chicana feminism and the representation of Chicanx identity in children's literature. Maria has an Ed.M. in Curriculum and Instruction.

Pejman Habibie is an Assistant Professor of TESOL at the University of Western Ontario, Canada. He is also a founding co-editor of the *Journal of English for Research Publication Purposes* and the book series *Routledge Studies in English for Research Publication Purposes*. His research interests and scholarly publications focus on the geopolitics, socio-economics, and scientometrics of knowledge construction and dissemination, writing for scholarly publication, and academic literacies. His work has been published in international journals such as *The Annual Review of Applied Linguistics* and *The Journal of Second Language Writing*, among others.

Sandra Jack-Malik is a recently retired, Associate Professor at Cape Breton University, Department of Education. Prior to academia she worked as a K-12 school administrator in remote, northern Canadian communities. As well, she was the sole proprietor of a literacy clinic for 13 years. Her qualitative research focussed on literacies as a shaping influence on identities.

Jeong-Hee Kim is a Professor and Chair of the Department of Curriculum and Instruction at Texas Tech University. Kim's research interest includes interdisciplinary curriculum making through narrative, linking education with the field of engineering and medicine. She received the 2017 Outstanding Publication Award for her book, *Understanding Narrative Inquiry* (2016) from AERA's narrative research group, which is also translated in Chinese.

Janet L. Kuhnke is an Associate Professor in the School of Nursing at Cape Breton University. She spent more than 30 years working alongside First Nation communities. Her research focuses on exploring wellbeing when living with chronic illnesses. Her research methodology is qualitative, with a focus on lived experiences as represented and shared through stories and art.

Luke Lawrence is an Assistant Professor in the College of Commerce at Nihon University, Japan. His research takes an intersectional approach to identity in the English Language Teaching field. His work focuses on native-speakerism as well as gender, race, sexuality and multilingualism as it relates to translingual practices.

Robert J. Lowe is an Associate Professor in the Department of Languages and Culture, Ochanomizu University. His research focuses on critical qualitative inquiry in English language teaching. His publications include the monograph *Uncovering Ideology in English Language Teaching* (2020), and papers in journals including the *Journal of Language, Identity, and Education, The Journal of Multilingual and Multicultural Development*, and *ELT Journal*.

Jessica Masterson is an Assistant Professor of teaching and learning at Washington State University Vancouver, where her work involves examining the interrelationship of literacies, democratic practices, and youth studies.

Ellie Nik, with a PhD from the University of New South Wales, is driven by a resolute focus on equity and social justice. Currently based at the University of Technology Sydney, Ellie is dedicated to empowering marginalized individuals and communities, giving voice to their experiences. Her research interests encompass migration, equity in education, identities, multilingualism, and autoethnography.

Hanako Okada is an Associate Professor of rhetoric and composition in the Faculty of Liberal Arts at Sophia University in Tokyo, Japan. Her academic interests include illness and disability narratives and other reflexive personal narratives and multilingual identities. She is particularly drawn to work infused with *life*, using methods such as narrative inquiry and ethnography.

Matthew T. Prior is an Associate Professor of English (Linguistics, Applied Linguistics, & TESOL) at Arizona State University, USA. His research interests include language and emotion, socio-psychological dimensions of language learning and use, multilingualism and identity, qualitative methods, narrative and discursive-constructionist approaches, and methodographic perspectives. He has authored and edited a wide range of publications in international journals and edited collections.

Richard D. Sawyer is a Professor of Education at Washington State University. He has published widely on curriculum theory and dialogic methodologies, including duoethnography (which he co-developed). With Joe Norris in 2011 he received The American Educational Research Association's Division D Outstanding Book Award for *Duoethnography: Understanding Qualitative Research*. He is a co-editor of the *Northwest Journal of Teacher Education*.

Jing Tan is a Ph.D. candidate in the Educational Leadership program at Miami University. She teaches *Sociocultural Studies in Education* at Miami. Her research interests are language education, curriculum and instruction, and educational policy analysis. She earned an M.A. in Teaching English to Speakers of Other Languages, and an M.Ed. in Student Affairs in Higher Education from Wright State University in 2019.

Wanying Wang is currently a visiting Assistant Professor at the School of Education at St. John's University. She acquired her PhDs from the University of Hong Kong in Curriculum Innovation and Leadership Studies and University of British Columbia in Curriculum Studies. Her research areas include curriculum studies, teacher education, spirituality of education, attunement, and sociology of education.

Shain Wright (they/them) graduated with a doctorate in Cultural Studies and Social Thought in Education from Washington State University. Shain has a research interest in queer families, specifically family planning, fertility, birth work and building community. Shain is a parent to three small children; their family is the impetus for much of their research and scholarly work.

Zhe (Zoey) Zheng is a PhD researcher at the University of Stirling. Her research interests lie in multilingualism, teacher identity and discourse analysis. She has worked as an English teacher and a teacher educator in China and the UK at the tertiary level. Her recent publications and projects adopt a teacher's perspective to explore translingual practices in various contexts.

CHAPTER 1

Reflectivity and reflexivity in qualitative research and scholarship

Richard D. Sawyer & Pejman Habibie
Washington State University | University of Western Ontario

In this chapter, we first introduce four reflexive methodologies: autoethnography, duoethnography, narrative inquiry, and *currere*. Although these four approaches vary, they all involve inquirers telling stories about self and culture. Researchers working with these methodologies explore subjective yet socially situated, personal yet relational, and discursive yet emancipatory questions and topics. Describing these methodologies, we refer both to published accounts and literature and to specific chapters in this book. Central to these methodologies are the related concepts of reflection and reflexivity. Given their multiple levels, reflection and reflexivity assume a range of profiles, both individually and collectively. As a framework for "reading" reflection and reflexivity in this chapter, we consider the following structure: (a) what they are, (b) how they are enacted and mobilized within inquiry, and (c) what they yield within and from inquiry. Finally, we present an overview of the subsequent chapters in this volume.

Introduction

As the field of qualitative research responds to the political, environmental, and cultural upheavals of the 21st century, researchers in different academic disciplines have turned to dialogic and reflexive methodologies. Recently, for example, Consoli and Ganassin (2023) published a book examining the use of reflexivity in Applied Linguistics. In Applied Linguistics, as well as other fields such as social work, education, criminal justice, medicine, nursing, and business, researchers are examining the ethics and value of personal/collective voice and agency in situated, collaborative forms of self-study. For example, Okada (Chapter 9) mentions the importance of virtue ethics to research in Applied Linguistics to understand the complexities of another person's life as it unfolds. In this book, we examine four of these methodologies — autoethnography, duoethnography, *currere, and* narrative

https://doi.org/10.1075/rmal.8.01saw

inquiry — in this expanding landscape of reflexive methodologies. Although these methodologies vary, they all engage stories between self and culture. Stories create new ways of seeing and being: as they explore culture, they create culture. Patti (2012, p.159) reminds us that story-based research ultimately increases not only knowledge and understanding, but also "compassion and sympathy, and a sense of connection with others" (Freeman, 2004, p.79).

As subjective approaches, these methodologies reject modernist notions of an objective, single, fixed, and stable reality, grounded in grand-narratives and generalizable to all groups, cultures, traditions, or races. Eschewing a mind-body split, they instead provide a synthetic view of knowledge and its relationship to experience as a transactive process (Benozzo, 2018; Rosenblatt, 1978). Story-telling, story-listening, and story-interpretation interweave and mutually expand as researchers make sense of their experiences and develop knowledge about self, others, and society (Clandinin, 2004). Researchers working with narrative, autoethnography, *currere*, and duoethnography explore subjective yet socially situated, personal yet relational, and discursive yet emancipatory questions and topics. In some studies, researchers' examination of self occupies the foreground; while in others, personal examination moves behind that of other people's experiences of phenomena. Successful studies are complex, layered, and dynamic, as inquirers bend emergent meanings back to their perceived positionality in relation to both dominant discourses of power and to the relationship of their methodology to these representations of power. Sometimes researchers examine central yet unresolved situations from the past, as Francyne Huckaby and Molly Weinburgh (2016) did in their duoethnographic investigation of their relationship to the song Dixie, the informal Confederate anthem in the 19th century American Civil War, which blasts to this day from car horns in Southern American towns and cities. Other times researchers examine erasures and gaps, as Courtney R. Allen (2018) did in his *currere* of his public school experience as a young black student.

Both of these studies examined power, where it lay, and how it moved. Echoing topics of self-reflexive researchers, Karen Barad (2003) mentioned, "Discourse is not what is said; it is that which constrains and enables what can be said" (p.819). At a time of cultural, political, and environmental reckoning amid an expanded call for ethics in research, researchers face themselves (and others) and ask, "Who is afforded — or [who] appropriates — this power to see and speak about what is seen as well as what is hidden from scrutiny [...] in a time of ideological assault on the poor" (Fine et al., 2000, p.109). In this book we explore *some* possible affordances and limitations of these methodologies — things that are said and things that are not said-highlighting reflexivity as a central dynamic within them. We start with the assumption that multiple forms of qualitative (and quantitative) research are necessary in Applied Linguistics research in order to explore a range of questions, uncover important findings, and even generate ways of see-ing life in a new way. We have selected two relatively new methodologies (*currere* and duoethnography) to balance two well-established ones (narrative inquiry and autoethnography). Although focusing on four methodologies limits the scope of the book, it does provide the opportunity to examine the affordances and limi-tations of these four specific methodologies in more detail. Still, we present and examine the examples in this book as illustrative of broader themes within these approaches as related to Applied Linguistic.

A brief introduction to narrative, autoethnography, *currere*, and duoethnography

As the various authors in this book examine these four methodologies in depth, in this chapter we limit our discussion to brief introductions of them. With nar-rative research, researchers examine "the unity, continuities and discontinuities, images and rhythms in our lives. [....] The storied quality of experience is both unconsciously restoried in life and consciously restoried, retold and relived to processes a reflection" (Connelly & Clandinin, 1990, as cited in Clandinin, 2004, pp. 124–125). Narrative allows researchers to make sense of narrative wholes in which the pieces of experience are embedded. They involve a "narrative identity thesis", an organization that socially constitutes and shapes our lives (Bochner & Herrmann, 2020, p. 290). This thesis provides a setting for meaning making: ref-erencing Donald Spence-who helped found narrative as a viable methodology in the social sciences in the early 1980s-Bochner and Herrmann (2020) state:

> it was not the events themselves but the meanings attributed to events that shaped a person, and these meetings could be refrained and reshaped into a story that gave new hope and promise to a despondent individual plagued by doubt, despair and or dejection.　　　　　　　　　　　　　　　　　　　　　　　　(p. 287)

The researcher is situated into this process, as narrative researchers inquire into the meaning making of themselves as much as their participants or co-participants.

Autoethnography, in contrast somewhat to narrative inquiry, "refers to re-search, writing, stories, and methods that connect the autobiographical and per-sonal to the cultural, social, and political" (Ellis & Adams, 2020, p. 359). Researchers "bring cultural interpretation to [their] autobiographical data [...] with the intent of understanding self and its connection to others" (Chang, 2016, p. 56). Examining others, autoethnographers focus more centrally on themselves, using the interpretation of their experiences as a frame for inquiry into how par-ticipants make sense within their cultural worlds. Since 1982, different traditions have evolved in autoethnography, including evocative, analytical, and collabora-tive. All three of these strands often take a critical orientation. And within these strands a wide range of types of studies exist, from self narratives, to poetic com-mentaries, epiphanies, dialogues, exploratory work, and short stories (Bocangra-Valle, Chapter 6).

The third methodology we present, *currere*, has evolved from curriculum the-ory (Pinar, 1975; 2012). Emphasizing the intersections between subjective lived experience and educational experience (Pinar, 2012), *currere* asks inquirers to situate their educational experience historically, socially, and subjectively in the interest of self-understanding and social reconstruction (Pinar et al., 2000). Its critical examination process unfolds as a trans-temporal (regression and pro-gression) and trans-conceptual (analysis and synthesis) endeavour, premised on the recognition that conceptualization is a construction that changes over time (Cell, 1984; Sawyer, 2022). With *currere*, inquirers dialogically intersect and jux-tapose the four steps to ideally create liminal and heteroglossic spaces. This dia-logic process helps to scaffold a disruption of discourses regulating conceptions of experience. The use of free-association, especially within the regressive step, plays a central role in this re-entering-and-restorying process.

Finally, the fourth methodology we present is duoethnography, initially con-ceived by Norris and Sawyer in 2005 (Norris et al., 2012; Sawyer & Liggett, 2012; Sawyer & Norris, 2013). As a collaborative research methodology (usually with inquirers working in pairs) falling within a tradition of ethnographic research prac-tices, duoethnography draws from the work of Mikhail Bakhtin (1981), William Pinar (1975), and a range of educational researchers. It facilitates stratified, nested auto-ethnographic accounts of a given research context or question designed to emphasize the complex, reflexive, and aesthetic aspects of the work in process and product. Duoethnography seeks to promote new perspectives and change (in com-plex interconnected research ecologies) by engaging the researcher in a multi-dialogic process that supports a shattering of preconceived views. Employing Oberg and Wilson's (2002) adage that researchers who use the autobiographical method should be the site, not the topic, of their research, duoethnography allows researchers to explore how their lives have been situated socially and culturally. Duoethnographers seek to discover and explore their overlapping gray zones and in-between perspectives as intertwined intersections that create hybrid identities, instead of binary opposites. *Currere* is a central tenet in duoethnography. It is worth mentioning that a number of threads run through these four methodologies: researchers consider themselves part of the research transaction, foreground sub-jectivity, maintain an ethical framing, consider critical dimensions of power not just related to the inquiry topic but also to the method, examine not just past events but build on emergent processes to engage future possibilities, and consider the reader as a co-participant, not spectator. These methodologies do not follow prescribed or scripted steps, but are framed by tenets or principles: their "findings" are part of a fluid and lived process. Although each of them is different, they all share ideal precepts of, as Bochner and Herrmann (2020) described narrative inquiry, a "reflexive, relational, dialogic, embodied, and collaborative process" (p. 289).

Identifying reflection and reflexivity

Central to these methodologies are the related concepts of reflection and reflexivity. Given their multiple levels, they assume a range of profiles both individually and in combination. And, as with the diverse range of researchers and their goals, a multiplicity of approaches to reflection and reflexivity exist. We consider reflection and reflexivity on three levels: (a) what they are; (b) how they are enacted and mobilized within inquiry; and (c) what they yield within and from inquiry. Although the terms reflection and reflexivity are often used interchangeably, key differences between them exist. Reflection is often understood as a process of inquirer self-examination in relation to culture. For example, referring to autoethnography and personal narrative, Ellis and Bochner (2000) described reflective researchers as primarily using "their own experiences in the culture reflexively to bend back on self and look more deeply at self-other interactions" (p. 740). Engaging in reflection, looking at themselves looking at others-zooming in and then zooming out in their research (Chang, 2016; Ellis & Bochner, 2000)-inquirers examine how they are positioned to the personal, the practical, and the societal within their study (Clandinin et al., 2007).

Forms of reflection range along a fairly wide continuum. At one extreme, problematic forms of reflection may reinforce uncritical views of self or lay claim to a neutral contextualization (i.e., teaching in a classroom with objective subject matter), justifying a maintenance of dominant discourses and the status quo. In contrast, deeper forms of reflection shape and are shaped by inquirers' interrogation of their own complicity in structures of privilege, propelling new conceptualizations and plans for collective change. The depth of interpretation contributes to the depth of the reflection. Ivković (2015) described "first-order" reflection (in the related field of language studies) as remaining on a more surface, detonative level. "Second-order" reflection involves a semiotic/affective engagement, an intersection of meaning making and affective/emotional connections. In more critical forms of reflection, inquirers excavate their socialization into not only regulatory discourses of power and behavioural norms, but also how such norms influence their study (Pino Gavidia & Adu, 2022). For some, this critique might reveal uncomfortable personal complicity with dominant and self-serving traditions. For others, it might surface hope and a re-storying and re-centering of narratives of resistance to norms of oppression (Huckaby & Weinburgh, 2016). For all, ideally, "it is becoming aware of the limits of our knowledge, of how our behavior plays into organisational practices and why such practices might marginalise groups or exclude individuals" (Bolton, 2010, pp. 13–14). Becoming aware of the limits of one's knowledge demands narrative ways of knowing how we have engaged in knowledge production. It asks us to surface and examine how our multi-faceted, layered, and at time contradictory intersections of identity and patterns of behaviour have reinforced and continued and/or resisted and disrupted power dynamics.

For example, Allen et al. (Chapter 5) discuss how reflexivity in narrative research is a part of the inquirer's interpretive process. It is an analysis of oneself and one's assumptions and beliefs, especially in relation to truth claims and grand truth narratives. They mention that it involves a meta level, with which the researcher reflects on their reflection-how they have structured their inquiry. Referring to autoethnography, for example, Bilgen (Chapter 2) notes that reflective practice when combined with social critique helps a researcher know how their identity, background assumptions, politics, relationships, privileges, and marginalities impact aspects of their analysis, knowledge building and subjective truth telling throughout their inquiry. Building on Bilgen's chapter, Bocanegra-Valle (Chapter 6) more specifically applies autoethnography to Applied Linguistics, examining how personal beliefs and institutional practices act as an interpretive context both for language development and awareness about it. Bilgen and Bocanegra-Valle's more theoretical discussion is then amplified by Nik (Chapter 10), who explores relationships between migration, language, and power. Her study provided her with a means not only to investigate, but also to gain self-knowledge and agency within her situation.

Related to reflection, the concept of reflexivity requires a critical, dialogic, and metacognitive element. With reflexivity, researchers reflect on their reflection (Allen et al., Chapter 5) as part of their inquiry. As Chiseri-Strater's (1996) stated, "to be reflective does not demand an 'other', while to be reflexive demands both an other and some self-conscious awareness of the process of self-scrutiny" (p. 130). Critically considering an "other" demands that the inquirer unpack their perception of the power of "the gaze," patterns in how they consider and represent others as well as conceptualize how they perceive others considering and representing themselves — again, in relation to power (Denzin & Lincoln, 2000). Matthew Prior (Chapter 14) examines the connection to power in reflexivity on two levels. He distinguishes between the inquirers' critical consciousness in first-order reflexivity and, in second-order reflexivity, their examination of the "norms of the field more broadly and common taken-for-granted practices" (Kester, 2022, p. 52). Engaging in both levels of reflexivity is challenging, with "reflexivities of discomfort" (Pillow, 2015, p. 3) confronting lodged epistemic patterns-routine and taken-for-granted ways of thinking and producing knowledge. Acting as a spring-board for praxis, discomfort may scaffold a subsequent commitment to action for self-and-societal change. Sawyer and Wright (Chapter 3) discuss how reflexivity in duoethnography develops from a dialogic and ethical relationship between the duoethnographic partners.

Reflexive criticality can run throughout all the stages of inquiry, from initial planning, to analysis and mode of representation, and to the form of storytelling (Davids & Willemse, 2014). Textual features such as narrative structure, underlying arguments, and textual layout are also created and animated by the writer's epistemological history and stance, thus benefiting from the researcher's critique into the mutual connections between self and methodology. Applying collaborative, iterative processes which structure critical consciousness, Paulo Freire (1970) introduced the concept of "decoding in circles" (p. 100). This interpretive process facilitates the development of a critical consciousness on the part of those examining a problem, leading to a commitment to engage in structural change to self and society: "Participants externalize their thematics and make explicit their real consciousness of the world" (Freire, 1970, p. 90). Ideally, decoding in circles creates a process akin to hermeneutic circles (Buber, 1958), spirals connecting inquirer praxis — their reflection, critical consciousness, and action for liberation. Inquirers engage in reflexivity then as an iterative (not linear) process involving a number of movements: (a) a cognitive/affective/emotional engagement in the inquiry process, (b) a dislodging of routines and taken-for-granted ways of knowing, (c) a creation of imaginative reconceptualizations, and (d) a development of a sense of praxis. In the following discussion, we review a framework that scaffolds these goals. They include inquirers' ethical, open, and critical stance toward the study, engagement of difference, use of dialogue and heteroglossia, use of criticality, and inclusion of the reader/viewer.

Lowe (Chapter 7) underscores this need for a structural and critical stance in duoethnographies of Applied Linguistics, arguing that such a stance "challenges inequitable social hierarchies, questions the politics of representation of self and other in text, and attempts to move away from the extractive and exploitative nature of much social and ethnographic research" in Applied Linguistics. Zheng and Lawrence (Chapter 11) work in a critical vein to apply duoethnography to translanguaging situations in relation to native and non-native English teachers of English. In their work they highlighted larger ideologies and power dynamics at play, showing how monolingualism and native-speakerism in their local communities greatly complicated their adoption of a translingual disposition. This critical focus also involves a personal dimension: Jack-Malik and Kuhnke (Chapter 13) in their narrative investigation of how grade 3 First Nation's children in

Canada learned to write, showed how as researchers they repeatedly adapted their method as they became aware of the impact of larger structures of inequity to their participants' views as well as to their own. A critical theme runs through these methodologies. Garcia and Masterson (Chapter 8) show, for example, how *currere* can help illuminate the web of power dynamics between the researcher and their lived experience. Tan and Chang (Chapter 12) illustrate this process as they examined in their collaborative *currere* the power dynamics centered on accountability structures (i.e., testing), which structured how they learned English as a second language in their native China.

How are they utilized: Iterative dynamics

A lived critical stance: Self, others, and society

Over 25 years ago Michelle Fine et al. (2000) presented criteria in support of "ethical injunctions" (p. 125) in research. These responsibilities include connecting the voices and stories of individuals back to the set of historic, structural, and economic relations in which they are situated; considering how data can be used for progressive, conservative, or repressive social policies; remaining vigilant not to decouple personal responsibility from study interpretations; and, considering how the analysis offers an alternative to the taken-for-granted dominant discourse (pp. 126–127). We also hold a responsibility to stories: Do we tell other people's stories for them (Said, 1993), or do we allow them to represent themselves? These injunctions remain important in reflexive inquiry, in which the process is often the "product". Here researchers hold a special responsibility to remain open, connected, flexible, and critical throughout their studies. From the start, before beginning an inquiry, they consider a number of questions. For example, what is our purpose in the research? Are we hoping to leave a positive impression of ourselves or are we open to uncomfortable self-interrogation? Are we willing to act on insights and reconceptualizations to form new ways of being with others? How will we take a critical approach to discourses of power that run through our lives and our views of research? What are our methodological framings: will we bracket ourselves into our study (Sawyer & Norris, 2013) and embrace subjectivity as a lived approach in which identity and method are mutually shaped and the boundaries of the study remain close to our own situated experience? Or will we bracket ourselves out of the inquiry and seek generalizable findings and universal understandings? How will we learn from difference? From others? From dialogic spaces? Finally, how do we consider our own identities — as layered and emergent or closed and defined?

As we examine these questions and bracket ourselves into the inquiry, unconscious processes are also at play. Wang (Chapter 3), for example, discusses how a goal of one's use of *currere* is to illuminate the researcher's inner world. This illumination follows a recursive process, involving transactions between one's inner and outer worlds. The ethics of self-accountability come into play here. As the author of the text, what gives us the authority to narrate other people's stories or even guide them methodologically? (Barton, 2011; Josselson, 2011). How are we responsible to others and society? How will we let others tell their own stories? How do we actively listen to the stories of other people as pedagogical frames for self-understandings? The answers to these questions underscore a responsibility to self, others, and society (Buber, 1958). They ask us to engage "narratives of discomfort" (Pillow, 2015) in our responsibility to self and other (Buber, 1958).

Difference as heurism

In reflexive methodologies, the concept of difference expands perception. It provides a lens for the interrogation of the self, guiding us into new knowledge construction and scaffolding reconceptualization. As Sawyer and Norris (2013) stated, "the gaps that lie between the different perspectives and different voices create space for the exploration of the fluidity of identity, the layered recursive often inconsistent layers of who we are" (p. 37). Engaging difference pushes us to unpack the mythologies that regulate the taken-for-granted perceptions within our lives. For example, when we hear another person's story, the temptation is to compare it and find similarities to our own story. However, in order to promote reflexivity, it's more helpful to look into difference as a light passing through a diamond, refracting, illuminating adjacent surfaces, and bending in on itself. It's important to note that differences are examined as existing not just between people. Multiple forms of difference that animate the inquiries include ways of understanding, ways of being among people, stories from different time periods, local narratives, metanarratives, internally persuasive arguments, and externally persuasive arguments, to mention a few. They are conceptual as well as concrete.

Dialogue and heteroglossia

In self-reflexive research dialogue mediates consciousness and scaffolds imagination and perspective. This imagination unfolds along the hyphen separating different perspectives. Reviewing Bakhtin, Holquist (1981) stated that "dialogue may be external (between two different people) or internal (between an earlier and a later self), as well as spatial (A to B) or temporal (A to A)" (p. 427). It is between these conflicting possibilities that a third space of cultural translation emerges

(Bhabha, 1994). Here, Bhabha (1994) clarified a process of cultural translation: "With the notion of cultural difference, I try to place myself in the position of liminality, in that productive space of the construction of culture as difference, in the spirit of alterity or otherness" (p. 209). He continued:

> ... If [...] the act of cultural translation (both as representation and a reproduction) denies the essentialism of a prior given original or originary culture, then we see that all forms of culture are continually in a process of hybridity. But for me the importance of hybridity is not to be able to trace two original moments from which the third emerges; rather, hybridity to me is the "third space" which enables other positions to emerge. This third space displaces the histories that constitute it, and sets up new structures of authority, new political initiatives, which are inadequately understood through received wisdom.   (p. 211)

In these third spaces, dialogue involves both trans-temporal and trans-conceptual crossings. These dialogic spaces sit, for example, between an examination of past/present-day vantage points. This involvement of time deepens the relationship of the inquirer to the inquiry, exposing discursive framings of their narratives over time. Inquirers also create dialogues from their present-and-past (re)conceptualizations related to themes, such as displacement (Bodle & Loveless, 2016), identity and equity (McLellan & Sader, 2012), and methodology itself within academic settings (Formenti & Luraschi, 2017). For example, constructing a polyvocal autoethnography, Patti (2012) explored the wonder and humanity of his departed father, re-animating "shadowy, unconscious complexities" (p. 153) in a dialogic layering of stories about his father, myths (e.g., Navajo), and the "compassionate feminism" (p. 159) from his mother, aunts, and grandmothers. He stated, "Through sharing in the complex symbolic stew of myth, we spark possibility, insight, compassion, and communion [...]" (Patti, 2012, p. 157). Engaging specific details of his adult and childhood experiences, Patti also shows how reflexive inquiry mixes the personal with the meta, the situated with the mythic, and the present with the past as dialogic frames.

Criticality

Foucault (1972) discussed tensions subjects experience between agency (desires to act and change) and regulation (pressures maintaining the status quo and taken-for-granted). The temporal and physical setting of the study itself relays messages, internalized and usually normative symbolic codes people are socialized into, which are thought to mediate thought and action within a particular space (Bourdieu, 1983). This exploration of the tension between regulation and agency and between internally persuasive and externally persuasive speech

(Bakhtin, 1981) lends a special, and at times discomforting, layer of heteroglossia to the study.

Adopting a critical lens, inquirers use their studies to surface, unpack, and reconceptualize these normative discourses, which are often related to equity and justice. Using self as a site, not a topic (Oberg & Wilson, 2002) and adopting a (dialogic) process of conscientization (Freire, 1970), inquirers surface and examine their patterns of socialization into larger meta-narratives related to normative traditions and ideologies. In this process, knowledge production changes from distant, abstract and objective, to embodied, lived, and organic.

Interaction/transactions with reader

Dialogue in reflexive studies involves not only the inquirer(s), but also the reader(s) and/or viewer(s) who conduct their own transactive readings of the study (Rosenblatt, 1978). This dynamic underscores a purpose of reflexive inquiry as being more about its ongoing dynamic process than about a final product. Furthermore, readers help contribute to and expose the underlying infrastructure of reflexivity. Ellis et al. (2011), for example, emphasized the important role that the reader plays in evaluating and accepting underlying assertions and levels of credibility within the study.

What do they yield: Subjectivity, transactive knowledge, and praxis

Almost one hundred years ago, Kurt Lewin stated, "Research that produces nothing but books cannot suffice" (1948/1994, p. 203). Now, framed by the growing political, environmental, and cultural inequities of the 21st century, Lewin's words emphasize a need to move from researching the other in valid ways to researching one's self in relational ways. The focus on subjectivity within reflexive and dialogic research contributes not only to new understandings about the critical and cultural topics under investigation, but also about how to actually conduct research in ethical and socially just ways. Benefits from research that focuses primarily on participants, such as narrative inquiry, include a deeper and more holistic understanding of the participants, as framed by the researchers situating themselves into the text and acknowledging their own presence. In more self-study forms of reflexive research, such as autoethnography, duoethnography, and *currere*, benefits include subjective and humanistic findings and insights related to cognition, affect, and emotionality about self and others.

These methodologies offer imaginative spaces of cultural translation. Within multivoiced texts, inquirers balance new perspectives and insights with deconstruction and reconstruction in emotional and cognitive reckonings with culture, power, and self (Ahmed & Morgan, 2021). Working with multiple, overlapping texts, inquirers layer and interweave critical analyzes of positionality, multivocal dialogues, temporal juxtapositions, critiques of norms and traditions, and critiques of self in relation to these norms and traditions. Inquirers also, within such contexts, identify and study phenomenon. Ideally, these forms of engagement lead to hermeneutic circles, generative cycles of meaning-making and understanding in which identity and methodology change and shape each other (Mueller-Vollmer, 1988). Ethical stances and performativity within the methodologies ideally reframe the studies in developmentally, culturally, critically, and environmentally meaningful ways. These methodologies do more than reveal findings; they present, ideally, performative models for engagement and a reconceptualization of practice and action, becoming pedagogical. And although they are not therapy, participants have expressed a sense of relief and even emancipation as they lift the weight of the null curriculum — their present-absent memories and experiences (Flinders et al., 1986). After this introduction of these reflective and reflexive methodologies, now let's take a brief look at the structure of the volume and synopses of its constituent chapters.

Overview of the book

Aside from this introductory chapter, the book comprises 13 chapters thematically organized into three different yet related parts (Chapters 2–13) and a Coda section (Chapter 14).

Part I.   Reflectivity and reflexivity in research

The chapters in Part I (Chapters 2–5) present a general introduction of autoethnograpy, duoethnography, *currere*, and narrative inquiry. More specifically, they address topics including but not limited to: (a) contributions of those methodologies to scholarship in general; (b) their boundaries and central tenets/elements; (c) theoretical and methodological affordances, challenges, and limitations; and (d) their pedagogical dimensions and implications and ethical issues involved.

In Chapter 2, Wendy Bilgen examines autoethnography as an increasingly popular yet controversial methodology that draws on the practices of autobiographical writing, narrative inquiry, and ethnography, to interrogate aspects of the researcher's own life experiences in order to illuminate and critique personal, social, and cultural phenomena. Following a brief historical view of autoethnography, Bilgen explains the ways in which one might interrogate their own reality, seen as a construct highly dependent on their cultural environment and social interactions, using the tools of *self-reflexivity, subjectivity/intersubjectivity, emotionality, and storytelling* to make connections between the *inner world* of the self and the socio-cultural *world out there*. Looking at how autoethnographers use a range of narrative forms to tackle sensitive topics and controversial positions sometimes ignored, distorted, or silenced in traditional research, the author then discusses some of the discourses around orientations to *analytic, critical, interpretive, evocative,* and *artistic* styles of autoethnographic research. Finally, Bilgen presents the overall purpose of autoethnography as a transformative pedagogical practice.

In Chapter 3, Richard D. Sawyer and Shain Wright provide an overview of duoethnography, highlighting its evolution as a living, reflexive, self-study methodology. The authors introduce duoethnography, present its tenets, and examine its affordances and limitations. Then, the authors present examples of how duoethnography facilitates the researcher's critical examination of knowledge production and dissemination, as well as how his/ her own positionality discursively frames the inquiry. They explain how that duoethnographers work in pairs (or occasionally trios), juxtaposing and intertwining storytelling with story-listening in trans-conceptual (analysis and synthesis) and trans-temporal (past, present, and future) ways. They discuss that duoethnography facilitates stratified, nested autoethnographic accounts of a given research context or question designed to emphasize the complex, reflexive, and aesthetic aspects of the work in process and product. They highlight that a goal of duoethnography is researcher change and praxis, as well as self-understanding.

In Chapter 4, Wanying Wang presents *currere* as a research methodology and a key concept in curriculum. The author explains that *currere* emphasizes not only the lived experience of curriculum but also includes the social, political, and cultural enactment of experience through conversation. Wang discusses regression, progression, analysis, and synthesis as the four steps of *currere* to engage the individual in both temporal and reflective movements, thus enabling one's understanding of what operatives have been at work in an individual's educational experience. The author explains that as a key method and concept in curriculum studies, *currere* is to understand one's lived experience as it presents itself, an experience as encountered with alterity, as surfaced from potentiality, as structured toward adequacy.

In Chapter 5, Annie R. Allen, Jeong-Hee Kim, and Jeasik Cho introduce narrative inquiry as a means to gain profound insights into the diverse aspects of society, culture, and human actions. They present an overview of its central tenets and elements as well as limitations as a research methodology, delving into the ethical considerations and reflexive aspects necessary to ensure the responsible and careful exploration of human experiences. Then, the authors examine the pedagogical implications of narrative inquiry, highlighting its potential to enrich educational practices and enhance student engagement. Finally, they propose *"Posthuman Narrative Inquiry"* as a potential future direction and elucidate how stories shape realities and inspire a deeper understanding of the human condition, inviting researchers and students alike to appreciate the power of narratives and their transformative influence on the world.

Part II.   Reflectivity and reflexivity and Applied Linguistics Research

The chapters in Part II (Chapters 6–9) examine the above-mentioned method-ologies in relation to disciplines of Applied Linguistics and Language Education. With a more narrow scope and focus, these chapters discuss topics and issues such as (a) the potential and contributions of those methodologies to research and scholarship in Applied Linguistics and Language Education, (b) methodological boundaries in relation to those fields of research, (c) affordances and limitations of those methodologies for research in those disciplines, and (d) ethical consider-ations and issues involved in adopting those methodologies in Applied Linguistics and Language Education research and scholarship.

In Chapter 6, Ana Bocanegra-Valle discusses the affordances and limitations of autoethnography as a research methodology in Applied Linguistics. The author examines whether the current literature within the fields of English Language Teaching (ELT)/TESOL and academic literacies enhances or questions auto-ethnography as a research method. Accordingly, the author focuses on the main approaches to autoethnography and then moves on to consider the ways in which autoethnographically-oriented studies from major publications in Applied Lin-guistics meet the goals of those approaches. Finally, the author highlights some ethical challenges that autothnographers may encounter in both conducting and writing their narratives.

In Chapter 7, Robert J. Lowe examines the role that duoethnography could play in a research program oriented around the post-Marxist critical theory of the early Frankfurt School. Drawing on a conception of critical theory as a form of self-reflexive social science focused on ideology critique and emancipatory praxis, the author explores the ways in which the dialogic nature of duoethnography can inform and contribute to theoretical development and consciousness raising. The author suggests that through processes of immanent critique, duoethnography could be used to evaluate the internal coherence of claims within a critical pro-gram of research in ELT, as well as identifying starting points for ideology cri-tique. Finally, the author highlights the accessibility of duoethnographic work as a possible route for transforming research into praxis.

In Chapter 8, Maria García and Jessica Masterson discuss the ways in which *currere* can contribute to research in Applied Linguistics. Drawing on *currere*-based research in the field, they present some guidelines for those interested in using *currere* as their methodology which aim to ensure that the *currere's* methodological structure and approach to drawing conclusions is preserved throughout a *currere*-based research project. Lastly, the authors address the affordances, limitations, and ethical considerations of using *currere* in Applied Linguistics research, especially as researchers begin to embark on studies that discuss power dynamics used within language.

In Chapter 9, Hanako Okada highlights the appeal of a good story to everyone including increasing number of scholars in Applied Linguistics and particularly novice scholars who may be interested in doing research on people's lives and experiences with languages, such as learning and teaching second and foreign languages. By the same token, the author presents a brief background and history of narrative inquiry in Applied Linguistics. Then, the author addresses the pleasures and perils involved in conducting and writing narrative inquiry, with the goal of making a case for the value of carefully done narrative inquiry in Applied Linguistics research.

Part III.   Reflective and reflexive studies

The chapters in Part III (Chapters 10–13) each demonstrates and reports on a study that has used the afore-mentioned methodologies to explore and examine a research area / topic within the fields of Applied Linguistics and Language Education. These chapters discuss topics and issues such as (a) the centrality of methodology to investigation, (b) applied and theoretical challenges and assets with use of method relevant to Applied Linguistics and Language Education, (c) the connection between theory and method/practice, (d) method's contribution to Applied Linguistics and Language Education in particular, and (e) ethical issues regarding the use of method.

In Chapter 10, Elli Nik uses critical autoethnography to examine the phenomenon of English linguistic imperialism and explore the influence of power structures and social imaginaries on her language choices as a migrant non-native English speaker residing in Australia. The chapter aims to contribute to enhancing the understanding of sociolinguistic challenges confronted by migrants and the influence of dominant language ideologies on their linguistic practices. By providing insights that foster increased awareness and empathy, the author offers a pathway towards promoting a more inclusive and equitable language environment within multicultural societies.

In Chapter 11, Zhe (Zoey) Zheng and Luke Lawrence adopt a two-stage duo-ethnographic approach to explore the experiences of two multilingual migrant English teachers; one a "non-native speaker" teaching in the "native" English environment of the UK, and the other a "native speaker" teaching in the "non-native" environment of Japan. The authors highlight that monolingualism and native-speakerism in the local communities have heavily influenced their willingness to claim a bilingual identity, preventing them from adopting a translingual disposition. The authors also discuss that those issues have constrained their autonomy in professional identity negotiation and resulted in them de-emphasizing or concealing their national origins. However, their stories also indicate that teachers' small acts of resistance can afford them the possibility to challenge existing ideologies.

In Chapter 12, Jing Tan and Xiali Chang demonstrate how to apply *currere* in developing critical pedagogy for language educators by deconstructing the past, co-constructing the present, and reconstructing the future. Through this collaborative research, the authors advocate for *currere* as a research methodology and argue that the trans-temporal and trans-conceptual steps within *currere* can bring an inner critical perspective for researchers and educators in the field of Applied Linguistics and Language Education to advance their teaching pedagogy and related research.

In Chapter 13, Sandra Jack-Malik and Janet L. Kuhnke report on a study involving children in grade three, labelled as struggling readers. In this study, they adopted narrative inquiry and designed a structured literacy intervention. The authors aimed to come alongside children, families, and teachers through time to deepen understandings of how they experienced learning to read and reading remediation. They were interested in understanding efforts to shift away from struggling reader identity stories. Although the authors had planned to complete the study over a span of two years, the plan was interrupted by the global pandemic and related restrictions on school access.

Coda

Finally, in Chapter 14, Matthew T. Prior offers some reflection on the discourses and discussions of the preceding chapters and their contributions to reflective and reflexive research in Applied Linguistics and Language Education. The author presents a brief historical overview of developments across the field to locate this volume in relation to ongoing scholarly discourses and conversations. Then, the author explores and examines some of the ways reflectivity and reflexivity have been defined and applied in qualitative inquiry. Finally, the author concludes the chapter with some reflections for advancing both theory and practice.

References

Ahmed, A., & Morgan, B. (2021). Postmemory and multilingual identities in English language teaching: A duoethnography. *The Language Learning Journal, 49*(4), 483–498.

Allen, C. R. (2018). Diary of an angry black man: My *currere* journey within the curriculum of hip hop culture and the life of Malcolm X. *Currere Exchange Journal, 2*(2), 60–68. https://www.currereexchange.com/uploads/9/5/8/7/9587563/10allen.pdf

Bakhtin, M. M. (1981). *The dialogic imagination.* The University of Texas Press.

Barad, K. (2003). Post humanist performativity: Toward an understanding of how matter comes to mater. *Signs: Journal of Women in Culture and Society, 28*(3), 801–831. https://www.jstor.org/stable/10.1086/345321?origin=JSTOR-pdf

Barton, B. (2011). My auto/ethnographic dilemma: Who owns the story? *Qualitative Sociology, 34,* 431–445.

Benozzo, A. (2018). Poststructuralism. In C. Cassell, A. L. Cunliff, & G. Grandy (Eds.), *The Sage handbook of qualitative research methods in business and management* (pp. 86–101). Sage. https://lccn.loc.gov/2017939759

Bhabha, H. (1994). *The location of culture.* Routledge.

Bochner, A. P., & Herrmann, A. F. (2020). Practicing narrative inquiry II: Making meanings move. In P. Leavy (Ed.), *The Oxford handbook of qualitative research* (2nd ed., pp. 285–328). Oxford University Press. https://global.oup.com/academic/product/the-oxford-handbook-of-qualitative-research-9780190847388?q=leavy&lang=en&cc=us

Bodle, A., & Loveless, D. J. (2016). (Un) becoming the I: A duoethnography of displacement. In R. D. Sawyer & J. Norris (Eds.), *Interdisciplinary reflective practice through duoethnography* (pp. 103–120). Palgrave Macmillan.

Bolton, G. (2010). *Reflective practice: Writing and professional development.* Sage.

Bourdieu, P. (1983). The field of cultural production, or the economic world reversed. *Poetics 12*(4–5), 311–356.

Buber, M. (1958). *I and thou* (R. G. Smith, Trans.). Charles Scribner's Sons, MacMillan Publishing Company.

Cell, E. (1984). *Learning to learn from experience.* State University of New York Press. https://citeseerx.ist.psu.edu/document?repid=rep1&type=pdf&doi=af56cf98e484349274d9a79ad48566ba5c03d81b

Chang, H. (2016). *Autoethnography as method* (Vol. 1). Routledge.

Chiseri-Strater, E. (1996). Turning in upon ourselves: Positionality, subjectivity, and reflexivity in case study and ethnographic research. In P. Mortensen & G. E. Kirsch (Eds.). *Ethics and representation in qualitative studies of literacy* (pp. 115–133). National Council of Teachers of English.

Clandinin, D. J. (2004). Narrative and story in teacher education. In T. Russess & H. Munby (Eds.), *Teachers and teaching: From classroom to reflection* (pp. 124–124). Routledge.

Clandinin, D. J., Pushor, D., & Orr, A. M. (2007). Navigating sites for narrative inquiry. *Journal of Teacher Education, 58*(1), 21–35.

Connelly, F. M., & Clandinin, D. J. (1990). Stories of experience and narrative inquiry. *Educational Researcher, 19*(5), 2–14. https://scholarpractitionernexus.com/wp-content/uploads/2019/12/Connelly-Clandinin.pdf

Consoli, S., & Ganassin, S. (2023). *Reflexivity in applied linguistics*. Routledge.

doi   Davids, T., & Willemse, K. (Eds.). (2014). Embodied engagements: Feminist ethnography at the crossing of knowledge production and representation — An introduction. *Women's Studies International Forum, 43*, 1–4.

Denzin, N. K., & Lincoln, Y. S. (Eds.). (2000). *The Sage handbook of qualitative research* (2nd ed.). Sage.

doi   Ellis, C., & Adams, T. E. (2020). Practicing autoethnography and living the autoethnographic life. In P. Leavy (Ed.). *The Oxford handbook of qualitative research* (2nd ed, pp. 359–396). Oxford University Press. https://global.oup.com/academic/product/the-oxford-handbook-of-qualitative-research-9780190847388?q=leavy&lang=en&cc=us

Ellis, C., Adams, T. E., & Bochner, A. P. (2011). Autoethnography: An overview. *Forum Qualitative Sozialforschung / Forum: Qualitative Social Research, 12*(1), Art.10.

Ellis, C., & Bochner, A. P. (2000). Autoethnography, personal narrative, reflexivity: Research as subject. In N. K. Denzin & Y. S. Lincoln (Eds.). *Handbook of qualitative research* (2nd ed. pp. 733–768). Sage.

Fine, M., Weiss, L., Weseen, S., & Wong, L. (2000). For whom? Qualitative research, representations, and social responsibilities. In N. K. Denzin & Y. S. Lincoln (Eds.), *Sage handbook of qualitative research* (2nd ed. pp. 107–132). Sage.

doi   Flinders, D. J., Noddings, N., & Thornton, S. J. (1986). The null curriculum: Its theoretical basis and practical implications. *Curriculum Inquiry, 16*(1), 33–42.

Formenti, L., & Luraschi, S. (2017). How do you breathe? Duoethnography as a means to re-embody research in the academy. In A. V. S. Wilson (Ed.), *Re-enchanting the academy* (pp. 305–324). Rubedo Press.

Foucault, M. (1972). *The archeology of knowledge*. Pantheon Books.

Freeman, M. (2004). Data are everywhere: Narrative criticism in the literature of experience. In C. Daiute, & C. Lightfoot (Eds.), *Narrative analysis: Studying the development of individuals in society* (pp. 63–81). Sage.

Freire, P. (1970). *Pedagogy of the oppressed*. Continuum.

Holquist, M. (1981). *Introduction to the dialogic imagination*. The University of Texas Press.

Huckaby, M. F., & Weinburgh, M. (2016). Alleyways and pathways: Our avenues through patriotic songs. In J. Norris, R. D. Sawyer, & D. Lund (Eds.), *Duoethnography: Dialogic methods for social, health, and educational research* (pp. 157–176). Routledge.

doi   Ivković, D. (2015). Towards a semiotics of multilingualism. *Semiotica, 207*, 89–126.

Josselson, R. (2011). Bet you think this song is about you: Whose narrative is it in narrative research? *Narrative Matters, 1*(1), 33–51. https://id.erudit.org/iderudit/nm1_1art02

doi   Kester, K. (2022). Global citizenship education and peace education: Toward a postcritical praxis. *Educational Philosophy and Theory, 55*(1), 45–56.

Lewin, K. (1948/1994). *Resolving social conflicts. Selected papers on group dynamics*. Harper.

McClellan, P., & Sader, J. (2012). Power and privilege. In J. Norris, R. D. Sawyer, & D. Lund (Eds.), *Duoethnography: Dialogic methods for social, health, and educational research* (pp. 137–156). Left Coast Press.

Mueller-Vollmer, K. (Ed.). (1988). *The hermeneutics reader*. Continuum.

Norris, J., Sawyer, R. D., & Lund, D. (Eds.). (2012). *Duoethnography: Dialogic methods for social, health, and educational research*. Left Coast Press.

Oberg, A., & Wilson, T. (2002). Side by side: Being in research autobiographically. *Educational Insights*, *7*(2), 4–16.

Patti, C. J. (2012). Split shadows: Myths of a lost father and son. *Qualitative Inquiry*, *18*(2), 153–161.

Pillow, W. S. (2015). Reflexivity as interpretation and genealogy in research. *Cultural Studies. Critical Methodologies*, *15*(6), 419–434.

Pinar, W. F. (1975). *Curriculum theorizing: The reconceptualists*. McCutchan.

Pinar, W. F. (2012). *What is curriculum theory?* (2nd ed). Routledge.

Pinar, W. F., Reynolds, W. M., Slattery, P., & Taubman, P. M. (2000). *Understanding curriculum*. Peter Lang.

Pino Gavidia, L. A., & Adu, J. (2022). Critical narrative inquiry: An examination of a methodological approach. *International Journal of Qualitative Methods*, *21*.

Rosenblatt, L. (1978). *The reader, the text, the poem: The transactional theory of the literary work*. Southern Illinois Press.

Said, E. W. (1993). *Culture and imperialism*. Alfred A Knopf.

Sawyer, R. D. (2022). Queer narrative theory and currere: Thoughts toward queering currere as a method of queer (curricular) self-study. *Journal of Curriculum Theorizing*, *37*(1), 23–38. https://journal.jctonline.org/index.php/jct/article/view/981

Sawyer, R. D., & Liggett, T. (2012). Postcolonial education: Using a duoethnographic lens to explore a personal curriculum of post/decolonization. In J. Norris, R. D. Sawyer, & D. Lund (Eds.), *Duoethnography: Dialogic methods for social, health, and educational research* (pp. 71–88). Left Coast Press. https://www.taylorfrancis.com/chapters/edit/10.4324/9781315430058-3/postcolonial-education-richard-sawyer-tonda-liggett

Sawyer, R. D. & Norris, J. (2013). *Duoethnography: Understanding qualitative research*. Oxford University Press.

Reflectivity and reflexivity in research

CHAPTER 2

Transformative possibilities of autoethnography

Wendy Bilgen
Cleveland State University

This chapter presents autoethnography, an increasingly popular albeit controversial research methodology that draws on the practices of autobiographical writing, narrative inquiry, and ethnography, to interrogate aspects of the researcher's own life experiences in order to illuminate and critique personal, social, and cultural phenomena. After presenting a brief history of autoethnography, this chapter will describe how one might interrogate one's own reality, seen as a construct highly dependent on cultural environment and social interactions, using the tools of *self-reflexivity, subjectivity/intersubjectivity, emotionality, and storytelling* to make connections between the *inner world* of the self and the socio-cultural *world out there*. Some of the debates around orientations to *analytic, critical, interpretive, evocative,* and *artistic* styles of autoethnographic research will be considered including how autoethnographers use a range of narrative forms to tackle sensitive topics and controversial positions sometimes ignored, distorted, or silenced in traditional research. Finally, the overall purpose of autoethnography — to *represent, break, and remake* our personal and shared understandings of individual experiences as well as systemic practices in need of change — is presented as a transformative pedagogical practice.

Introduction

I am not a novice autoethnographer, anymore. Yet I feel unsure of how to introduce autoethnography; I am sure that I enjoy doing autoethnography, and reading autoethnography, much more than writing about doing autoethnography. I
am sure I must start with my "self," my experiences of writing autoethnographi-
cally, layered with the experiences of others, and the literature. That's the story of
all good autoethnography   (Personal journal excerpt, 2022)[1]

---

1. I found it impossible to write about autoethnography non-autoethnographically. Thus, I
included short narrative drawn from personal writing as a means of *showing and telling* about
autoethnography. Autoethnographic narrative is italicized and centered throughout.

https://doi.org/10.1075/rmal.8.02bil
© 2025 John Benjamins Publishing Company

This chapter introduces autoethnography, the study of culture through one's own story. As a type of qualitative inquiry, autoethnography unites *autobiography,* a genre of writing about one's life, and *ethnography* a research genre methodology in the social sciences that studies culture through the lived experiences of individuals living in that culture (Adams & Herrmann, 2023; Harrison, 2023). Along with being a methodology that unites approaches to research writing, autoethnography is a bridging approach for researchers wanting to cross the expanses between writing inside the academy to writing beyond the academy (Poulos, 2014). The processes embedded in autoethnographic inquiry offer a "form of bricolage, a makeshift bridge... methodologically built" (Lowery & Gautam, 2023, p. 137), to give researchers a means of passage into new territories beyond the reach of academic writing. Through the use arts and first person narratives autoethnography has manages to "speak across gaps or chasms... building connections between our varied storehouses of experience, of thought, of understanding, of memory, of story" (Poulos, 2014, p. 276).

As a researcher-focused approach, autoethnography reveals and interrogates the self as research subject at every stage of the inquiry. An autoethnographer begins their inquiry with curiosity surrounding a lived experience. Then gathers autobiographical experiences, carefully chosen, as the primary data with the ultimate aim of gaining "sociocultural understandings of their lived experiences in relation to others and their contexts" (Hernandez et al., 2022, p. 3). Throughout the autoethnographic process the researcher's personal narratives are woven into stories that make connections between their own inner world and the outer world in which their experiences are situated.

While all autoethnographic inquiry starts with self, it never stops with the self; rather an autoethnographer's gaze moves continually inward and outward, gazing with a critical eye at themselves, interacting with others, and the cultures they inhabit with others (Ellis & Bochner, 2000; Jones et al., 2013). In that way, autoethnography also bridges a distance between the self as researcher, and reaches to the audience, who is invited to respond to the story.

And what is to be gained by this inward/outward gaze that ends with an author's culturally focused story? Autoethnography is premised on the belief that *writing* the self *changes* the self, relationships, organizations, and society. Indeed, this is a tall order for a research methodology. But as many autoethnographers have come to realize, autoethnography is as much a research methodology as it is a writing practice, a pedagogical praxis, a form of social activism, and a way of life (Bochner, 2020; Jones, 2016; Jones et al., 2013; Hernandez et al., 2022).

A short history of autoethnography

Autoethnography is one of many qualitative methodologies that gained influence during what has been called the *narrative turn* in social science research (Denzin & Lincoln, 2000). The narrative turn was characterized by a pivot away from centuries of scientific inquiry ruled by positivism and the belief that knowledge was best gained through unbiased empiricism, and a turn toward an emphasis on how our texts, and self-narratives among them, bring into being everything from identities to organizations and cultures themselves. One of the leading voices on the narrative nature of human experience, Jerome Bruner (1985), expressed the sentiment of those turning to narrative forms of inquiry when he wrote that "self is a perpetually rewritten story ... in the end we become the autobiographical narratives that we tell about our lives" (p. 15).

The narrative turn was not a sudden shift, rather, it emerged in a research context in which positivist forms of inquiry were already being challenged. The post-modern thinkers of the 20th century began embracing methods of inquiry such as phenomenology, interpretivism, and critical analysis, all of which were steeped in the ontological underpinnings of relativism and social constructionism. Social constructionist thinking was characterized by a view that reality is socially shaped and knowledge is developed, transmitted, and maintained in social situations (Berger & Luckmann, 1967). A social constructionist views human experiences as tied securely to embodied individual experiences that are influenced by myriad socio-cultural contexts and power structures in society. It is in our social interactions, full of language, symbols, and ascribed meanings that knowledge is developed, shared, and individual realities are understood. In the days that positivist inquiry was the golden standard, efforts to remove any hint of bias by the researcher were believed to bring one closer to a Truth about the world and those who inhabit it. As the positivist stance became less entrenched and the social construction of reality more accepted, the role of subjective representations of reality was strengthened in the research world. At the same time the role of the researcher as a central figure in inquiry was being re-examined.

Ethnographers, those who study culture, were among the first group of qualitative researchers to question the primacy of researcher objectivity. Ethnographers of the early 1900s suggested that perhaps an insider's view of a cultural phenomenon could tell us more than an objective and distanced outsider view (Chang, 2008). The insider view or *emic* approach to the study of culture was taken in the early 1900s as ethnography students at the University of Chicago were encouraged to conduct research that was connected to their own lives, where they worked, lived, and studied. This practice, known as the Chicago

School tradition, led to the expansion of qualitative research approaches in which the researcher's presence became a valuable means of understanding cultural experiences (Ellis, 2004). The recognition that researchers influence the research at every phase of investigation led to an increased attention to self, particularly among ethnographers. This early form of self-reflexivity, that is, the purposeful attending to one's own position in a cultural study, became an expected feature of ethnographic work.

By the mid-1970s ethnographers were publishing studies of their own cultures, reporting as full insiders, including self-narratives and insights into their own cultures alongside the experiences of other culture members (Chang, 2008). Some ethnographers took the emic approach a step further by looking exclusively at their personal experiences within the cultural context being studied. Findings of ethnographies based on one's own experiences were called *auto-ethnographies* (Ellis, 2004).

The core components of autoethnography, that is the *auto*, the *ethno*, and the *graphy* methodically woven together, must all be present for one's personal narrative account to be considered as autoethnography (Adams & Herrmann, 2023). The *auto* refers to the *I* standpoint or position which is the first-person perspective of the author(s). The *ethno* points to the cultural analysis that is always the focus of the study. And the *graphy* refers to the art and science of crafting the self-in-culture story, alive with vivid, concrete, and thick description (Adams & Herrmann, 2023, p.3).

The growth of autoethnography corresponded to a rise in research paradigms that highlighted the voices of previously marginalized people as well as a "wave of interest in more personal intimate and embodied writing" (Ellis & Bochner, 2000, p.734).

Autoethnography met a felt need among a new group of researchers to tell their own stories with an eye on cultural analysis, acknowledging that everyone's stories are full of nuance and complexity, and the *truths* we gain from those stories are best discovered by those who live them.

An early exemplar of autoethnographic work by Carol Rambo Ronai (1995) provided a unique layered account of her own experiences of child sexual abuse told as a retrospective participant observation steeped in deep sociocultural analysis. The impact of Rambo's work was profound as it unveiled the possibilities of research that is artfully and evocatively told and rich with critical social analysis. Rambo Ronai's early piece is just one example of many autoethnographic accounts emerging in the 1990s at a time when self-narrative accounts into complex cultural realities were springing up in the academic landscape (See Denzin, 2014 and Pelias, 2022 for a more complete list of works from this decade).

Today autoethnographic accounts across disciplinary lines have exponentially increased in numbers far too numerous to cite here.[2] One of the attractions drawing researchers to autoethnography is that no topic or human experience is off limits for investigation. Topics of autoethnographic inquiry focus around an endless range of human experiences such as: identity construction (Bilgen, 2018; Jones & Abes, 2013; Luckett, 2017), family relationships (Adams & Manning, 2015), sexuality (Javaid, 2020; Jones & Adams, 2010; O'Shea, 2019), loss and grief (Custer, 2022; Lengelle, 2021; Matthews, 2019), work place bullying (Higgins, 2023); drug addiction (Wakeman, 2021), mental health crises, race relations and privilege (Ettorre, 2017; Ridgway, 2022), breast feeding (Hemeon et al., 2023), professional athletics (Stamp, et al., 2023), mothering, fathering, sibling-ing, writing, sleeping, praying, living, and dying. Autoethnographic accounts offer readers stories that are embodied, visceral, and full of potential to shape identities and cultural understandings of complex issues.

Autoethnographic accounts can be found in nearly every discipline as researchers are led toward "more humanized and decolonized" (Keles, 2022, p. 466) story telling in which new and emancipated interpretations can flourish. The increase in the number of researchers and practitioners turning to autoethnography attests to the impulse among scholars to look to their own experiences as a potential source of rich data that might lead to knowledge creation as well as individual and societal change. We now turn our attention to exploring the nuances of autoethnographic method and what to consider if you are being drawn to this methodology.

Overview of the methodology

> As I began my dissertation journey the thought that I might use autoethnography as my research approach filled me with dread. I never imagined my dissertation defense might begin with "enough about you, let's talk about me." I was alarmed when a social work colleague warned me not to pursue autoethnography for my doctoral thesis; she thought it too controversial for a novice researcher to attempt to defend. "After all" she said, "this is not your life's work, it's just your dissertation." But what if this is my life's work? I want it to be authentically, me. I want it to do something good for others, and for the world. That's what I want my life's work to be. Can my story do all that?   (Personal journal excerpt, 2014)

---

2. In the most recent *Handbook of autoethnography,* editors Adams, et al. (2022) noted that over 15,000 sources mentioned autoethnography in a Google Scholar search and numerous university courses are solely devoted to autoethnographic processes.

In nearly every culture throughout history, people have been predisposed to telling their stories as a way of making sense of their experiences (McAdams, 2008).

Autoethnography as an approach to inquiry draws on the rich human tradition of story creation and joins with the qualitative research practices of narrative inquiry and ethnography. Autoethnography uniquely invites the narrative inquirer to pay attention to their own physical experiences, thoughts, sensations, emotions, and inclinations of the spirit in holistic inquiry that pushes past methodological dogmas that assert scholars should neither embrace nor examine their own experiences in the research setting (Amoroso, 2021; Bilgen, 2022; Cozart, 2010; Poulos, 2010).

The researcher's choice of telling the story of self must move beyond personal preference, although this is important (Nash & Bradley, 2012). From a researcher's interest around their own cultural experiences and topics of personal and universal consequence, autoethnographic work is motivated by a desire to tackle sensitive topics and controversial positions that are sometimes ignored, distorted, or silenced in traditional research.

The product of an autoethnography is often creative, artistic, evocative, and transformative story telling inviting new insights and understandings of what it means to be human in the particular context of interest. By joining the *auto+ ethno+graphy* in research and writing, one is able to create "critical spaces" for dialogical and inter-relational exchanges to be made "between the storyteller/ storymaker, her lived and embodied experiences, and the readers" (Metta, 2013, p. 494). Conducted in collaboration with others or individually, this unique form of inquiry is accomplished through specific attention to core methodological features of: *self-reflexivity, subjectivity/intersubjectivity, emotionality, and storytelling* (Bochner & Ellis, 2016).

Self-reflexivity

Self-reflexive processes are at the heart of autoethnography. Self-reflexivity refers to how one positions the self in their inquiry and requires a "careful consideration of the ways in which researchers' past experiences, points of view, and roles impact these same researchers' interactions with, and interpretations of, the research scene" (Poulos, 2021, p. 5). Self-reflexivity involves: (1) engaging deep examination of the self; (2) examining the self in relation to others within their social contexts; (3) making honest and transparent efforts to discover new insights about the self in deeper levels; and (4) motivating self-improvement and actionable changes.

Self-reflexive processes are everything an autoethnographer does in order to make the needed connections between *what is inside the self* and what is in the *world out there*. Ongoing personal reflection, for example asking themselves questions like, *what just happened there, what was I feeling, thinking, wanting, and how can I make sense of that experience* (Schön, 1987) is a starting point. Reflective practice when combined with social critique is the self-reflexivity that helps to make known the ways that researchers' own identities, background assumptions, politics, relationships, privileges, and marginalities impact aspects of analysis, knowledge building and subjective truth telling throughout their inquiry.

Sometimes referred to lightheartedly as a "methodological chat with self" (Egeli, 2017), self-reflexivity has been firmly anchored to the discursive tool of language. It is often described in terms of internal conversations that are made plain to readers in the form of confessionals, diaries, and other testimonial style literature. The inclusion of self-narrative in any of these forms is one of the ways that the reflexivity component of the autoethnographic process is made plain. Still, reflexive processes are not located only in the head, or in the pen, but in the whole body (Pelias, 2022).

While self-reflexivity in research writing leans heavily on the use of language as the primary tool for expression, self-reflexive processes are also fully embodied. That is, self-reflexive processes take place in particular physical bodies and spaces that are situated in specific cultural contexts. For example, awareness and responsiveness to one's bodily sensations (shallow breath, rapid heart, sweaty palms) can give researchers deeply personal and nuanced layers of interpretive possibility of their personal experiences. In my own autoethnographic work, I described my self-reflexive processes as dependent on paying attention to thoughts and reflections but also to "emotional responses in myself...which were sometimes surprising, inspiring, and frightening" (Bilgen, 2018, p.95). Analysis of autobiographical data depends on deep thinking and deep feeling around one's embodied responses to one's socio-culturally embedded and embodied experiences.

Subjectivity and intersubjectivity

The centering of personal embodied experiences in autoethnography creates multiple positions for the researcher; they are participant, analyzer, interpreter, and finally, the teller of their own story. A subjective stance is taken by autoethnographers as they move away from what has been called the "façade of objective research" (Spry, 2001, p.710) that results in detached third-person accounts. It is not that objectivity is rejected, rather the goal of objectivity is downplayed as the autoethnographer looks primarily to their subjective experiences for understanding.

Researcher experiences are not only subjective but "inter-subjective," including the voices and viewpoints of others into the meaning making process (Ellingson & Ellis, 2008). Subjective experience alone is not sufficient to understand all that

is contained in our human interactions. Autoethnographers also look to the inter-
subjective nature of our experiences. That is, they seek out collaborative relational
spaces for dialogical encounters where increased opportunities for meaning making can be found (Allen-Collinson, 2013; Poerwandari, 2021).

Insight and meaning are gathered through reciprocal interactions that could
not be gained had we relied only on our own interpretations of subjective experience. In conjunction with the practice of self-reflexivity, that is, knowing how to
dialogue with self, we are continuously in dialogue with others. We engage in both
the subjective and intersubjective interrogation of our experience throughout the
self and culture interrogation. This entails the exchange of thoughts, feelings, and
experiences between individuals in one's story, between the researcher and the literature, and between the researcher and the consumers of the research product.
Autoethnographers regard their own reality as a construct highly dependent on
their social environment and their social interactions with others so much so that
autoethnographic narratives are thought to be co-constructed products, and what
becomes known "arises from the interaction of text and reader" (Poerwandari,
2021, p. 11). These interactions are sometimes invisible as my autoethnography
might be read by hundreds of others who I may never meet. Still, consumers, readers, watchers, of autoethnographic work, will be in some way stimulated toward
meaning making about the cultural phenomenon in question as the personal experiences autoethnographers share reveal insight and knowledge about their individual world that will inevitably connect to some collective experience (Anderson
& Glass-Coffin, 2016).

Emotionality

Autoethnographers generally blend the rational and emotional paths toward
knowledge creation, paying attention to what is seen, heard, thought, and felt. A
rejection of hierarchical separation between rational and emotional accounts of
individual experience is called for as another bridge is made, that is a connection of the rational and emotional. Autoethnographers approach their experiences
with as much attention to what is empirically observable as to the emotions that
move them toward meaning making.

Perhaps it can be said that one's thoughtful descriptions create the setting of
the story, but "reading emotions of self and other often forms a necessary precur-
sor for rational action" (Ellingson & Ellis, 2008, p. 452). In that way, the emotions
of the narrative can be seen as that which move us (they motion us) to action.
The amount of emotion that features into an autoethnographic work depends on
the preferences of the author. Some may intentionally limit the use of emotion
and sensory detail in their research writing, believing it makes for sensationalized

writing, perhaps not fitting for a research report. Still other autoethnographers rely heavily on capturing the emotion of a moment, as a key mechanism in which social analysis comes alive.

The autoethnographer's intent is to capture moments of epiphany, crisis, change, and learning; these moments are naturally full of emotional and evocative qualities and are seen as necessary to portray the full range of human experiences (Adams & Herrmann, 2023). The emotional content within a personal experience is real, authentic, and human. It is often what readers connect to most, and in a visceral way. Autoethnographer and poet Ron Pelias (2022) says that when "writing the personal, I speak from the body" hoping for a "sensual scholarship" (p.123) that links body, mind, emotion, creativity, all that is common to humanity.

Personal narrative and story telling

From the belief that stories are a primary way that humans make sense of and re-imagine their worlds, autoethnographers craft their personal experiences as fully embodied emotional narratives. The same cultural experiences reported in a distal third person account may give some insight into social realities, but it is stories that "awaken us to the existence and experience of others — especially those others who are different from us." (Jones, 2016, p.230). What Jones described is empathy being fostered, or as McIlveen (2008) characterized it, a sharing of humanity through story "that reaches across, touches; and in feeling with the other, we become our own self — the human intertextuality of existence" (p.19).

The experience of an autoethnographic story (i.e., product) should convey a commitment "to linking analysis and action as they unfold together in a material and ethical practice — by creating bridges between analytic, practical, and aesthetic modes of inquiry and representation" (Jones, 2016, p.231). Balancing emotionally rich subjective storytelling and the use of rigorous research methods is the sweet spot that good autoethnographers aim for.

Questions of methodological boundaries

Clearly story telling is key, but it is not the only mechanism involved in the knowledge building and transformative impact of autoethnographic work. Rather, stories of autoethnographers are what move listeners in meaningful ways, connect individual experience to common experience, and motivate a way forward together. Jones (2016) suggested that autoethnographic work is story telling, activism, and research with its value understood by how well it evokes a response, catalyzes dialogue, builds relationships, and changes communities and institutions. Its value is in its ability to disrupt oppressive norms and create visions for what is possible in our lived worlds. It takes both art and science to fill that tall order; and autoethnography is both.

Still autoethnography as a way of doing research across disciplines has been the subject of countless debate. Debate surrounds its highly subjective and emotionally-based nature, as well as the sometimes unconventional artistic nature of the finished product. Some have called autoethnography a *hopelessly blurred genre* (Denzin, 2018), clouded by opaque distinctions between what counts as good autoethnography, and what is simply a researcher writing a memoir or producing a work of art. Autoethnography does not fit neatly into the traditional framework of qualitative inquiry and autoethnographers must be comfortable straddling traditions. This reality draws some researchers to the method and repels others. And despite countless attempts to create clear and firm boundaries around what counts as autoethnography, definitions and usage of the method remains elusive.

Common qualifiers distinguish variations in process, product, context, and the reasons for using autoethnography. For example *critical autoethnography* (Boylorn & Orbe, 2020) has an essential aim to critique power structures in culture, *evocative autoethnography* (Bochner & Ellis, 2016) to evoke emotional engagement and response to lived cultural realities, *analytic autoethnography* (Anderson, 2006) to apply theory, *performative autoethnography* (Spry, 2016) to produce embodied experience of cultural realities, *artistic autoethnography* (Bartleet, 2022) to blend artistic forms into inquiry, *poetic autoethnography* (Pelias, 2022) to draw on the art of poetics that involve soul work, *interpretive autoethnography* (Denzin, 2014) to focus on connecting the dots between what is lived, performed, and understood about own's life story, *organizational autoethnography* (Herrmann, 2020) to situate the inquiry in organizational contexts, *transformative autoethnography* (Hernandez et al., 2022) to draw on the meaning making of initial autoethnographic work and extend the process in the direction of transformative learning. Other descriptors refer to the number of individuals involved in the autoethnographic inquiry, for example, *solo, duo, collaborative, community* (Chang, 2022).

This overly simplified summary of variants of autoethnography is not meant to capture the nuances of each one. It is merely to portray the varied ways that individuals practice, talk about, and think about autoethnography. The use of self and individual preferences lead the way in this methodology and that is one of its beautiful inviting attributes.

The many distinctions reveal two realities. First, that the methodology is itself malleable. Creativity, personalization, and adaptation are all welcome and accommodated within autoethnographic inquiry. Secondly, and perhaps more concerning, is the tendency toward dichotomous thinking in the research community that is present within the autoethnographic genre as well. Some of the unhelp-ful dichotomies associated with autoethnography in the past have been high-lighted by Ellingson and Ellis (2008) and included: (a) researcher-researched; (b) objectivity-;subjectivity (c) process-product; (d) self-others; (e) art-science; (f) personal-political. Rather than becoming encumbered with the task of reconcil-ing these dichotomies, Ellingson and Ellis (2008) suggested autoethnography can instead "operate[s] as a bridge" between a range of research approaches by mak-ing "necessary connections between seemingly polar opposites" (p. 445).

Perhaps the most polarizing debate has been between those who champion either *evocative* or *analytic* autoethnography. Those at the analytic side of the spectrum fear that an overemphasis on the story could lead to what some call "narrative imperialism" (Watson, 2009, p. 428) in which the narrative as told evocatively outweighs the use of analytic method. The underlying fear is that autoethnography may simply evoke an emotional response within the reader, but not stimulate new meaning making. In support of autoethnographic accounts that lean on the evocative side of the spectrum, some autoethnographers point out that it is precisely the emotional, evocative quality of storytelling that is necessary to portray the full range of human experiences from which meaning arises (Adams & Herrmann, 2023; Bochner & Ellis, 2016).

What has become clearer over the years of autoethnographic growth is that all forms of *true autoethnography* will contain evocative elements (response in the body, soul and spirit) as well as analytic characteristics (layered with analysis and theory). While some are still engaging in the *analytic* or *evocative* debate, oth-ers have come to see that "key features of autoethnographic inquiry are similar no matter where along the spectrum from evocative to analytic one stands" (Anderson & Glass-Coffin, 2016, p. 65).

Autoethnographers need not flail in a predicament in which they feel "caught between two camps — hard social science and interpretive/imaginative/humanistic inquiry" (Bochner & Ellis, 2016, p. 30). Rather they can straddle the analytical-evocative continuum, creating their own version of autoethnography that positions their work precisely at the intersection that their own story demands. Regardless of the approach one aligns with, or the style in which one presents their work, "…autoethnography should be ethnographic in its methodological orientation, cul-tural in its interpretive orientation, and autobiographical in its content orientation" (Chang, 2008, p. 48). And despite one's orientation with regard to how they will tell their story (performatively, sensually, artistically, musically, evocatively, analyt-ically etc…), the uniting intention of autoethnographers is to use their personal experiences, narratively told, as an opportunity for them to engage in representing, breaking, and remaking their own understanding of personal experiences as well as systemic practices in need of change (Jones et al., 2013).

Ethical issues

As qualitative researchers, autoethnographers must address ethical considerations along the lines of both *procedure* and *practice* (Guillemin & Gillam, 2004). The methodological challenges and ethical considerations of the autoethnographer will always involve how the researcher goes about accessing her own story, and toward what end. Even though what is being interrogated is one's own story, "...the self is porous, leaking to the other..." (Tolich, 2010, p. 1608). Therefore, autoethnographers must stay cognizant that sharing stories about self always involves others, but this need not silence the autoethnographer (Grant & Young, 2022). Rather care should be taken to tend to what Ellis (2007) calls *relational ethics*.

Relational ethics refer to the effects on personal, professional, and family relationships that will undoubtedly be felt as the author's self story will naturally involve an array of others. As researchers, autoethnographers must be concerned with our "ethical responsibilities toward intimate others who are implicated in the stories we write about ourselves" (Ellis, 2007, p. 5). Relational ethics, sometime also called an "ethics of care", is demonstrated through invitations to those others in our stories to participate in aspects of interpretation of our stories. For example in my own autoethnographic study, I invited those who were characters in my story and participants in my research to speak freely into my writing and to critique my interpretations (Bilgen, 2018). At various points in my study, I shared my writing with participants, asking questions like "Did I get that right?" and "Is there anything more you want to say about that?". In this way the relationships themselves were given equal importance with the story in which relationships were lived. Participants could weigh in, add insight, request detail be redacted, or add detail they felt missing. But as the final story teller, the autoethnographer has the power and the responsibility to create their own version of the story, one that seeks verisimilitude, all the while taking steps to make sure they got it right while also ensuring that they do no harm to others in the process of telling their story.

Also important to consider is an "ethic of the self" (Edwards, 2021, p. 3), in which the auotethnographer considers the harm that may be done to self in the course of writing about and revealing personal experiences to an increasingly growing community of consumers of autoethnography. By revealing intimate stories in which vulnerabilities are revealed, one risks judgment, threats to reputation, relationships, and even mental health (Edwards, 2021).

The autoethnographer may face difficulty balancing the competing claims of *the right to be heard* by telling one's story with *oppressive silencing* that may result from the repercussions of telling one's story (Lee, 2018). Additional risk includes revisiting traumatic events in one's life that may re-traumatize them, making "risky revisiting" (Berry, 2021, p. 34) a tension not easily solved, but openly acknowledged. As autoethnographers tend to the competing ethical demands arising from "the tension between the relational ethic and the ethic of the self" (Edwards, 2021, p. 5) they are developing "the critical autoethnographic knowledge, skills, awareness and reflexive abilities" (Grant & Young, 2022, p. 22) that makes individual and community inquiries possible and powerful.

Pedagogical value

Individual and collaboratively produced autoethnography is on the rise across disciplines as a mechanism of teaching, learning, development, and transformation. This is occurring as individuals experience the impact of autoethnography as it moves them from personal and collaborative exploration of a topic, to reflection, analysis and action (Denzin, 2018; Hernandez et al., 2022; Tombro, 2016). While autoethnography is widely used as a method of inquiry by teachers and educational leaders to explore their own experiences (Hernandez et al., 2022), the "utility of autoethnography in the classroom remains underexplored" (Barr, 2019).

As a social work educator my interest in autoethnography often intersects with my teaching. I incorporate autoethnographic assignments with the aim of helping students develop an awareness of their social positions and privileges, cultural biases, and the role that past experiences, including family and generational trauma, might have on their social work practice. Course content centers around problems such as racism, violence, modern day slavery, hunger, international terrorism, and economic inequality and students are encouraged to draw on their real-life experiences with an eye toward strategies for social action. This is done as I cultivate a safe classroom environment, sometimes through sharing my own story, and inviting inquiry, dialogue, and multiple perspectives to be voiced. Gleanings from course evaluations have informed me that autoethnographic assignments are particularly powerful for minority students whose voices and experiences are marginalized in academia and society in general. The telling of one's own story allows space for attention to physical experiences, thoughts, feelings, emotions, and the spirit, aspects seldom regarded as important in education (Palmer, 1983). Using autoethnographic assignments to stimulate self-narrative writing is a powerful means to interrogate self, other, relationships, culture and societal structures as well as build empathic connection with others (Hernandez et al., 2022; Jones & Abes, 2013).

An example assignment I use in an undergraduate social work course is based around having students participate in the well-known online *Harvard Implicit Bias* test, and then engaging in critical self-reflexive exercises about the experience. The below excerpt from my social work course syllabus provides one example of an autoethnographic assignment in higher education:

Part 1: Taking the Implicit Bias Test

– Follow this link to take the Implicit Bias test at https://implicit.harvard.edu/implicit/aboutus.html.
– Consider the following questions and respond in your weekly class *Reflections Journal*

   What was your reaction (feelings, thoughts, bodily sensations) to the content and results of the test?

   Do the test results seem accurate? Give examples of how you do/do not see the results of the test played out in your life.

   What did you learn about yourself?

Part 2: Self-Narrative Writing

– Readthe article by Vazquez (2022) titled *A Reflection on Supporting Students with Racial Trauma as I Endure Racial Re-Traumatization* (pp. 73–80)that is featured in the social work journal *Reflections; Narratives of Professional Helping.*
– **Then,** write a two-page self-narrative essay describing a moment of "critical consciousness and empathy emerging" when you realized the presence of some kind of bias in your life and how this might relate to your social work practice. You could use the consciousness-raising format of "I heard, I saw, I smelled, I tasted, I felt…" to describe this moment.
– Choose a theoretical perspective to help you describe/do some critical analysis of what was going on in that moment. This moment may have been stimulated by a significant event, or it may have dawned on you as you were taking the Implicit Bias test. You might choose to write in the style of the piece by Vazquez, but you are invited to use your own unique style.
– End the essay by commenting on how your own story helps you connect empathically with the story of others.

Autoethnographic explorations such as this one from my social work classroom invite students to "write bridges built of autoethnographic words" (Poulos, 2014, p. 276), that move students closer to seeing how their belonging to social groups within communities is closely tied to their identities, and their place in the world they hope to change.

The critical components inherent in autoethnography are increasingly recognized as processes with "potential to revolutionize" learning and teaching as a means of questioning oneself in relation to the social and political worlds they studied (Barr, 2019, p. 9). In line with the exhortation of Paulo Freire (1996) to create pedagogies around the ultimate goal of liberation or *conscientization*, Diversi and Moriera (2016) consider the practice of autoethnography "as a way of being and writing ourselves into the history of resistance against oppression, injustice, and exclusion" (p.581). Perhaps we have come back to the bridging capability of autoethnography.

My own understanding of autoethnography portrayed in this chapter is not the only way to view it or to use it in research. As a methodology full of nuances and possibilities, it pushes many boundaries in qualitative research (Ellis, 2004; Short et al., 2013) and will continue to do so. I am among the researchers who turn to autoethnography out of a yearning for a flexible methodology that engages the whole self and allows one to reject many of the false dichotomies in the research community created by over-zealous adherence to one particular way of knowing (Denzin & Lincoln, 2000; Ellingson & Ellis, 2008). In that way, it is a liberating research writing approach for me.

Autoethnography is transforming the way researchers approach writing, language, the use of self, and the aim of research, as well as stretching our vision of what we expect of ourselves and our research. Autoethnography has become many things to many people: a way of life (Bochner, 2020), social activism (Bilgen, 2018; Jones, 2016), an expression of solidarity (Bochner & Ellis, 2016), an act of resistance (Pławski et al., 2019), truth telling (McIvor, 2010), therapeutic (Custer, 2022), transformative (Custer, 2022; Hernandez et al., 2022), soul work (Callier & Hill, 2021). Perhaps the time has come to let autoethnography change how we teach, learn, and transform our societies.

Conclusion

I just joined another book club. My sister learned I had a free evening and invited me to join her. On Wednesday she gave me the book and by Thursday I had finished it, in time for the Friday evening gathering. It was an easy read, a murder mystery. I skipped through a lot of it, the predictable, unbelievable, far-fetched scenarios that didn't ring true. The whole time I was reading it I was thinking "I would rather be reading a good autoethnography." I read autoethnography, a lot, just for fun, and for learning, and because I know what it does to me. It challenges my thinking, evokes in me empathic responses as I bear witness to the lovely stories of humanity in this universe we share. Reading and writing autoethnography makes me a better social worker, learner, teacher, partner, colleague…a better person: "Perhaps that is the work of autoethnography as a mode of inquiry: creating sensuous, affective, spiritual, and cognitive shifts through evocation and provocation".

(Bhattacharya, 2022, p.117)

What more could I want from a story?   (Personal journal excerpt, 2023)

References

Adams, T. E., & Manning, J. (2015). Autoethnography and family research. *Journal of family theory & review*, *7*(4), 350–366.

Adams, T. E., & Herrmann, A. F. (2023). Good autoethnography. *Journal of Autoethnography*, *4*(1), 1–9.

Adams, T., Holman, S. H., & Ellis, C. (2022). *Handbook of autoethnography* (2nd ed.) Routledge.

Amoroso, L. A. (2021). Walking as a way of knowing: An autoethnography of embodied inquiry (Doctoral dissertation, Portland State University). Publication No. 28319189, ProQuest Dissertations Publishing.

Allen-Collinson, J. (2013). Autoethnography as the engagement of self/other, self/culture, self/politics, selves/future. In S. Holman Jones, T. Adams, & C. Ellis (Eds.), *Handbook of autoethnography* (pp. 281–299). Left Coast Press.

Anderson, L. (2006). Analytic autoethnography. *Journal of Contemporary Ethnography*, *35*(4), 373–395.

Anderson, L., & Glass-Coffin, B. (2016). I learn by going. In S. H. Jones, T. Adams, & C. Ellis (Eds), *Handbook of autoethnography*. (pp. 57–83). Routledge.

Barr, M. (2019). Autoethnography as pedagogy: Writing the "I" in IR. *Qualitative Inquiry*, *25*(9–10), 1106–1114.

Bartleet, B. L. (2022). Artistic autoethnography. In T. Adams, S. H. Jones, & C. Ellis (Eds.) *Handbook of autoethnography* (2nd ed., pp.133–145). Routledge.

Berry, K. (2021). Meditations on the story I cannot write: Reflexivity, autoethnography and the possibilities of maybe. In T. Adams, S. H. Jones, & C. Ellis (Eds.) *Handbook of autoethnography* (2nd ed., pp. 29–40). Routledge.

Berger, P. L., & Luckmann, T. (1967). *The social construction of reality: A treatise in the sociology of knowledge*. Anchor Books.

Bhattacharya, K. (2022). Nepantleric traveling: Writing and reading autoethnographies as a mode of inquiry. In T. Adams, S. H. Jones, & C. Ellis (Eds.) *Handbook of autoethnography* (2nd ed., pp. 117–120). Routledge.

Bilgen, W. A. (2018). Constructing a social justice leadership identity: An autoethnography of a female Jewish Christian social worker living in Turkey (Doctoral dissertation, Eastern University). Publication No. 13859267, ProQuest Dissertations Publishing.

Bilgen, W. A. (2022). Looking to autoethnography as spiritual practice. *Religions*, *13*(8), 699.

Bochner, A. P. (2020). Autoethnography as a way of life: Listening to tinnitus teach. *Journal of Autoethnography*, *1*(1), 81–92.

Bochner, A., & Ellis, C. (2016). *Evocative autoethnography: Writing lives and telling stories*. Routledge.

Boylorn, R. M., & Orbe, M. P. (2020). *Critical autoethnography: Intersecting cultural identities in everyday life*. Routledge.

Bruner, J. (1985). Narrative and paradigmatic modes of thought. In E. Eisner (Ed.), *Learning and teaching the ways of knowing* (pp. 97–115). The University of Chicago Press.

Callier, D. M., & Hill, D. C. (2021). Autoethnography that moves the soul: Activating the creative in troubled times. *International Review of Qualitative Research 14*(2), 283–287.

Chang, H. (2008). *Autoethnography as method*. Left Coast Press.

Chang, H. (2022). Individual and collaborative autoethnography for social science research. In T. Adams, S.H. Jones, & C. Ellis (Eds.) *Handbook of autoethnography* (2nd ed., pp.53–65). Routledge.

Cozart, S.C. (2010). When the Spirit shows up: An autoethnography of spiritual reconciliation with the academy, *Educational Studies, 46*(2), 250–269.

Custer, D. (2022). A father's death: The therapeutic power of autoethnography. *Qualitative Report 27*(2), 340–347.

Denzin, N.K. (2014). *Interpretive autoethnography* (2nd ed.). Sage.

Denzin, N.K. (2018). *Performance autoethnography: Critical pedagogy and the politics of culture*. Routledge.

Denzin, N.K., & Lincoln, Y.S. (2000). *Handbook of qualitative research* (2nd ed.). Sage.

Diversi, M., & Moreira, C. (2016). *Betweener talk: Decolonizing knowledge production, pedagogy, and praxis*. Routledge.

Edwards, J. (2021). Ethical autoethnography: Is it possible? *International Journal of Qualitative Methods, 20*, 1–6.

Egeli, C. (2017) Autoethnography: A methodological chat with self. *Counseling Psychology Review, 32*(1), 5–15.

Ellingson, L.L., & Ellis, C. (2008). Autoethnography as constructionist project. In J. Holstein & J. Gubrium (Eds.), *Handbook of constructionist research* (pp. 445–466). The Guilford Press.

Ellis, C. (2004). *The ethnographic I: A methodological novel about autoethnography*. Rowman Altamira.

Ellis, C. (2007). Telling secrets, revealing lives: Relational ethics in research with intimate others. *Qualitative Inquiry, 13*(1), 3–29.

Ellis, C., & Bochner, A.P. (2000). Autoethnography, personal narrative, reflexivity: Researcher as subject. In N.K. Denzin & Y.S. Lincoln (Eds.), *Handbook of qualitative research* (pp. 733–68). Sage.

Ettorre, E. (2017). Feminist autoethnography, gender, and drug Use: "Feeling about" empathy while "Storying the I". *Contemporary Drug Problems, 44*(4), 356–374.

Friere, P. (1996). *Pedagogy of the oppressed* (2nd ed.). Penguin Press.

Grant, A., & Young, S. (2022). Troubling Tolichism in several voices: Resisting epistemic violence in creative analytical and critical autoethnographic practice. *Journal of Autoethnography, 3*(1), 103–117.

Guillemin, M., & Gillam, L. (2004). Ethics, reflexivity, and "ethically important moments" in research. *Qualitative Inquiry, 10*(2), 261–280.

Harrison, M.E. (2023). Self as subject. Retrieved on 1 June 2023 from https://theautoethnographer.com/what-is-autoethnography/

Hemeon, J., Norris, D., Stahlke, S., & Lordly, D. (2023). Unintended consequences of "Breast Is Best" messaging on mothers: An autoethnography. *Canadian Journal of Dietetic Practice and Research, 23*(11), 1–10.

Hernandez, K.A., Chang, H., & Bilgen, W. (2022). *Transformative autoethnography: Change process for individuals and groups*. Myers Education Press.

Herrmann, A. F. (Ed.). (2020). *The Routledge international handbook of organizational autoethnography*. Routledge.

Higgins, P. (2023, March 23). "I don't even recognize myself anymore": An autoethnography of workplace bullying in higher education. *Power and Education*, 16(1).

Javaid, A. (2020). Reconciling an irreconcilable past: Sexuality, autoethnography, and reflecting on the stigmatization of the 'unspoken'. *Sexualities*, 23(7), 1199–1227.

Jones, S. R., & Abes, E. S. (2013). *Identity development of college students: Advancing frameworks for multiple dimensions of identity*. John Wiley & Sons.

Jones, S. H., & Adams, T. E. (2010). Autoethnography is a queer method. In K. Brown & C. J. Nash (Eds.), *Queer methods and methodologies* (pp. 195–214). Routledge.

Jones, S. H., Adams, T., & Ellis, C. (2013). *Handbook of autoethnography*. Routledge.

Jones, S. H., Adams, T. E., & Ellis, C. (2015). *Handbook of autoethnography*. Routledge.

Jones, S. H. (2016). Living bodies of thought: The "critical" in critical autoethnography. *Qualitative Inquiry*, 22(4), 228–237.

Keles, U. (2022). Autoethnography as a recent methodology in applied linguistics: A methodological review. *The Qualitative Report*, 27(2), 448–474.

Lee, C. (2018). Culture, consent and confidentiality in workplace autoethnography. *Journal of Organizational Ethnography*, 7(3), 302–319.

Lengelle, R. (2021). *Writing the self in bereavement: A story of love, spousal loss, and resilience*. Routledge.

Lowery, C. L., & Gautam, C. (2023). Collaborative autoethnography as a bricolage: An authentic approach to constructing the eastern-western bridge in educational research. In E. A. Samier & E. S. Elkaleh (Eds.), *Culturally sensitive research methods for educational administration and leadership* (pp. 137–149). Routledge.

Luckett, S. D. (2017). *Young gifted and fat: An autoethnography of size, sexuality, and privilege*. Routledge.

Metta, M. (2013). Putting the body on the line. In S. Holman Jones, T. Adams, & C. Ellis (Eds.), *Handbook of autoethnography* (pp. 486–509). Routledge.

Matthews, A. (2019). Writing through grief: Using autoethnography to help process grief after the death of a loved one. *Methodological Innovations*, 12(3), 1–10.

McAdams, D. P. (2008). Personal narrative and the life story. In L. A. Pervin & O. P. John (Eds.), *Handbook of personality: Theory and research*, (3rd ed., pp. 242–262). Guilford Press.

McIlveen, P. (2008). Autoethnography as a method for reflexive research and practice in vocational psychology. *Australian Journal of Career Development*, 17(2), 13–20.

McIvor, O. (2010). I am my subject: Blending indigenous research methodology and autoethnography through integrity-based, spirit-based research. *Canadian Journal of Native Education*, 33(15), 137–151.

National Association of Social Workers (2021). NASW Code of Ethics. Retrieved on 15 October 2023 from https://www.socialworkers.org/about/ethics/code-of-ethics

Nash, R. J., & Bradley, D. L. (2012). The writer is at the center of the scholarship: Partnering me-search and research. *About Campus*, 17(1), 2–11.

O'Shea, S. C. (2019). My dysphoria blues: Or why I cannot write an autoethnography. *Management Learning*, 50(1), 38–49.

Palmer, P. J. (1983). *To know as we are known: A spirituality of education.* Harper & Rowe.

Pelias, R. J. (2022). Writing autoethnography: The personal, poetic, performative as compositional strategies. In T. Adams, S. H. Jones, & C. Ellis (Eds.), *Handbook of autoethnography* (2nd ed., pp.121–132). Routledge.

Pławski, M., Szwabowski, O., Szczepaniak, C., & Wężniejewska, P. (2019). Friendly writing as non-inquiry: The problems of collective autoethnographic writing about collective autoethnographic writing. *Qualitative Inquiry, 25*(9–10), 1002–1010.

Poerwandari, E. K. (2021). Minimizing bias and maximizing the potential strengths of autoethnography as a narrative research. *Japanese Psychological Research, 63*(4), 310–323.

Poulos, C. N. (2010). Spirited accidents: An autoethnography of possibility. *Qualitative Inquiry, 16*(1), 49–56.

Poulos, C. N. (2014). Writing a bridge to possibility. *International Review of Qualitative Research, 7*(3), 342–358.

Poulos, C. N. (2021). *Essentials of autoethnography.* American Psychological Association.

Rambo Ronai, C. (1995). Multiple reflections of childhood sex abuse: An argument for a layered account. *Journal of Contemporary Ethnography 23*(4), 395–426.

Ridgway, A. (2022). Love, loss and a doctorate: an autoethnography of grieving while writing a PhD. *Higher Education Research & Development, 42*(1)1–14.

Schön, D. A. (1987). *The reflective practitioner: How professionals think in action* (1st ed., Kindle for Mac). Basic Books.

Short, N. P., Turner, L., & Grant, A. (2013). *Contemporary British autoethnography.* Sense Publishers.

Spry, T. (2001). Performing autoethnography: An embodied methodological praxis. *Qualitative inquiry, 7*(6), 706–732.

Spry, T. (2016). *Body, paper, stage: Writing and performing autoethnography.* Routledge.

Stamp, D. M., Potrac, P. A., & Nelson, L. J. (2023, March 6). 'It's not all about me': Negotiating the transition out of (semi-) professional football from an autoethnographic perspective. Open Select. Retrieved on 39 May 2023 from https://researchportal.northumbria.ac.uk/en/publications/its-not-all-about-me-negotiating-the-transition-out-of-semi-profe

Tolich, M. (2010). A critique of current practice: Ten foundational guidelines for autoethnographers. *Qualitative Health Research, 20*(12),1599–1610.

Tomboro, M. (2016). *Teaching autoethnography: Personal writing in the classroom.* Open SUNY.

Vazquez, E. (2022). A reflection on supporting students with racial trauma as I endure racial re-traumatization. *Reflections: Narratives of Professional Helping, 28*(3), 73–80.

Wakeman, S. (2021). Doing autoethnographic drugs research: Some notes from the field. *International Journal of Drug Policy, 98,* 103504.

Watson, T. J. (2009). Narrative, life story and manager identity: A case study in autobiographical identity work. *Human Relations, 62*(3), 425–452.

CHAPTER 3

Duoethnography

A collaborative, organic self-study methodology for personal and societal reconceptualization

Richard D. Sawyer & Shain Wright
Washington State University

In this chapter we provide an overview of the inquiry method of duoethnography, highlighting its evolution as a living, reflexive self-study methodology. We introduce duoethnography, present its tenets, and examine its affordances and limitations. We give examples of how it facilitates researchers' critical examination of knowledge production and dissemination, as well as how their own positionality discursively frames the inquiry. Falling within a tradition of ethnographic research practices, duoethnography draws from the work of diverse educational researchers, including Mikhail Bakhtin and William Pinar. Duoethnographers work in pairs (or occasionally trios), juxtaposing and intertwining storytelling with story-listening in trans-conceptual (analysis and synthesis) and transtemporal (past, present, and future) ways. It facilitates stratified, nested auto-autoethnographic accounts of a given research context or question designed to emphasize the complex, reflexive and aesthetic aspects of the work in process and product. A goal of duoethnography is researcher change and praxis, as well as self-understanding.

Introduction

As a collaborative story-based methodology falling within a tradition of ethnographic research practices, duoethnography draws from the work of Bakhtin (1981), Pinar (1975), and a range of educational researchers. It facilitates stratified, nested, and entangled auto-ethnographic accounts of a given research context or question. By engaging the researcher with a multi-dialogic process that supports a reconceptualization of preconceived views, it furthermore seeks to promote new perspectives and praxis within complex research ecologies. Duoethnographers seek to discover and explore their overlapping gray zones and in-between perspectives to open new possibilities for becoming and interacting within their cultural worlds.

https://doi.org/10.1075/rmal.8.03saw

Working together in pairs, duoethnographers juxtapose and intertwine — conceptualize and reconceptualize — their stories of lived cultural engagements (Norris & Sawyer, 2020; Norris et al., 2012; Sawyer & Norris, 2013). In duoethnography, the dialogic story-telling process is generative, with stories begetting more stories (Sawyer & Norris, 2013), moving practitioners more deeply into webs of meaning. Simultaneously, while writing in script format and maintaining difference as a heuristic of discovery, practitioners deconstruct the discursive frames that surround and regulate their perceptions of their stories. In its fifteen years as an active methodology, inquirers have experimented with it, focusing on the affordances (and challenges) of dialogue, voice, agency, criticality, and personal-awareness as integral aspects of the inquiry process.

Duoethnographies elude neat categorization. In the early duoethnographies, practitioners conducted studies related to personal questions (e.g., learning to write), professional issues (e.g., personal/professional boundaries of therapy), teaching/pedagogical studies (e.g., becoming an elementary school teacher), and structures of power within relationships and society (e.g., gay/straight alliances).

In addition to the earlier studies, the newer studies also explore more critical intersections related to, for example, race and patriotism (Huckaby & Weinburgh, 2015), race and society (Ashlee & Quaye, 2021), methodology and wellness (Valdez et al., 2022), and race and learning contexts (Fallas-Escobar & Herrera, 2022). A study by Garcia and Cifor (2019), for example, explored "collaborative possibilities for examining socio-technical systems [i.e., computers] using duoethnography" (p. 190–1). In addition, many duoethnographers have built on relational aspects of the methodology to promote solidarity as they examine potentially traumatic issues or situations.

In this paper, we discuss the complexities of duoethnography, including its tenets and general methodological boundaries, affordances, limitations and challenges, ethical considerations, and future directions.

Methodological roots

Duoethnography is rooted in autoethnography and post-reconceptualization curriculum theory. It shares with autoethnography an emphasis on research into the relationship between self and culture, as researchers use their own lived experiences, beliefs, and practices as a lens to interpret and understand cultural phenomena. As with autoethnography, duoethnographers use self as the site, not the topic, of their inquiry (Oberg & Wilson, 2002). However, duoethnography differs in key ways from autoethnography. In duoethnography, the researcher (the duoethnographer) is not the narrator of another person's story, but rather of their own story and its conception (Norris & Sawyer, 2020), as they bracket themselves *into* the inquiry. Also, the two differ in that duoethnography is explicitly dialogic: Duoethnographers create dialogues between persons, artifacts, concepts, time periods, and self and art within their polyvocal texts. These texts then become contexts for analysis, interpretation, and reflexivity. As a newer form of research, duoethnography has not yet developed clear branches of inquiry, as has autoethnography, although professional, critical and evocative (arts-based) strands appear to be emerging.

Duoethnography is also grounded in post-reconceptualist curriculum theory In the mid-1970s William Pinar and others called for curriculum to be a site of both the examination of power inequities and the promotion of liberation (Pinar, 1975). To highlight the pedagogical dimensions of reconceptualization, Pinar developed *currere*, a lived curriculum emphasizing the praxis between narrative and curriculum (Pinar, 1975; Sawyer, 2021a, 2022). *Currere* plays a major methodological role in duoethnography.

Before outlining the central tenets of duoethnography, an example of one study might help to illustrate duoethnography's central dynamics.

A place walking trioethnography on a college campus

In "Biracial Place Walkers on Campus," Agosto et al. (2015) explored the active participation of place on their identities as biracial faculty members and graduate students at universities in the Southern United States. In what they called a "place walking" inquiry, they literally walked through the physical space of their campus-describing a liminal awareness of how that space both foreclosed some narratives and aspects of identity, while opening others up. As part of their conceptual framing, they built on the concept of the "3Ss" of understanding (Henderson & Gornik, 2007), which highlight the intersections of self, society, and subject matter.

Their walk, which they described in the study, forms the narrative structure of the inquiry. Throughout their paper, they wrote with a script format to separate their different voices, including in their summary reflections. Zooming in, they organized their walk thematically and episodically around their descriptions of their entering different campus spaces, for which they provided rich, concrete details. Zooming out, they followed each of these concrete episodes (described through photography, conversations, sounds, and memories) with a summary reflection. In these reflections, they unpacked their responses to the episodes and apply each other's analytical lens to their own analysis, highlighting emerging meanings and understandings.

In their study, they take the viewer on their walk (which also acts as a performative device). Initially they described being hesitant to walk through the campus, echoing a sense of vulnerability, both as faculty and students. Vonzell Agosto, a professor, wrote:

> ... I walked with Rica [Ramirez] and Travis [Marn] through stairwells in the College of Education that I did not know existed. They showed me routes that left me asking: Where are we? I grew painfully aware there were places I had not traveled because there were few invitations for me to know the landscape more thoroughly and therefore few opportunities to develop a deep sense of belonging.

During the walk, in a later episode, they encountered for the first time another professor on campus, "Professor X." They find that Professor X's space is in itself pedagogical, with posters of Gloria Anzuldua (1987) and Billie Holliday taped to the walls, personal books available to students around library tables, comfortable living room furniture inviting students to stay, and a blue cloth dimming harsh overhead florescent lights. His space communicated to the trioethnographers that knowledge can be embodied, soulful, and lived (Anzaldúa, 1987), and that all people are welcome and meaningful.

In their study, they then contrasted this space of possibilities with their own offices on campus, spaces which do the occupying, including them. Their walk helped them to surface meanings within the inhospitable spaces they encounter, envision new possibilities through their encounter with Professor X, and feel a greater sense of resistance within their individual spaces as deepened by their collective voice. Agosto wrote toward then end of the walk:

> [We seek] to share and nourish our cultural selves through a relationship to the campus that is symbiotic rather than parasitic. Rather than be deadened into walkers by an institutional culture and climate that breeds alienation, intolerance, and neglect of cultural difference we seek places and people that imbibe the campus with social, epistemological, and physical hybridity, intersectionality, and eclecticism. We are place walkers eating (away/our way out of) cultural starvation. We came to this trioethnography talking from a victim's stance but have learned from one another's stories how to talk back from a survivor's stance.
>
> (Agosto et al., 2015, p. 125)

In their study, as they simultaneously told about, listened to, and interpreted meanings generated by their walk, they structured and engaged in multiple levels of dialogue. As each of them told their story, they listened and learned not only from each other, but also from Professor X. And they also storied and listened to the messages from the spaces and structure of their inquiry. As they literally considered their next steps, their awareness was grounded in the reflexivity within themselves and within their changing study. Agosto et al. illustrate how dialogue in duoethnography — in this specific case involving language, time frames, con-

ceptual spaces, photography and art, free association, deconstruction, and reconstruction. — may be layered, generative, and heteroglossic.

This example also illustrates how storying and then restorying can scaffold
an emancipatory process. In their study they move from a sense of oppression
to, if not emancipation, at least a renewed awareness of an existing and emergent
community that comes from a collective voice (a community often submerged by
institutional factors within universities).

Central tenets

Duoethnography has methodological guidelines — core tenets — but not prescribed steps. These evolving tenets continue to be interpreted in multiple ways
by its practitioners. Telling stories about their lives, duoethnographers use these
tenets in grounded and flexible ways. They fold inquiry, analysis, synthesis, and
representation (and their constructions) into the story telling process.

To highlight duoethnography's methodology, we first discuss key tenets. Following this discussion, we examine the affordances and limitations of duoethnography within specific studies.

Naming their narrative: Duoethnographers tell their own story

Edward Said once famously wrote about the relationship of narrative to colonial-
ism. He said that "the power to narrate, or to block other narratives from forming and emerging, is very important to culture and imperialism, and constitutes
one of the main connections between them" (Said, 1993, xii–xiii). An important
tenet in duoethnography is that duoethnographers tell their own stories. In their
story-telling they select the forms of representation strategically layering language,
images, sounds, artifacts, memories, and performativity. And in this story-telling
in duoethnography, given that they attempt to listen to their stories through the
conceptual lens of their duoethnography partner, they are simultaneously storyteller, story-listener, and story-interpreter.

This openness to the text helps duoethnographers avoid reinscribing in their
story presentation the very ideologies and norms they are unpacking and destabi-
lizing in their analysis. By choosing to tell stories in a juxtaposed and dialogic way,
duoethnographers can create texts that are epistemologically more consistent with
the critical goals of the inquiry (Koro-Ljungber et al., 2009). Instead of presenting
stories with a Western story arc that reinforces independent and positivist "truth"
claims, they construct relational inquiries grounded in emergent questions.

Centering dialogue and creating heteroglossia

In addition to selecting their own forms of representation, duoethnographers create dynamic, dialogic interactions. Dialogue in duoethnography is a means for inquirers to begin to deconstruct their own interpretive lens based on the lived interpretive lens of another person. In dialogue (Sawyer, 2021b) duoethnographers create heteroglossia — a process of meaning generation — within dynamic third spaces (Bhabha, 1994; Holquist, 1981). Engaging in dialogue, as opposed to authoritative discourse, an inquirer creates a context in which an expression, representation, and analysis become "relativized, de-privileged, aware of competing definitions for the same things" (Holquist, 1981, p. 427). These polyvocal spaces are a context for inquirers to question stable and unified meanings and explore varied perspectives of phenomenon. They exist between stories, temporal-spatial contexts, past/present views of artifacts, ways of thinking, and notions of performativity, for example.

Dialogue is also created with the juxtaposition of text within the document. Sometimes this dialogue is between the back-and-forth, interactive conversations (the "showing") and the thematic analysis and/or summary reflection (the "telling") (see, for example, Karasa & Uchilara, 2021; Lowe & Kiczkowiak, 2016; Rose & Montakaniwong, 2018). Other times, this dialogue is framed more formally, with duoethnographers' use of, for example, "bulk dialogues." With bulk dialogues, both speakers' comments are presented separately and in totality, followed by short sections of analysis. This order presents the conversations more holistically and with less analytical constriction. Often this structure identifies and discusses themes within more traditional "findings" and "discussion" sections (Fallas-Escobar & Herrera, 2022).

With these and other dialogic arrangements, duoethnographers strive to surface and critique the symbolic power of codes — the habitus (Bourdieu, 1983, 1991) embedded within their lives and their inquiry. Bourdieu views habitus as the "socially constituted system of cognitive and motivating structures" (Bourdieu, 1977, p. 76), the codes embedded within situations and places (Lefebvre, 1991). It creates "a mutually mediating field, with the setting itself relaying social structures that guide thought and practice, and with individuals interpreting these internalized codes" (Sawyer, 2021b, p. 97). In duoethnography, researchers attempt to excavate the codes related to "that invisible power which can be exercised only with the complicity of those who do not want to know that they are subject to it, or even that they themselves exercise it" (Bourdieu, 1991, p. 164).

In all cases, duoethnographers use a script format to underscore and make explicit the dialogue. They attempt to differentiate and highlight — not blend —

their diverse voices as a foundation toward their reconceptualization of meaning. Meanings are extended, validated, and disrupted simultaneously by juxtaposed texts, artwork, and artifacts. The resulting dialogue is unstable and even at times contradictory as multiple meanings are reflected upon and understood by the duoethnographers (and readers).

Restorying: A reflective pedagogical intent and stance

Lévinas (1984) maintained that the dynamic nature of self-understanding comes from seeing oneself through the lens of another person. And in duoethnography, the voice of another person is central to the inquiry. The storytelling partner provides not only a new conceptual lens for self-analysis and awareness, but also an ethic of accountability. In duoethnography, inquirers imagine a range of responses to their stories based on their interaction with their partner. These responses often stem from their partner's patterns of cognition and problem-solving. But they also stem from their positionality and engagement within discourses of justice (and injustice). Given that the inquiry is written in script format, duoethnographers also consider their audience or reader as playing an active transactional role (Rosenblatt, 1978) in the restorying process. In duoethnography, this dynamic self-understanding helps drive a process of inquirer reflexivity — a reconceptualization of one's positionality to values and ideologies, leading to a change in action and practice. Part of reflexivity is an inquirer's development of a critical stance (also known as reflectivity) or heightened conscientiousness (Freire, 1970) toward events framed by power, such as sexism, racism, homophobia, ableism. Foremost in duoethnography is a goal to open an awareness of how one is positioned to continuums of power, such as oppressor/liberator. It is also about how one then acts on these reconceptualizatons to begin to form and live within new possibilities of justice and liberation.

   It should be noted that an open and critical stance on the part of the duoethnographer facilitates this generative polyvocal process. Duoethnographers acknowledge that stories, especially their own personal stories, are not neutral or value-free, but are mediated by human encounter and interactive dialogue and that meaning is emergent, organic, holistic, generative, and historically situated.

Mixing transtemporal and trans-conceptual meanings: The use of *currere*

Duoethnography builds on *currere's* post-modern dynamic. As a curriculum of self, *currere* frames inquiry as pedagogical, shaping conceptualizations and actions. Without their intentional use of *currere* within duoethnography, inquirers often stay on the descriptive surface of their self-study and fail to make deep-seated analyses and reconceptualizations.

Currere is organized around four moments (or steps): the analytical (deconstructing), the synthetical (reconstructing), the regressive (engaging past memories and experiences), and the progressive (reconceptualizing) (Pinar, 2012). Guided by these steps, inquirers juxtapose multiple temporal and conceptual vantage points between and within themselves to examine the critical influences of their conceptions and memories of specific themes and events (Sawyer, 2017, 2022). As part of this process, they focus on transtemporal relationships (e.g., using non-linear sight-lines to interpret conceptions of the past, present, and future) and trans-conceptual relationships (conceiving topics from multiple perspectives and vantage points).

As part of an analytical lens on the socialization and enculturation process, Pinar (2005, 2012, 2017) mentioned the use of the psychoanalytic technique of "free association." Free association triggers inquirers' recollections of repressed material and memories. This generation of repressed memories opens possibilities for inquirers to re-experience engagement within past events without the hegemony of historical memory (Brown & Au, 2014; Flores, 2002; Gramsci, 1971), helping them to reconceptualize past events, including narratives of resistance and of trauma.

It is important to note foreground-and-background differences between *currere* and duoethnography. As discussed in Chapter 4 (this volume) *currere* foregrounds transtemporal and trans-conceptual psychoanalytic processes such as free-association and memory retrieval. Duoethnography, in contrast, foregrounds dialogic and polyvocal storytelling with memory retrieval, with *currere* intertwined with its other tenets. A central methodological difference between *currere* and duoethnography is that duoethnography is conducted by at least two people telling stories to each other, while with *currere* inquirers usually, but not always, work individually. (Although recently there have been duo-*curreries*.)

Additional tenets include writing in a script format, considering the audience as an inquiry partner, engaging in a quest for understanding outside binaries (such are hero/victim), adopting a post-modern stance toward identity as fluid, flexible, layered, and non-binary, and acknowledging that meaning is emergent and constructed. Together, these tenets ask duoethnographers to break assumptions about their own understandings of experiences and reconceptualize them. They ask them to acknowledge that the complex interplay between identities, positionalities, and experiences result in complex and varied understandings of a phenomenon (Sawyer & Norris, 2013).

Unpacking for understanding: Affordances of duoethnography

At the risk of oversimplifying a complex and situated process, we briefly summarize the affordances of duoethnography — both to the inquirers as well as to the readers of their studies. We ground this summary within illuminative examples. These benefits follow a pattern of inquirers' increasing meaning construction embedded in a reflexive process.

Starting with an openness in telling their story, duoethnographic inquirers have ownership over their own narrative. Their narrative form typically emerges slowly — sometimes painfully — over the course of the dialogue, but when it does become apparent, instead of regulating traditional meanings and findings, it facilitates deeper and more unique meanings (Norris & Sawyer, 2020).

It should be noted that duoethnographers' positionalities to normative discourses differ and their pathways to constructed understandings diverge (sometimes within the same studies). Some duoethnographers are able to "erase the erasure" (Poetter, 2022) and surface at times long-buried-counter-narratives, thus triggering a shift in peripheral/center meanings. Other duoethnographers come face-to-face with a personal positionality complicit with oppressive traditions. Within both of these pathways, duoethnographers are able to begin a process of (re)storying their conceptualizations. This restorying may involve reclamation, for example, of erased experience. Other times it opens unexpected avenues of becoming. Ideally, these journeys lead to personal reflexivity. Grounded in new conceptions of past experience, inquirers shift their positionality and agency in relation to new possibilities for the future — for themselves and others.

The following examples show that the affordances of duoethnography are holistic and synergistic: they emerge together in recursive and layered ways. These benefits include, among others, generative storytelling, the exploration of differences leading to new understandings, a reclamation of once submerged counterstories and critical understandings, a greater sense of identity, agency, and wellness within their socially mediated lives, and, importantly, a personal process of reflexivity. We present and discuss these examples here as illustrative, not definitive.

As mentioned, duoethnographers select multiple forms of representation for their narratives. For example, Huckaby and Weinburgh (2015) explicitly focused on music and textual formatting as they examined and told their stories in *"Spark like a Dialectic" Difference Inbetween Feminisms/Duoethnography*. In this study they examined their past-and-present relationship to a complex song — the well-known "ice cream-truck song" that leaves a catchy melody as it drives through neighborhoods and draws children to its treats. However, the song is deeply complicit with a history of oppression in America. It is both a subtle reminder of racism and a catchy jingle in its promotion. For them, the song was both a trigger into deeper memories as well as a context of analysis of the meanings packed between themselves and the song. They state, "...the ice cream truck song, though public, carries hidden meanings neither of us knew" (p. 52).

They told their story with contrasting anecdotes underscored by a creative layout of print on the page. Working within in-between spaces, they layered music, contrasting textual elements, back and forth dialogue, and contrasting time periods and associations. Huckaby's dialogue was blocked with white letters against a black backdrop, while Weinburgh used black letters against a white backdrop. These contrasts created in-between spaces, unhinging the song from its childhood associations and allowing them to examine it as decontextualized text. They stated:

> We problematize race, ethnicity, and gender as expressed in public and private spaces. Instead of conceptualizing these concepts as antagonistic, we turn to intersectionality and the third space to not only understand, but also inter-stand the inbetween. We piece together the tenants of duoethnography, black feminism, and feminism to highlight the gifts and challenges each offers the other.
>
> (Huckaby & Weinburgh, 2015, p. 49)

As seen in the above example, differences are exploited by duoethnographers as dialogic third spaces and guides to discovery (Bhabha, 1994). In Huckaby and Weinburgh (2015), Huckaby surfaced a historical yet personal narrative of resistance in relation to subliminal racism, embedded into seemingly appealing music. Weinburgh, in contrast, disrupted her socialization into a dominant racist narrative, developing her own form of resistance in the process.

A different example of the power of dialogic storytelling is found in Fallas-Escobar and Herrera's (2022) study about structural inequities in an educational institution. In their study they played creatively with the text and narrative. Where we might expect the dialogue to shift between each speaker quickly, each one adding directly to each other's comments, they instead took turns sharing short stories centered on a location separate from that of their collaborator. Their bulk dialogues allowed them to explore — within a dialogic transaction operating more in the background — a more focused *currere* of their lives, With this formatting, they collapsed the duoethnographic process, de-centering iterative cycles of dialogue by emphasizing the difference between each other and their complex, layered identities. Their stories did not include a beginning and middle, nor did they present a tidy, "happy" ending. This break allowed them to reconsider their stories in a new way.

Karasa and Uchihara's (2021) *In Silence: A Duoethnography* also benefited greatly from its dialogic method of presentation. In their study, they examined a process of being culturally silenced in English language learning classes. They discovered that their openness to play with the form of their story telling — sidestepping binary and traditional Western narrative forms — opened their inquiry to new perspectives. In the following example, they explore an underlying bias from one of their classes, reinforced by multiple binaries within the situation:

> Karasa: Was speaking emphasized in your English language classes? Some of the readings we have done (e.g., Bao, 2014; Ellwood & Nakane, 2009) discuss the "silent east" and a more "talkative west" and note that there is often a dichotomizing between the two. I think we were guilty of this dichotomizing as well at first when we broadly discussed Japan and Canada. However, we don't really fit this stereotype. We have been together in many social and academic settings, and I find you usually speak much more often than I do and without much hesitation.
> (Karasa & Uchihara, 2021, p. 68)

Notably, their new understandings were not only about language teaching. It was also about forces operating in class to both silence their voices and regulate their identity — to have them internalize a sense of themselves as being from the "silent east." This process helped them to reclaim a counternarrative of themselves that decentered the story being told about them by the instructor. And, on a methodological level, the break from a Western narrative form helped resolve epistemological tensions that contradicted and limited their inquiry. They were able to explore and then re-represent in non-binary ways their own experience of silence and its role in teaching and learning English.

The above examples suggest that — although duoethnography is not a therapy — it is therapeutic. While it emphasizes difference, it also builds solidarity. In many if not most studies, different ways of working together and telling stories ideally create stronger bonds between the participants. This process is seen in *"The Power of Sum: An Accountability Sistah Circle"* (McLane-Davison et al., 2018). The authors engaged in a co-mentoring inquiry about normative expectations that accompany university positions. As part of their method, they told their stories from within a circle that facilitated equity, shared voice, and engagement.

An additional benefit is that duoethnography invites the reader to transact with the text (Rosenblatt, 1978) as a co-participant and active witness (Sawyer & Norris, 2013). The goal is to allow readers to draw their own conclusions and determine connections independently through exposure to new perspectives, meanings, and shifting temporality related to their existing understandings (Ahmed & Morgan, 2021). In *Examining Raciolinguistic Struggles in Institutional Settings*, Fallas-Escobar and Herrera (2022) explored their own experiences as teachers of English (and Spanish) of Other Languages (ESOL). The authors first asked the reader to examine the stories through the "zone of non-being" (p. 2), which they used as their theoretical framework. Then, the reader is presented with each author's raw story, followed by the collective, thematic understandings of the stories in the summary discussion section. Finally, the reader is asked to consider parallels in their own experiences in educational institutions. Thus, the readers are encouraged to engage in reflexively exploring their perceptions of their own experiences related to race and language instruction.

Perhaps duoethnography's largest affordance is its facilitation of inquirer reflexivity. Since most duoethnographers work in professional fields (e.g., as teachers, psychologists, mentors, nursing education practitioners, language teachers), it is probably not surprising that its reflexivity often takes a professional turn. For example, Sawyer and Liggett's findings in their study (2012) on postcolonial teaching allowed them to reconceptualize their teaching practice and facilitate a sense of praxis. Applying Liggett's post-feminist lens to his own conceptualizations, Sawyer realized how he was in many ways "gender blind" in his teaching, leading to his conceptualization of how gender courses through the curriculum, underscoring the need to decolonize curriculum from the norming and normative framing of patriarchal forms (Sawyer & Liggett, 2012).

Fallas-Escobar and Herrera's study (2022) provides a slightly different example of reflexivity. Becoming aware of their conflicting emotions in relation to their uneven responses to structures of inequity, the authors first became critical of their initial emotions, which on the surface appeared to stymie and prevent them from acting to challenge structures of inequity. But their subsequent discussion and reflection revealed to them that their emotional responses actually propelled them to act in other instances of inequity. They then realized that their inertia in the face of inequity operated as a defense mechanism, trapping them in the very dynamic they wished to change. With this realization, they began to restory their view of their narrative, revealing their actions as strategic acts of courage and agency under duress. They then began to nurture their actions as assets, not deficits or failings.

Limitations to duoethnography

As a complex and relational methodology, duoethnography offers abundant challenges. In duoethnography, the meanings that inquirers develop are situated within relational encounters. These encounters are not only between the two duoethnographers who juxtapose their stories, but they involve other individuals and their stories. Although the voice, agency, and self-representations of the duoethnographers are central, duoethnographers still tell and represent other people's stories within their research. This complexity underscores the need for such inquirers to ground their interactions within a lived sense of ethics related to the research setting.

Given complexities of situated research, Kubanyiova (2008) has suggested a balance between both macro and micro methodological and ethical considerations. Macro guidelines as formalized within institutional review boards and professional frameworks are important, but they may be inadequate by themselves for more holistic and situated ethnographic forms of inquiry. Specifically, the situated dilemmas and complexities in research involving lived interactions (micro situations) call for a grounded ethical responsiveness involving both value and care ethics. Drawing from the work of Haverkamp (2005), Kubanyiova (2008) has called for the use of virtue ethics, in which a researcher develops the ability to discern ethical situations and make ethical situation in research. She pairs virtue ethics with care ethics, in which a researcher recognize the relational character of research.

Furthermore, given its story-telling base, the methodology appears seductively easy: anyone can tell a story. However, core tenets often elude duoethnographers and their inquiries fall short. For example, if inquirers do not include *currere* — the examination of past events, concepts, and socialization — into the investigation, then the depth and quality of the inquiry is severely limited. Snapshot views of experience tend to privilege momentary, possibly decontextualized meanings. They also shield the inquirer from developing deeper understandings to the embodied meanings within their lives. A superficial snapshot lens not only limits the depth of the inquiry, it forecloses possibilities of praxis and reflexivity.

Another challenge is related to Bourdieu's (1991) concept of habitus. To begin to dislodge the "invisible power" of regulatory codes, a critical self-awareness is needed. One's relationship to structures of privilege and power — one's history of hegemony — may frame and neutralize the very stance needed to reconceptualize one's position to structures of privilege and power. Many seemingly liberatory goals are undermined by self-serving and narcissistic stances that continue to privilege power imbalances. A critical self-awareness of subject positions in relation to structures of power may become necessary for hegemonic dynamics not to appropriate voice and perpetuate privilege.

Another challenge in duoethnography is the complexity of selective data presentation. Although uncensored-and-unedited dialogue is integral to the meaning of the stories, many inquirers present duoethnographies thematically (i.e., reorganizing raw dialogue into thematic categories). Duoethnographers have perceived and questioned this approach as a possible limitation. Breault et al. (2012), for example, have claimed that the removal of dialogue from its original context reduces the transparency of the duoethnographic process. Furthermore, it has been suggested that academic restraints may exasperate this process, erasing or obscuring the duoethnographic process (Ahmed & Morgan, 2021; Breault et al., 2012). Breault et al. discuss, however, that this challenge may be overcome by inquirers' posting all data, including conversational transcripts, to an online location.

It has also been thought that the final published form, in conformity with academic conventions, can appear far more cohesive and purpose-driven than the reality of its emergence as a messy, reiterative process. Ahmed and Morgan (2021) state, for example, that "our research process was notably non-linear and recursive, at times, featuring interactions and thought trajectories far more rhizomatic and free flowing (cf. Deleuze & Guattari) than dialectical and goals/telos-oriented (cf. Hegel & Marx)" (p.5). In response to this complication, they chose not to include interpretations outside of dialogues within each theme in order to avoid creating a meta-narrative.

Duoethnographers are also at times confronted with more traditional notions of academic research — what counts as research — in their institutions (Habibie et al., 2021) and experience constraints to their inquiries. For example, Fallas-Escobar and Herrera's (2022) bulk dialogues contrast with traditional western dialogue and story-telling. However, they also found that they were relatively restricted by expectations and traditions in academia to produce "valid" research, possibly creating internal tensions within their study.

Pedagogical dimensions and potentials?

As curriculum, duoethnography provides educators a student-centered and developmental context with which to promote their students' learning. On a classroom level, educators have used duoethnography in student-centered, experiential ways. For example, educators have taught English to special education Japanese students (Kasparek & Turner, 2020), critical race theory to nurses (Dekker, 2016), social justice activism to teacher preparation students (Latremouille, Lee, Shergill, & Lund, 2014), and American higher education history to curriculum students (Nicolazzo & Marine, 2016). It has also given educators opportunities to begin to understand their relationship to important educational topics within their own fields. For example, Woods and Sebok (2016) critiqued the developmental portfolios they created as nursing and education students, respectively, as artifacts of their professional training.

But the pedagogical potential of duoethnography goes beyond classroom applications. With a reflective intent, it examines and builds on the pedagogical possibilities of everyday life, providing a way for people to begin to outline, learn from, and share their personal life curriculum. Perhaps its central value is how it scaffolds inquirers' examination of their patterns of socialization as well as of resistance to dominate normative (and norming) discourses. For example, in their duoethnography on relational whiteness, Toyosaki and Hummel (2015) became aware of deeply engrained personal assumptions: Hummel stated to Toyosaki,

> I have been learning to recognize that my white body is a benefactor of whiteness. I have been trying to become sensitive to how whiteness is perpetuated through multiple dominant systems and state apparatuses. Recognizing some of the ways whiteness functions in/through marginalized bodies is a fascinatingly disheartening yet hopeful process for me. (p. 35)

Another powerful example is found in how Johansson and Jones (2019) identified forces that classed and gendered their identity construction in an academic workplace. They write:

> Focusing on academia, which we view as a classed and gendered field, [...] we, as women of working-class origin, have experienced 'breaches' through which we have come to understand ourselves in classed and gendered terms. Coming from different cultural backgrounds, we also reflect on how understandings of class are context-specific. (p. 1527)

In the above and additional examples, inquirers' new understandings are accompanied by a growth in their emotional learning. And while this process is not therapy, per se, duoethnography can facilitate "a process of integration" and open a "therapeutic space" (Bolton & Delderfield, 2017, p. 190).

Finally, as a pedagogical space, duoethnography contributes a new frame for ethical ways of engagement. Based on dialogue and the acceptance of difference, it scaffolds inquirers' situated, organic interaction with others.

Ethical considerations

As Kubanyiova (2008) has noted (discussed above), tensions exist between macro and mirco levels of ethics with situated research. Traditionally, ethical principles in research are premised on a researcher-other relationship. In ethical research, researchers refrain from deception, produce no harm (physically or mentally), do not exploit participants, fully inform participants of pertinent risks, receive informed-consent from participants, and guard participants' agreed-upon confidentiality or anonymity (The American Anthropological Association, 2023). These principles apply as well to duoethnography, but as self-study research, duoethnographers follow many of them inherently within the course of their study.

However, as dialogic research between two people which encourages and intertwines personal stories, duoethnography adds an extra layer to the complexity and perhaps urgency of ethics. For example, the concept of "do no harm" holds special meaning in a study involving disclosure, personal history, and even traumatic events. Duoethnographers need to listen closely and respectfully to each other and allow their research partner full control over any personal disclosures. Partners should not deceive each other or manipulate the conversation for personal gain or intentional pain of their collaborator. While partners should encourage each other's reflection, they should also respect boundaries and know when not to ask questions. With their own responses, they have an obligation to be honest and respectful. Where power dynamics frame the inquiry — for example between an academic advisor and their student — both partners but especially the more "powerful" one needs a commitment to fairness and equity in the relationship. Finally, even given the importance of the script format and the separation of voices within the inquiry, the two researchers do create a shared investigation and text: they thus need to commit to a shared veto-power over the contents of the inquiry and not default to an imbalanced consensus of meaning.

Conclusion

As a dialogic method, duoethnography scaffolds participants' awareness of unexpected perspectives, experiences, and meanings within their cultural worlds. As they publish and share their stories, readers also experience these new perceptions and are able to expand their own thinking. Central to participants' reconceptualization is their growth of a "dialogic imagination" (Bakhtin, 1981). Free to tell their own stories with evocative representations, inquirers engage in an excavation of their socialization patterns and the formation of their beliefs. In the process, they often break scripted ways of understanding self, others, and society and highlight long-hidden strategies of resistance or, conversely, patterns of complicity to social injustice.

Duoethnography's contributions to research emerge from intertwined intra-personal and inter-personal dynamics. Individually, participants learn about themselves: they gain self-understanding, agency over their personal stories, psychic awareness and well-being (grounded partly in *currere*), and even a personal sense of praxis and reflexivity. Collectively, they learn about others: through dialogue, they begin to excavate and unpack their socialization process through the mirror of their very different collaborator. The contributions of the study — the meanings, new understandings, and challenging moments of wide-awake awareness (Greene, 2017) — stem from these intertwined dynamics. Engaging in a collaborative organic process, duoethnographers do not seek stable findings or a finished product: rather, the process is the product, the journey the conclusion.

References

Agosto, V., Marn, T., & Ramirez, R. (2015). Biracial place walkers on campus. *International Review of Qualitative Research, 8*(1), 109–126.

Ahmed, A., & Morgan, B. (2021). Postmemory and multilingual identities in English language teaching: A duoethnography. *The Language Learning Journal, 49*(4), 483–498.

American Anthropological Association Code of Ethics. n.d. Web. 9 June 2023. Retrieved on 6 October 2024 from https://ethics.americananthro.org/

Anzaldúa, G. (1987). *Borderlands: The new mestiza = la frontera*. Aunt Lute Books.

Ashlee, A.A., & Quaye, S.J. (2021). On being racially enough: A duoethnography across minoritized racial identities. *International Journal of Qualitative Studies in Education, 34*(3), 243–261.

Bakhtin, M.M. (1981). *The dialogic imagination*. The University of Texas Press.

Bao, D. (2014). *Understanding silence and reticence: Ways of participating in second language acquisition*. London: Bloomsbury.

Bhabha, H. (1994). *The location of culture*. Routledge.

Bolton, G., & Delderfield, R. (2017). *Reflective practice: Writing and professional development*. Sage.

Bourdieu, P. (1977). *Outline of a theory of practice* (R. Nice, Trans). Cambridge University Press. (Original work published in 1972). https://d1wqtxts1xzle7.cloudfront.net/55192846/Pierre_Bourdieu_Outline_of_a_Theory_of_Practice_Cambridge_Studies_in_Social_and_Cultural_Anthropology_1977.pdf?1512387071=&response-content-disposition=inline%3B+filename%3DOUTLINE_OF_A_TFIEOFY_OF_PRACTICE.pdf&Expires=1734129582&Signature=e0FjxFITr1xF-timkGX6k91Tq5VHP-MJ~eQxLyFwJuCEO5IFMLY-ubdLoSp-WJ7Y8ffoc1JMza~nSHwL7RCQRZOzQrgmbTJm-Faji4bfNVCBj7EBiQdr4nfLX2gswDHNph9jCZO1OMMe1i7rkQHIWcr~SbUkc~F4OUDAyGa9ro537sE-rLRg5yDBY9KEdOvgJuyDO6ApKQZ63KwhEkNMLarTMFXQwK1sV8YIl6epjn-Fd-7sMtsoaZ1uM8A6PgQLj9naUdnvGC2ypzPSKIqrTB-Sy70PdYlPK4WArWFnsd4~UWF~ZK-FiRmeBly~v99-qm7iNkmADsnwZBjamd9VzQ__&Key-Pair-Id=APKAJLOHF5GGSLRBV4ZA

Bourdieu, P. (1983). The field of cultural production, or the economic world reversed. *Poetics 12*(5–6), 311–356.

Bourdieu, P. (1991). On symbolic power. In J.B. Thompson (Ed.). *Language and symbolic power* (G. Raymond & M. Adamson, Trans), (pp. 163–170). Harvard University Press. (Original work published 1979).

Breault, R., Hackler, R., & Bradley, R. (2012). Seeking rigor in the search for identity: A trioethnography. In J. Norris, R.D. Sawyer, & D. Lund (Eds.), *Duoethnography: Dialogic methods for social, health, and educational research*. Left Coast Press.

Brown, A.L., & Au, W. (2014). Race, memory, and master narratives: A critical essay on US curriculum history. *Curriculum Inquiry, 44*(3), 358–389.

Dekker, L. (2016). Cultural safety and critical race theory: Education frameworks to promote reflective nursing practice. In H. Brown, R.D. Sawyer, & J. Norris (Eds.), *Forms of practitioner reflexivity. Critical, conversational, and arts-based approaches* (pp. 91–116). Palgrave Macmillan.

Ellwood, C., & Nakane, I. (2009). Priviligeing of speech in EAP and mainstream university classrooms: A critical evaluation of participation. *TESOL Quarterly*, 43(2), 203–230.

Fallas-Escobar, C., & Herrera, L.J.P. (2022). Examining raciolinguistic struggles in institutional settings: A duoethnography. *Linguistics and Education*, 67, 101012.

Flores, R. (2002). *Remembering the Alamo: Memory, modernity, and the master symbol.* University of Texas Press.

Freire, P. (1970). *Pedagogy of the oppressed.* Seabury Press.

Garcia, P., & Cifor, M. (2019). Expanding our reflexive toolbox: Collaborative possibilities for examining socio-technical systems using duoethnography. *Proceedings of the ACM on Human-Computer Interaction*, 3(article 190), 1–23.

Gramsci, A. (1971). *Selections from the prison notebooks of Antonio Gramsci.* International Publishers.

Greene, M. (2017). Wide-awakeness and the moral life. In A.R. Sadovnik, P. Cookson, Jr., S. Semel, & Ryan Coughlan (Eds.), *Exploring education* (pp. 219–224). Routledge. https://dshutkin253.education/wp-content/uploads/2018/08/greene2018morallife.pdf

Habibie, P., Sawyer, R.D., & Norris, J. (2021). Thinking beyond ourselves: Career reflections on the Trojan Horse of hegemonic discourses. In P. Habibie (Ed.). *Scholarly publication trajectories of early-career scholars* (pp. 299–320). Palgrave.

Haverkamp, B.E. (2005). Ethical perspectives on qualitative research in applied psychology. *Journal of Counseling Psychology*, 52(2), 146–155.

Henderson, J.G., & Gornik, R. (2007). *Transformative curriculum leadership.* Pearson Merrill/Prentice Hall.

Holquist, M. (1981). *Introduction to the dialogic imagination.* The University of Texas Press.

Huckaby, F.M., & Weinburgh, M. (2015). Spark like a dialectic. Difference in-between feminisms/duoethnography. *International Review of Qualitative Research*, 8(1),49–67.

Hummel, G.S., & Toyosaki, S. (2015). Duoethnography as relational whiteness pedagogy: Human orientation toward critical cultural labor. *International Review of Qualitative Research*, 8(1), 27–48.

Johansson, M., & Jones, S. (2019). Interlopers in class: A duoethnography of working-class women academics. *Gender, Work & Organization*, 26(11), 1527–1545.

Karasa, M., & Uchihara, T. (2021). Silence: A duoethnography. *Journal of Silence Studies in Education*, 1(1), 64–75.

Kasparek, N., & Turner, M.W. (2020). Puzzling about special educational needs in EFL teacher development: A duoethnographic inquiry. In L. Lawrence & R.J. Lowe. (Eds.), *Duoethnography in English language teaching* (pp. 112–132). Multilingual Matters.

Koro-Ljungber, M., Yendol-Hoppey, D., Smith, J.J., & Hayes, S.G. (2009). (E)pistemological awareness, instantiation of methods, and uninformed methodological ambiguity in qualitative research projects. *Educational Researcher*, 38(9), 687–699.

Kubanyiova, M. (2008). Rethinking research ethics in contemporary applied linguistics: The tension between macroethical and microethical perspectives in situated research. *The Modern Language Journal*, 92(4), 503–518.

Latremouille, J., Lee, L., Shergill, S., & Lund, D. (2014). Pedagogy for justice: An intersectional dialogue exploring critical conversations involving pre-service teachers and youth social justice activists. In P. Preciado Babb (Ed.). *Proceedings of the IDEAS: Rising to Challenge Conference* (pp. 121–131). Werklund School Education, University of Calgary.

Lefebvre, H. (1991). *The production of space* (D. Nicholson-Smith, Trans). Blackwell. (Original work published in 1974).

Lévinas, E. (1984). Emmanuel Lévinas. In R. Kearney (Ed.), *Dialogues with contemporary continental thinkers* (pp. 47–70). Manchester University Press.

Lowe, R. J., & Kiczkowiak, M. (2016). Native-speakersim and the complexity of personal experience: A duoethnographic study. *Cogent Education, 3,*(1), 1–16.

McLane-Davison, D. R., Quinn, C. R., Hardy, K., & Smith, R. L. (2018). The power of sum: An accountability sistah circle. *Journal of Social Work Education, 54*(1), 18–32.

Nicolazzo, Z., & Marine, S. B. (2016). Teaching the history of US higher education: A critical duoethnography. *Journal for the Study of Postsecondary and Tertiary Education, 1,* 215–231. https://scholarworks.merrimack.edu/soe_facpub/81

Norris, J. & Sawyer, R. D. (2020). Duoethnography: A polytheoretical approach to (re)storing, (re)storying the meanings that one gives. In P. Leavy (Ed.), *Oxford handbook of qualitative research* (2nd ed., pp. 397–423). Oxford University Press.

Norris, J., Sawyer, R. D., & Lund, D. (Eds.). (2012). *Duoethnography: Dialogic methods for social, health, and educational research.* Routledge.

Oberg, A., & Wilson, T. (2002). Side by side: Being in research autobiographically. *Educational Insights, 7*(2), 4–16. Retrieved on 6 October 2024 from http://ccfi.educ.ubc.ca /publication/insights/v07n02/contetualexplorations/wilson_oberg/

Pinar, W. F. (Ed.) (1975). *Curriculum theorizing: The reconceptualists.* McCutchan.

Pinar, W. F. (2005). Curriculum. In S. J. Farenga & D. Ness (Eds.), *Encyclopedia of education and human development* (pp. 3–47). M. E. Sharpe.

Pinar, W. F. (2012). *What is curriculum theory?* Routledge.

Pinar, W. F. (2017). That first year. *Currere Exchange Journal, 1*(1), 1–10.

Poetter, T. S. (2022). Of course, my own teacher education impacts others: The quest toward erasing "erasure". *Northwest Journal of Teacher Education, 17*(3).

Rose, H., & Montakantiwong, A. (2018). A tale of two teachers: A duoethnography of the realistic and idealistic successes and failures of teaching English as an international language. *RELC Journal, 49*(1), 88–101.

Rosenblatt, L. (1978). *The reader, the text, the poem: The transactional theory of the literary work.* Southern Illinois Press.

Said, E. W. (1993). *Culture and imperialism.* Alfred A Knopf.

Sawyer, R. D. (2017). Tracing Dimensions of aesthetic *currere*: Critical transactions between person, place, and art. *Currere Exchange Journal, 1*(1), 89–100.

Sawyer, R. D. (2021a). Queer narrative theory and *currere*: Thoughts toward queering *currere* as a method of queer (curricular) self-study. *Journal of Curriculum Theorizing, 37*(1), 23–38. https://journal.jctonline.org/index.php/jct/article/view/981

Sawyer, R. D. (2021b). Life history inquiry into the dynamic ecology of person and place: Dialogic ethnographies as public engagement. In A. Bainbridge, L. Formenti, & L. West (Eds.), *The ecology of living: A biographical construction* (pp. 95–106). Sense Publishers.

Sawyer, R. D. (2022). Confronting normative autobiography conventions at the intersection of queer literary theory and currere: A fluid high school homecoming. *Curriculum Exchange Journal, 6*(1), 2–14.

doi   Sawyer, R. D., & Liggett, T. (2012). Shifting positionalities: A critical discussion of a duoethnographic inquiry of a personal curriculum of post/colonialism. *International Journal of Qualitative Methods, 11*(5), 628–651.

Sawyer, R. D., & Norris, J. (2013). *Duoethnography: Understanding qualitative research.* Oxford University Press.

doi   Toyosaki, S., & Hummel, G. (2015). Duoethnography as relational whiteness pedagogy: Human orientation toward critical cultural labor. *International Review of Qualitative Research, 8*(1).

doi   Valdez, N., Carney, M., Yates-Doerr, E., Saldaña-Tejeda, A., Hardin, J., Garth, H., & Dickinson, M. (2022). Duoethnography as transformative praxis: Conversations about nourishment and coercion in the COVID-era academy. *Feminist Anthropology, 3*(1), 92–105.

doi   Woods, J., & Sebok, S. (2016). Promoting professional conversations and reflective practice Among educators: Unpacking our portfolios using duoethnography. In H. Brown, R. D. Sawyer, & J. Norris (Eds.). *Forms of practitioner reflexivity. Critical, conversational, and arts-based approaches* (pp. 63–87). Palgrave Macmillan.

CHAPTER 4

Toward an understanding of *currere* as a research method

Wanying Wang
St. John's University

This chapter introduces and explicates *currere* as a research method as well as a key concept in curriculum, which was first invoked by William Pinar during the 1970s to understand how one's educational experience can contribute to academic study and vice versa. The method of *currere* emphasizes the lived experience of curriculum — to run the course — but also includes the social, political, and cultural enactment of experience through conversation. Employing psychoanalytical technique, *currere* allows one to turn inward. As argued by Pinar (2019), the understanding of lived experience involves working from within as one encounters self, others, and world. The method of *currere* renders self knowledge that is never still, self-identical, making oneself a subject in a recursive process between self and the world, past and future. Pinar delineates four steps (regression, progression, analysis, and synthesis) to engage the individual in both temporal and reflective movements, thus enabling one's understanding of what operatives have been at work in an individual's educational experience. Eventually, through understanding oneself, the whole world unfolds in front of us (Wang, 2020).

Introduction

The concept of *currere*, the infinitive form of the noun curriculum, was first invoked by William Pinar during the 1970s to denote a shift from curriculum defined as syllabus (or objectives) to "curriculum conceived as the educational experience of 'complicated conversation'" (Pinar, 2015, p. 1). As a key concept in the Curriculum Reconceptualization movement, *currere* underscores the lived, embodied experience of curriculum, potentially educational experience structured by the past, present, and future (Pinar, 2019). The concept of *currere* redefines curriculum as complicated conversation, which includes the lived experience of curriculum — *currere*, to run the course — but also includes the social, political, and cultural enactment of experience through conversation (Wang, 2020). *Currere* is a paradigm

https://doi.org/10.1075/rmal.8.04wan

shift in the way we speculate about educational experience (Morris, 2015). It addresses the inner world in relation to the larger society for in-depth understanding (Morris, 2015), not only through a complicated conversation among students and teachers in classrooms but also within oneself in solitude. *Currere* offers a method, "by means of which students of curriculum could sketch the relations among school knowledge, life history and intellectual development in ways that might function self-transformatively" (Pinar et al., 1995, p. 515). Pinar delineates four steps (regression, progression, analysis, and synthesis) to reveal educational experience that enables one's understanding of what principles and patterns have been at work in an individual's educational experience (Cortazzi, 2014, p. 13). The autobiographical inquiry of educational experience engages one in both temporal and reflective movements and describes the dynamic, cognitive relationality between knower and known and unknown, that is the underlying structure of educational experience.

The method of *currere* provides a primary creative direction for reconceptualization (Carson, 2017). *Currere*, after all, is a turn toward the subject, whereby the self is transformed, through remembering and recalling, contingent upon the social and cultural, attuned to one's inner voice including one's anticipation, memory, mistakes, and attempts. It, then, binds and unbinds each of us. Eventually, the path ahead illuminates itself and hope grows. The path and hope are what *currere* renders us.

In this chapter, I will provide a brief discussion on the concept and the tenets of *currere*, its practice, and other related issues including its comparison to other methods, challenges and ethical issues. And hopefully, it can further our understanding of *currere* theoretically, and how to employ it practically in educational research.

Central tenets of *currere*

Currere gives momentum to run the course between the "temporal and conceptual" (Pinar, 1994, p. 19), between a personal and academic life, which is a perpetual and recursive movement. It is, simultaneously, trans-temporal and trans-conceptual (Pinar, 1975). In the following, I offer an overview of the central tenets of *currere*.

Currere as complicated conversation

Curriculum "reconceptualized" as *currere* denotes the running of the course (Pinar, 1975/2004). "In this sense, *curriculum* does not mean the syllabus, the content, the textbook, or the objectives of learning" (Morris, 2015, p. 103). The method of *currere* re-conceptualizes curriculum from course objectives to a complicated conversation, which includes both the lived experience of curriculum and the social, political, and cultural enactment of experience through conversation:

> Curriculum becomes a complicated, that is, multiply referenced, conversation in which interlocutors are speaking not only among themselves but to those not present, not only to historical figures and unnamed people and places they may be studying, but to politicians and parents alive and dead, not to mention to the selves they have been, are in the process of becoming, and someday may become.
> (Pinar, 2019, p. 23)

Curriculum as complicated conversation takes people far beyond the conception that curriculum is simply a body of academic knowledge separated from those who study it; on the contrary, curriculum as complicated conversation emphasizes the ongoing reconstruction of knowledge — subjective reconstruction of academic knowledge and life experience which courses through one's life (Wang, 2020). This method of *currere* understands curriculum as a lived path as well as an object and a course of study. Curriculum is not merely a "thing" to be studied; it is a path that is lived. It is a conversation threaded through academic knowledge. In other words, the method of *currere* seeks to understand the interaction between academic study and life history in the interests of self-understanding and social reconstruction (Pinar, 2019). Pinar says:

> It is a conversation with oneself (as a private person) and with others threaded through academic knowledge, an ongoing project of self-understanding in which one becomes mobilized for engagement in the world. Conceived as a complicated conversation, the curriculum is an ongoing effort at communication with others that portends the social reconstruction of the public sphere.   (p. 26)

Currere is a conversational process, threaded through the study of academic knowledge, in which participants reactivate the past, reconstruct the present, and look to the future by talking with themselves, and with figures across time and space (Wang, 2020). Therefore, it transcends the boundaries of classrooms or schools since it involves working from within. To sum up, "the running of the course — *currere* — occurs through conversation, ongoing dialogical encounter among students and teachers in classrooms but also within oneself in solitude" (Pinar, 2012, p. 1). Curriculum as complicated conversation "invites students to encounter themselves and the world they inhabit through academic knowledge, popular culture, grounded in their own lived experience" (Pinar, 2004, p. 208).

Currere as temporality — past, present, and future

Currere provides a "sketch of subjectivity-structured temporality" (Pinar, 2012a, p. 6). In the autobiographical method of *currere*, the student of curriculum situates simultaneously in the past, present, and future, which allows a "reconstruction of the present through the reactivation of the past, differentiating present-mindedness into the co-extensive simultaneity of temporal attunements, expressed individually in social context through academic knowledge" (Pinar, 2012a, p. 51). Through understanding temporality of *currere*, an individual can access one's past and future, presented by certain moments embedded in the past or present. Time is no longer linear in this sense. Huebner (1999) critiques the scientific view of time: "Man, has constructed his scientific view of time as something objective and beyond himself, in which he lives." (p. 137). Magrini (2011), however, argues that time is non-linear, and neither the clock nor wristwatch appropriately displays time. An authentic temporal existence, according to Huebner, requires examination of the past, along with the "identification of forms of existence or aspects of life considered worthy of maintenance, transmission, or necessary for evolution; and the projection of these valued forms into the future..." (p. 137), which is akin to Heidegger's notion of ecstatic temporality that enables particular configuration among past, present and future. "Our humanity, or ontological self-hood," Magrini (2011) posits, "is inextricably grounded in ecstatic temporality" (p. 137), which represents the inseparable aggregation of one's past, present, and future, embodied as a moment of coherence.

For Heidegger, the traditional sense of time, which is measurable in length, manifested through the clock, misses "the more substantial ontological-existential matter of how time is, which is to say, the way in which we enact our time when living as temporal, existential beings" (Magrini, 2011, p. 137). Magrini (2011), thus, contends that with such a false understanding of time, educators accommodate the curriculum and the learning experience toward the future, which is envisioned as predictable and determinate. Such a linear model that considers students as "products" simplifies students as passive recipients of knowledge, reduces learning into linear progression, ignoring their subjectivity. Contrariwise, the authentic understanding of temporality "makes possible moments of resolute openness wherein students choose to enact their authentic possibilities" (Magrini, 2011, p. 139). For *currere*, it is to explore each student's inner temporality, or ecstatic temporality in which general temporal structure exists as unparallel to one's growth. Pinar calls for a different language in which this temporality would become part of the curriculum reconceptualized as *currere* (Doerr, 2004).

Currere as lived experience

Currere is about exploring lived experience as it is associated with a deep understanding of education (Morris, 2015). As argued by Pinar et al., 1995, the method of *currere*, which stems in part from Husserlian phenomenology, exhibits an interest in describing immediate, pre-conceptual experience. Compared to other forms of educational research, *currere* embraces this conceptual structure:

> Unlike mainstream educational research which focuses upon the end products of the processes of consciousness as described by Husserl, those end products we call concepts, abstractions, conclusions, and generalizations we, in accumulative fashion, call knowledge, *currere* seeks to slide underneath these end products and structures to the pre-conceptual experience that is their foundation.
>
> (Pinar et al., 1995, p. 415)

Currere is committed to describing pre-conceptual experience lying underneath those end products and structures such as concepts, abstractions, and generalizations. Pre-conceptual is, in the famous phenomenological phrase, back to "the things themselves" (Pinar et al., 1995, p. 416). For Merleau-Ponty, in brief, lifeworldly or pre-conceptual meaning precedes philosophical or conceptual meaning. *Currere* acts as the phenomenological epoche "slackening the intentional threads which attach us to the world and thus bring them to our notice" (Merleau-Ponty, 1962, p. xii). By portraying these pre-conceptual experiences, a more essential picture might be presented, which then follows a thorough understanding of these experiences. As argued by Grumet (1976), *currere* is a phenomenological description of the subject's situatedness, which involves the intersection of one's historical, social, and physical life world.

In order to approach the pre-conceptual in *currere*, attention to "biographic situation" is needed first. The concept of "biographic situation" points to "where I conceptually and ontologically am now" (Pinar, 1975, p. 53). As Pinar (2011) makes explicit, biographic situation invites the self-restructuring of lived meaning that originates from past situations, a connotation that encompasses, perhaps unarticulated, contradictions of that past and of the present as well as anticipation of a possible future. To attend to one's biographic situation, Pinar (1975) encourages students to record questions and answers that come to mind, then analyze them asking why these questions and answers arise. The process is both pre-conceptual and conceptual. The reason why it is both pre-conceptual (ontological) and conceptual is that both views and problems derived from the situation are inherently produced by one's conceptual apparatus or *Gestalt*. In phenomenology, the pre-conceptual precedes language, and language (or the conceptual) is derivative from the things themselves, reality prior to language and being. This biographic situation acknowledges the interplay between the two dimensions — pre-conceptual and conceptual. Pinar (1975) posits that one comes to understand how the conceptual is an integral part of the biographic situation as one moves into the past. Autobiographical writing thus mediates between the two realms: pre-conceptual and conceptual (Wang, 2017; Wang, 2020). When one writes autobiographically, one can record the complex interaction and reciprocity between the two dimensions of being human; it requires taking on the role of artist and the epistemological posture of the phenomenologist (Pinar, 1975). Pinar appears to agree that all conceptualization is a manifestation of a pre-conceptual substratum but suggests that finding the relationship between pre-conceptual and conceptual could become dialectical, a sort of dynamic middle ground between a view that is "I think therefore I am" and phenomenological — "I am therefore I think." Through the description of biographic situation, the pre-conceptual becomes accessible. *Currere* is to understand one's lived experience, the writing of which mediates between pre-conceptual and conceptual.

In addition, in *currere*, the individual is stressed. The method is phenomenological and self-hermeneutical (Pinar, 1975). The field of curriculum studies, Pinar (1975) contends, had forgotten the existing individual. In its fixation with the public and the visible, with curriculum design, sequencing, implementation, evaluation, and in its preoccupation with curricular materials, the curriculum field ignored the individual's experience. While acknowledging society, culture, and history, the concept of *currere* underscores an individual's experience. *Currere* emphasizes the everyday experience of individuals and their capacity to learn from experience, to reconstruct experience through thought and dialogue as a means of enabling understanding (Pinar, 2012a). For Doerr (2004), curriculum must call forth individual experience and value it. If we do not use our personal experiences, Grumet (1988) posits that we risk turning away from the "places where we were most thrilled, most afraid, most ashamed, and most proud...our experience gathers up its convictions and its questions and quietly leaves the room" (xvii). This is where *currere* can be so effective (Doerr, 2004). It brings experience into the picture and renders it voice, as suggested by Grumet (1988).

Currere as working from within

Currere reveals the inner "psychic speech" (Doll, 2017). For Pinar (1976), "the psyche is the source of outward activity; it is the integrative center from which the hidden reveals itself; that which is given and that which we may transmute" (p. 21). As Graham (1991) has observed: "Autobiography has everything to learn from psychoanalysis" (p. 101).

For Pinar, living a more full and meaningful life commences with attending to one's interiority and examining the self in relation to academic knowledge and psychic well-being (Morris, 2015). Psychoanalytically, *currere* summons interpretation of educational experience, examining manifest and covert meaning, conscious and unconscious content of language, as well as the political implications of such refection and interpretation (Pinar et al., 1995). In this regard, Grumet (1976) writes that *currere* "is what the individual does with the curriculum, his active reconstruction of his passage through its social, intellectual, physical structures" (p. 111). Grumet is thus interested in the psychological "passages" students make while engaging with the various school subjects (Morris, 2015), the passage that exists invisibly, however functioning in its own way. In so doing, *currere* discloses new structures in the process of naming old ones.

Currere explores our interiority, "our inner lives in the broader context of education and in the context of our relations with others and the world" (Morris, 2015, p. 103). Interiority is of great concern to both Pinar and Doll (Morris, 2015). Doll (2017) illustrates this concern in her book *Mythopoetics of Currere*, in which she explores the mythopoetic nature of *currere*. She advances *currere* as mythopoetic expedition toward the inner world, through a recursive process between self and the world, to reveal the unconscious dimension of experience, the primitive self, enacted through writing autobiographically. *Currere* enables one to "unearth one's own foundational images" (Doll, 2017, p. xvi). If interiority is that "which is within all things" (Doll, 2017), *currere* recovers interiority, to enliven the coursing within, and to help us find "the constant" threaded throughout one's life (Casemore, 2019). Reaching toward to this interiority and "tapping" the coursing within animate our inner world, the world that awaits us (Casemore, 2019). Thus, *currere* is to enliven the inner current within oneself. *Currere* allows one to approach the core of oneself, the innermost part of a person.

To illuminate one's inner world, inspired by Jung, Pinar (1975) describes two forms of thinking: the free-associative and the directed. First, one "renders one's own educational experience into words, using the free-associative form of minding" (Pinar, 1975, p. 389). Second, one employs one's critical faculties to "understand what principles and patterns have been operative in one's educational life, hence achieving a more profound understanding of one's own educational experience, as well as illuminating parts of the inner world and deepening one's self understanding generally" (p. 389). Free association helps one see something under the surface or capture something beyond the realm of consciousness. This enables one to gain greater access to one's current lived experience. The individual can become conscious of something missed before and bring what is latent into consciousness. As a result, one becomes more existential. Being more existential means becoming more detached from the current situation and more reflective about multiple roles and selves (Pinar, 1975). This is a major moment or phase of the method of *currere*. It is not the entire method, as there are also analytic and progressive steps. By employing this examination of educational experience, Pinar (1975) contends that one can discover what factors are playing in the constitution of oneself as well as what fundamental structures underlie the educative process, the structure that may have been neglected before or beyond one's consciousness. One can come to understand how various factors work under certain circumstances and what consequences might be caused. In a sense, these structures would represent the last stop in the realm of the conceptual, the most fundamental level of analysis possible before entering the preconceptual, the *Lebenswelt* (Pinar, 1975). This analysis of educational experience, then, involves "working from within." Eventually one arrives at a place "where one experiences a continuity in educational experience, where normally most of us experience discontinuity and disjointedness" (Doerr, 2004, p.17). As argued by Pinar (1975),

> The method, as I conceive it now, would render two orders of consequences. It would yield information regarding the nature of educational experiences and their fundamental existential structures, and it would yield the researcher biographic information that would enhance "insight" and cultivate the innercenteredness and focus that are essential to psychic integration.   (p.390)

This process of turning inward, he stated, will lead to "a generalized innercenteredness and hopefully initiate or further the process of individuation, leading to the gradual formation of the transcendental ego" (p.410). For Pinar, to avoid psychic arrest, one must be watchful to keep the self-fluid and continue to have complicated conversations about the past, present, and future (Pacheco, 2009). Thus, this autobiographical theory of curriculum suggests a shift in focus "from external, behaviorally oriented learning objectives and predetermined subject matter content to the interrogation of students' and teachers' inner experiences and perceptions" (Miller, 2010, p.62).

   To sum up, *currere as a method* reveals the contribution of academic knowledge to one's understanding of life. *Currere* engages students and teachers in autobiographical writing that provokes reflection on how and why they have developed intellectually and emotionally. Rather than a reflective retreat isolated from the world, *currere* promotes a "heightened engagement with it through an examination of the relations between school knowledge, life history, and intellectual development" (Pinar et al., 1995, p.415). In this complicated conversation, academic knowledge and life experience are intertwined with each other, mutually informative and constitutive. Academic knowledge enables a more sophisticated understanding of the world. With academic knowledge, one can understand life experiences more deeply and can make connections that may not have been noticed or may not have been previously recognized as important. As a research method for studying the existing individual's lived experience of education, eventually, *currere* fosters self-understanding, as described by Pinar (2011), which is never self-identical, never still, requiring ongoing reconstruction. "In such reconstruction — simultaneously subjective and social — one activates agency as one commits to the ongoing study of the past, a 'regression' that enables one's entry into the future" (Pinar, 2012a, p.39). One, thus, engages in a subjective reconstruction during such an autobiographical inquiry.

Practice and pedagogy of *currere*

Currere consists of four stages: regression, progression, analysis, and synthesis. Regression looks at the past. In regression, the writer records a past experience and observes it. Self is the source of data. Since the focus is educational experience, the observations involve life in schools, life with teachers, life with learning. Through recording these observations, the writer brings the past to the present.

The second phase is progression. Pinar suggests a meditative method here and he encourages finding a coherence among past, present, and future through understanding lived experiences. The writer looks "at what is not yet the case, what is not yet present.... the future is present in the same sense that the past is present. It influences, in complicated ways, the present; it forms the present" (Pinar, 1994, p.24).

The third stage is analysis. At this point, the writer has produced three photographs of himself — one of his past, one of his future, and one of his present (Doerr, 2004). The writer searches for threading themes in these three photographs within and between these photographs (Pinar, 1975)?

The last phase is synthesis, which brings together the three photographs. Pinar concludes:

> The Self is available to itself in physical form. The intellect, residing in physical form is part of the Self. The Self is not a concept the intellect has of itself. The intellectual is an appendage of the Self, a medium, like the body, through which the Self and the world are accessible to themselves. Mind in its place, I conceptualize the present situation. I am placed together. Synthesis.   (Pinar, 1975, p.27)

Numerous studies employing the method of *currere* have been conducted. As pointed out by Doerr (2004), *currere* can be used to examine students' experience, teachers' experience, or solely used by the author. Upon reviewing Hyder's (1998) work in which a student teacher in an English teaching program worked with the professor to use *currere* to explore their educational life, Doerr (2004) advances "a curriculum for first-year college students in remedial writing that employs *currere* and critical pedagogy as its main structure" (Doerr, 2004, p. 19). Leslie Palmer (2019) also writes of her experience of using *currere* to explore her experience of working with student teachers. Daniel (1991) focuses on how fifth-grade teachers use *currere* for themselves to help analyze their teaching lives, and the planning of their own curriculum. In my work entitled *Chinese Currere, Subjective Reconstruction and Attunement-When Calls My Heart* (2020), I associate *currere* with elements of ancient Chinese philosophical thought. In so doing I testify to what I characterize as a cosmopolitan concept of spirituality, "a reverberating juxtaposition of concepts from West and East, a juxtaposition that carves an unfathomable space between them, providing a portal for a new and original conception: a Chinese *currere*" (Pinar, 2020, cited in Wang, 2020, p. v). Lastly, scholarship related to *currere* is growing. Examples include a provocative collection of reflections on *currere* edited by Teresa Strong-Wilson and colleagues and Jung-Hoon Jung and Saeed Nazari's book on *currere*. Ongoing is the *Currere* Exchange project — housed at Miami University in Oxford, Ohio and directed by Thomas Poetter and Denise Taliaferro Baszile, and Currere and Praxis directed by William Pinar and Sumer Atkin, which provides a home for those committed to understanding education through understanding themselves.

To teach *currere* may start with the four steps mentioned above. However, *currere* teaching may differ from person to person, from program to program. Pedagogically, *currere* does not require a universal protocol since as the method of self-understanding, *currere* may engage one in a distinctive way. It is to write one's own story, informed by literature writing. Essentially, it is to access one's life world through writing and contemplation. However, the four steps may work as the protocol for guidance.

Currere and curriculum studies

The method of *currere* has played a major role in the reconceptualization of U.S. curriculum studies, provoking a turning point in the field and opening the avenue for new scholarship (Pacheco, 2009). Through this method, Pinar articulates clearly the importance of the concrete subject: a flesh and blood person appears" (Murillo, 2019, p. 160). Hence, the field of curriculum studies comes back (Murillo, 2019). As pointed out by a large number of scholars (Pacheco, 2009; Morris, 2015; Schubert, 2009), *currere* gradually changed the countenance of the curriculum field from curriculum development to curriculum studies (as is evident in transformations within the American Educational Research Association's Division B).

At the initial stage, autobiography and *currere* — as a method of doing auto-biography — were introduced in curriculum studies, received scant attention (Morris, 2015). By the 1990s, however, things had altered. Morris (2015) posits that *currere* has spawned a variety of ways of doing autobiography as autobiography establishes itself as a suitable way of describing educational experience. *Currere* enlightens many educational scholars to write about their experiences in their own way (Morris, 2015). Pinar (2004) elaborates:

> At least four major projects employing autobiography in some form are underway on the North American continent: F. Michael Connelly and Jean Clandinin 's work on "personal practical knowledge," William Schubert and William Ayers' "teacher lore" and "student lore" projects, Richard Butt and Danielle Raymond's elaboration of collaborative autobiography, and Margo Figgins exciting theatrical work.   (p. 2)

It took almost 20 years for others in curriculum studies to appreciate the signifi-cance of this kind of work: "Without the notion of *currere* — as put forth by Pinar and Grumet — these other forms of autobiography would not have arrived on the scene. Pinar and Grumet opened an entirely new avenue of scholarship" (Morris, 2015, p. 108).

Pacheco (2009) seems to make a more systematic summary of what *currere* has led to and he contends at least three streams of scholarship emerged from this concept, the first of which is autobiographical theory and practice. Major concepts in this stream include *currere* itself, and other related concepts such as collaboration, voice, dialogue journals, place, as well as narrative, psychoanalyti-cal, and poststructuralist portraits of self and educational experience, and, finally, studies of myth, dreams, and the imagination (Pitt, 2003). The second stream — following *currere* and in tandem with his early work in gender studies — is femi-nist autobiography, major concepts of which include community, the middle pas-sage, and reclaiming the self. The third major category of studies are those efforts to understand teachers biographically and autobiographically, including collabo-rative biography and autobiographical praxis, the personal practical knowledge of teachers, teacher lore, and biographical studies of teacher lives. A large number of books and hundreds of articles report research on autobiographical studies in education, studies that have been informed by Pinar's idea of *currere* in the early 1970s.

To be noted, *currere* as an autobiographical inquiry is also political, as pointed out by Pinar (1978). *Currere* reveals hidden experiences and silenced voices, as shown in Denise Baszile's critical race/feminist *currere* (1995/2015). This *currere* is inspired by "the reality of one's absence and a quest to make oneself subject," seeking to understand "how the dynamics of race, gender, class, and other important architects of self and the ways in which they intersect and are inflected in the perpetually evolving question — Who am I?" (Baszile, 2015, p. 119). In her critical race/feminist *currere*, the others who are invited into the conversation embody the voices that have been "absent, ignored, misconstrued, distorted, repressed in the curriculum/s that shapes our lives — the curricula of schooling and media, in particular" (p. 120). Baszile's *currere* exalts the absent self and silenced voice(s). Thus, the method of *currere* is one means by which one can hear and see the hidden aspects of reality, enabling us to participate more consciously, with more agency and sensitivity, in the complicated conversation.

In summary, Pinar's reconceptualized notion of *currere* as a method has grown from "an opposition to the mainstream field and its tradition" (Pinar, 2004, p. 167) in the 1970s, to "become the field, complicated, with several centers of theoretical formation" (p. 167), to "an entire sector of curriculum studies scholarship" (Pacheco, 2009, p. 62). Miller (2017) suggests how the bringing of questions and new imaginings into the field and its theorizing can serve as part of the affirming practice of love itself. Perhaps it is also a practice of ethics. *Currere* might be the practice of love and ethics.

Currere and other methods

As elaborated previously, *currere* has spawned a variety of autobiographical methods. Here I focus on narrative inquiry, autoethnography, and duoethnography due to their relevancy.

Narrative inquiry is the study of Narrative inquir experience. Connelly and Clandinin (1990) first used the approach in education to describe the personal stories of teachers (Delmas & Giles, 2023). It focuses not only on individuals' experience but also "the social, cultural, and institutional accounts within which individuals' experience are constituted, shaped, expressed, and enacted" (Clandinin & Rosiek, 2007, pp. 42–43). "The story of the self is always already webbed inside a historical context; stories of the self are also stories of history" as interpreted by Morris (2015, p. 108). Such a character resonates with that of autobiography emphasized by Pinar: autobiography is always political, historical and contextual. Morris (2015) points out that Connelly and Clandinin emphasize the practical value of storytelling and narrative inquiry; Pinar, on the other hand, emphasizes the theoretical value of autobiography through the method of *currere* while acknowledging that sometimes there might not exist a fine line between the practical and the theoretical, but different theorists emphasize different aspects of autobiography. Additionally, in narrative inquiry, both teachers and researchers work toward shared meanings. However, for Willinsky (1989), the teacher's voice is kept distinct and subordinated in indented blocks as the research is being presented. This method may place the teacher in a position that is passive, one in which she does not possess theoretical knowledge that a researcher does Conversely, *currere* invites the teacher (sometimes a researcher too) to engage in writing their own stories, which highlights the particular voice of teacher.

Autoethnography is a research method that employs personal experience ("auto") to describe and interpret ("graphy") cultural texts, experiences, beliefs, and practices ("ethno") (Adams et al., 2017). Autoethnography focuses on the intersection of autobiography and ethnography. The process, principles, and practices of autobiography and ethnography guides the way we write and practice autoethnography (Adams et al., 2017). According to Ellis (2004), "Autoethnography is research, writing, and method that connect the autobiographical and personal to the cultural and social. This form usually features concrete action, emotion, embodiment, self-consciousness, and introspection … [and] claims the conventions of literary writing" (p. xix). Personal experience may work as the starting points in this research method.

For autoethnographers, there are numerous ways that personal experience influences the research process: "For example, a researcher decides who, what, when, where, and how to research, decisions necessarily tied to institutional requirement, resources and personal circumstances." (Ellis et al, 2010, para 3.). As a researcher, we need to be aware of it and consider it an essential characteristic of research. Autoethnography juxtaposes both personal experience and ethnographical methods such as interviews, observations and field notes to create particular, accessible, and evocative representations of the culture/cultural experience (Adams et al., 2017). Compared to *currere*, autoethonography seems to focus on articulating "insider knowledge of cultural experience" (Adams et al., 2017, p.3). However, *currere* may focus on the individual experience, which includes the social, political, and cultural enactment through complicated conversation.

According to Sawyer and Norris (2012), duoethnography is a collaborative research method in which two or more researchers are committed to a dialogue on their distinct histories in a given phenomenon. For them, through interrogating existing beliefs and engaging in a dialogue with their collaborative researcher, they can reconceptualize their beliefs regarding the given issue. Presenting layered nested, auto-ethnographic accounts of a given research context or question, duoethnography is formulated to emphasize the complex, reflexive, and aesthetic aspects of both the work in process and the product (Sawyer & Norris, 2012; Norris et al., 2012). As a curriculum making and a research method, as argued by

Sawyer and Norris (2012), duoethnography explores two seminal issues: representation in qualitative research (how to represent findings when findings are created within a dynamic phenomenological text); and praxis (how research contributes to personal transformation). Duoethnography allows researchers to explore how their lives have been situated socially and culturally when they are engaging in transformation. Recent duoethnographic studies have examined a range of topics, including forms of institutionalized racism, beauty, post-colonialism, multicultural identity construction, and professional boundaries between patient and practitioner in mental health professions. For Pinar, duoethnography is ethnography reconceptualized while acknowledging its self-reflexive character.

> Through juxtapositions of difference, educational experience's non-coincidence with itself is recast as a double, indeed, 'polyocular' consciousness, compelling an ongoing self-interrogation, thereby challenging interpellation, enabling subjective reconstruction in the 'polyvocal' presence of others. Through such dialogical encounter, key concepts — among them agency, identity, self-reflexivity — achieve renewed vitality and immediacy.   (Pinar, 2012b, back cover)

Compared to *currere* and autoethnography, duoethnography seems to emphasize collaborative work of researchers, during which they do autoethnographical, autobiographical, and ethnographical investigation simultaneously. The most important character, in relation to *currere*, is its focus on the dialogues between or among collaborative researchers, as well as its emphasis on the conceptual and temporal, which stems from *currere*. However, the emphasis of duoethnography is on the reciprocity of perspectives from participant researchers, which brings multi-voices to the surface, eventually fostering personal change and then social transformation.

Both autoethnography and duoethnography combine both perspective of self and other, connecting self to the larger culture and society, whereas *currere* emphasizes an individual's experience while acknowledging social and cultural influences since self is not isolated from which one is situated. For me, these various methods ostensibly emphasize understanding experiences, constituting an attuned togetherness with various perspectives, charged with feeling and textured with presence and encounters. However, my understanding on these methods is also tentative.

Difficulties and challenges — is *currere* solipsistic?

Is *currere* solipsistic since it focuses on the individual, that is, the self? As was mentioned earlier, there is nothing solipsistic about autobiography (Morris, 2015): "autobiography is more than someone simply telling their story" (Morris, 2015, p.

107). Edgerton (1991) acknowledges that autobiography is associated with many important issues:

> Autobiographical writing enables students to study themselves. Such study links self to place, and place is simultaneously historical, cultural, and racial. ... Via another's life one understands more fully one's own, as well as social and historical ties that link both lives to a particular place.   (p. 78, as cited in Morris, 2015)

The notion of autobiography involves the pressing concerns of history, culture, race, and place (Morris, 2015). Thus, the self situates in the various intersections and crossings. However, as Pinar (1975) points out, understanding at its deepest level must come from within: understanding the world implicates understanding self first according to phenomenologists. "Thinking more autobiographically, writing autobiographies or studying autobiographies means that one is always in relation to the other" (Morris, 2015, p. 106–107). In a sense, one has to understand the self before understanding the other. Reading others' autobiographies allows one to resonate with others, to understand oneself better. Quoting Kincheloe and Pinar (1991), "autobiography can confront the meaning of a given world, reject it, reformulate it, and reconstruct it with a social vision that is authentically the individual's" (p. 21). Morris (2015) argues that confronting the world might also result in changing that world (Morris, 2015). Confronting becomes possible only when one begins to understand one's situatedness. This understanding is achieved through writing autobiographically. Meanwhile, writing autobiographies changes oneself while engaging with others to consider how one is connected to each other. Pinar (2004) pointed out that "my work in curriculum theory has emphasized the significance of subjectivity [or thinking autobiographically] to teaching, to study, to the process of education. The significance of subjectivity is not a solipsistic retreat from the public sphere" (p. 4). What is private becomes available to the public through the writing of autobiographies (Miller, 2004). Autobiography is the bridge from which one connects to the other and the world. Grumet's theorization and employment of *currere* emphasize its social character and political potential (Morris, 2015). The most possible way to avoid solipsism might be writing autobiographically--the most profound way to understand self and world.

Thus, *currere* always includes relations with others, involving the double movement of self and society, of the personal and the political, a dialectic between "subjective risk and social reconstruction" (Pinar, 2004, p. 4). As Pinar emphasizes, *currere* is both a study of the subjective and the social; it is both about the self and the political. *Currere* allows us to arrive at a deeper understanding of the educative experience. Through understanding oneself, the whole world unfolds in front of us (Wang, 2020).

Ethical issues in *currere*

Currere is ethical in itself. First, *currere* allows one to study authentically. For Pinar (2015), study is "namely ongoing ethical engagement with alterity" (Preface, p. xi). A more authentic study, engendered by the exploration of *currere*, acknowledges and embraces alterity, allowing us to reconsider and reconfigure, thereby transcending what is given currently. Currere fosters self knowledge that facilitates our understanding about alterity. This self knowledge rendered by *currere* is the ethical work. Second, *currere* stresses care for students. For Noddings (2002), an ethic of care places students at the center of an educational process that focuses on nurturing and inspiring growth, which resonates with what *currere* is committed to, as shown in previous sections. Shapiro and Stefkovich (2011) note that empathy and compassion for manifold voices are at the heart of an ethic of care. In this sense, *currere* invites silenced, marginalized voices through looking into one's experiences that may have been neglected.

Third, *currere* is devised as self-scrutiny devoted to understanding paradox which captures intricacies and nuance that is integral to ethical understanding. According to Grumet (1976), *currere* reconciliates between objectivity and subjectivity in educational research, and it commits us to acknowledge the paradox, an essential part of our experience. In *The Ethics of Ambiguity* Simone de Beauvoir (1947/1970) praises paradox, its mysterious freedoms and awesome responsibilities: [T]he antimonies that exist between means and ends, present and future must be in a permanent tension. Quoting Beauvoir, Grumet (1976) argues that the self-scrutiny that *currere* requires helps examine the paradox between ends and means that is ethical in itself: "in setting up its ends, freedom must put them in parentheses, confront them at each moment with that absolute end which it itself constitutes, and contest in its name the means it uses to win itself" (as cited in Grumet, 1976, p. 19). To examine the paradox is to engage with particular situations which serve as a point of departure toward a new possibility of transcendence, during which one begets one's subjective reconstruction, then social reconstruction with oneself and the world. This special attention to "situatedness" is akin to the contexualized approach in the field of Applied Linguistics. Recently, a call for more contextualized approach to research ethics has been uttered in the field of Applied Linguistics (Dornyei, 2007). Such an approach extends the confines of macroethical principles, highlighting "a specific ethically significant moments for which macroethics holds ambiguous, contrasting, or no answer at all" (Kubanyiova, 2008, p. 515). *Currere* pays attentions to these moments. To address these moments appropriately, the researcher guided by *currere* may need to engage with them with ethical attentiveness, a concept proposed by Wang and Ness (2023) that may help illustrate this. Ethical attentiveness encourages educators and teachers to welcome students as a host, to embrace the wholly others, by which educators can make sense of and then transcend "those moments", not by avoiding them, but by leaving a space for others and othernesss (Wang & Ness, 2023).

Conclusion

This chapter describes *currere* as a research method that aims to understand one's lived experience as it presents itself, an experience as encountered with alterity, as surfaced from potentiality, as structured toward adequacy. By approaching one's existential experience as a data source and using the psychoanalytical technique, one can reconfigure one's lived autobiography, whereby the self engages in contemplation and transformation, through remembering and recalling; in so doing, educators (oneself and ourselves) can reconceptualize the meaning of curriculum (teaching and learning) through writing autobiographically. The method of *currere*, then, situates us both inside and outside, past and future — intersections that confront each of us. Eventually, the pathway ahead illuminates itself. The path and non-phenomenal possibilities are what *currere* renders us.

References

Adams, T. E., Ellis, C., Jones, S. H. (2017). Autoethnography. In J. Matthes, C. S. Davis, & R. F. Potter, (Eds.), *The international encyclopedia of communication research methods*. Wiley-Blackwell.

Baszile, D. (2015). Critical race/feminist *currere*. In M. He, M. Schultz, & W. Schubert (Eds.), *The Sage guide to curriculum in education* (pp. 119–126). Sage.

Carson, T. (2017). Crossing the continental divide. In M. A. Doll (Ed.), *The reconceptualization of curriculum studies: A festschrift in honor of William F. Pinar* (1st ed.). Routledge.

Clandinin, D. J., & Rosiek, J. (2007). Mapping a landscape of narrative inquiry: Borderland spaces and tensions. In D. J. Clandinin (Ed.), *Handbook of narrative inquiry: Mapping a methodology* (pp. 35–75). Sage.

Connelly, M., & Clandinin, J. (1990). Stories of experience and narrative inquiry. *Educational Researcher 19*(4), 2.14.

Cortazzi, M. (2014). *Narrative analysis*. Routledge.

de Beauvoir, S. (1970). *The ethics of ambiguity*. The Citadel Press.

Daniel, D. K. (1991). Teaching as hermeneutics (Unpublished doctoral dissertation). University of Alberta, Canada.

Delmas, P. M., & Giles, R. L. (2023). Qualitative research approaches and their application in education. In R. J. Tierney, F. Rizvi, & K. Ercikan (Eds.), *International encyclopedia of education* (4th ed., pp. 24–32). Elsevier.

Doerr, M. (2004). *Currere and environmental autobiography: A phenomenological approach to the teaching of ecology*. Peter Lang.

Doll, M. (2017). *The mythopoetics of currere: Memories, dreams, and literary texts as teaching avenues to self-study*. Routledge.

Dörnyei, Z. (2007). *Research methods in applied linguistics: Quantitative, qualitative and mixed methodologies*. Oxford University Press.

Edgerton, S. (1991). Particularities of otherness: Autobiography, Maya Angelou, and me. In J. Kincheloe & W. F. Pinar (Eds.), *Curriculum as social psychoanalysis: The significance of place* (pp. 77–79). State University of New York Press.

Ellis, C. (2004). *The ethnography I: A methodological novel about auto ethnography*. AltaMira Press.

Ellis, C., Adams, T. E., & Bochner, A. P. (2010). Autoethnography: An overview. *Forum Qualitative Sozialforschung / Forum: Qualitative Social Research, 12*(1), Art. 10. http://nbn-resolving.de/urn:nbn:de:0114-fqs1101108

Graham, R. (1991). *Reading and writing the self: Autobiography in education and the curriculum*. Teachers College Press.

Grumet, M. (1976). Existential and phenomenological foundations. In W. Pinar & M. Grumet (Eds.), *Toward a poor curriculum* (pp. 31–50). Kendall/Hunt.

Grumet, M. (1988). *Bitter milk: Women and teaching*. University of Massachusetts Press.

Huebner, D. (1999). *The lure of the transcendent*. Lawrence Erlbaum Associates.

Hyder, T. W. (1998). A model for remedial writing instruction based on autobiographical theory and informed by critical pedagogy (community colleges, composition, writing instruction) (Unpublished doctoral dissertation). University of Virginia, Charlotte.

Kincheloe, J., & Pinar, W. (Eds.), (1991). *Curriculum as social psychoanalysis: The significance of place*. State University of New York Press.

Kubanyiova, M. (2008). Rethinking research ethics in contemporary applied linguistics: The tension between macroethical and microethical perspectives in situated research. *Modern Language Journal, 92*(4), 503–518.

Magrini, J. (2011). Huebner's critical encounter with the philosophy of Heidegger in *Being and Time*: Learning, understanding, and the authentic unfolding of history in the curriculum. *KRITIKE, 5*(2), 123–155.

Merleau-Ponty, M. (1962). *Phenomenology of perception*. Routledge.

Miller, J. L. (2010). Autobiographical theory. In C. Kridel (Ed.), *Encyclopedia of curriculum studies* (pp. 61–65). Sage.

Miller, J. L. (2017). Generous interrogations and affirmations: Histories and trajectories. In M. A. Doll (Ed.), *The reconceptualization of curriculum studies: A festschrift in honor of William F. Pinar* (pp. 103–110). Routledge.

Morris, M. (2015). Currere as subject matter. In M. F. He, B. D. Schultz, & W. H. Schubert (Eds.), *The Sage guide to curriculum in education* (pp. 103–109). Sage.

Murillo, F. (2019). William Pinar responding to Elliot Eisner. *Encounters in Theory and History of Education, 20*(1), 159–164.

Noddings, N. (2002). *Starting at home: Caring and social policy*. University of California Press.

Norris, J., Sawyer, R. D., & Lund, D. (Eds.). (2012). *Duoethnography: Dialogic methods for social, health, and educational research*. Routledge.

doi Pacheco, J. (2009). *Whole, bright, deep with understanding.* Sense Publishers.

doi Palmer, L. (2019). *Intern teachers using currere: Discovering education as a river.* Peter Lang.

Pinar, W. F. (1975). *Curriculum theorizing: The reconceptualists.* McCutchan Publishing Corporation.

Pinar, W. F. (1994). *Autobiography, politics, and sexuality: Essays in curriculum theory, 1972–1992.* Peter Lang.

doi Pinar, W. F. (2004). *What is curriculum theory?* (1st ed.). Routledge.

doi Pinar, W. F. (2011). *The character of curriculum studies.* Palgrave Macmillan.

doi Pinar, W. F. (2012a). *What is curriculum theory?* (2nd ed.). Routledge.

doi Pinar, W. F. (2012b). Endorsement. In J. Norris, R. D. Sawyer, & D. Lund (Eds.), *Duoethnography: Dialogic methods for social, health, and educational research.* West Coast Press.

doi Pinar, W. F. (2019). *What is curriculum theory?* (3rd ed.). Routledge.

Pinar, W. F., Reynolds, W. M., Slattery, P., & Taubman, P. M. (1995). *Understanding curriculum: An introduction to the study of historical and contemporary curriculum discourse.* Peter Lang.

Pitt, A. (2003). *The play of the personal.* Psychoanalytic Narratives of Feminist Education.

doi Sawyer, R. & Norris, J. (2012). *Duoethnography: Understanding qualitative research.* Oxford University Press.

Schubert, W. H. (2009). Currere and disciplinarity in curriculum studies: Possibilities for education research. *Educational Researcher, 38*(2), 136–140.

doi Shapiro, J. P., & Stefkovich, J. A. (2011). *Ethical leadership and decision making in education: Applying theoretical perspectives to complex dilemmas (3rd ed.).* Routledge.

doi Wang, W. (2017). Currere, subjective reconstruction and autobiographical inquiry. *Transnational Curriculum Inquiry, 14*(2), 110–141.

doi Wang, W. (2020). *Chinese currere, subjective reconstruction and attunement: When calls my heart.* Palgrave Macmillan.

doi Wang, W. & Ness, D. (2023). Aporias, transcendence and a curriculum of hospitality. *Northwest Journal of Teacher Education, 18*(2), Article 4.

doi Willinsky, J. (1989). Getting personal and practical with personal practical knowledge. *Curriculum Inquiry, 19*(3), 247–26.

CHAPTER 5

Telling stories matters

An introduction to narrative inquiry

Annie R. Allen,[1] Jeong-Hee Kim[2] & Jeasik Cho[2]
[1] New Mexico Highlands University | [2] Texas Tech University

Narrative inquiry has emerged as a distinct and valuable research methodology within the human and social sciences. This chapter introduces the concept and significance of narrative inquiry as a means to gain profound insights into the diverse aspects of society, culture, and human actions. It begins by providing an overview of its central tenets and elements as a research approach, delving into the ethical considerations and reflexive aspects necessary to ensure the responsible and careful exploration of human experiences. The limitations of narrative inquiry are also discussed, including the "Rashomon effect" and the challenges of conducting "backyard research." The chapter then examines the pedagogical implications of narrative inquiry, highlighting its potential to enrich educational practices and enhance student engagement. Looking toward the future, "Posthuman Narrative Inquiry" is proposed as a potential direction for the field. This chapter concludes by elucidating how stories shape realities and inspire a deeper understanding of the human condition, inviting researchers and students alike to appreciate the power of narratives and their transformative influence on the world.

Narrative inquiry has emerged as a distinct and valuable research methodology within the human and social sciences. This chapter introduces the concept and significance of narrative inquiry as a means to gain profound insights into the diverse aspects of society, culture, and human actions. It begins by providing an overview of its central tenets and elements as a research approach, delving into the ethical considerations and reflexive aspects necessary to ensure the responsible and careful exploration of human experiences. The limitations of narrative inquiry are also discussed, including the "Rashomon effect" and the challenges of conducting "backyard research." The chapter then examines the pedagogical implications of narrative inquiry, highlighting its potential to enrich educational practices and enhance student engagement. Looking toward the future, "Posthuman Narrative Inquiry" is proposed as a potential direction for the field. This chapter concludes

https://doi.org/10.1075/rmal.8.05all

by elucidating how stories shape realities and inspire a deeper understanding of the human condition, inviting researchers and students alike to appreciate the power of narratives and their transformative influence on the world.

Narrative inquiry, a storytelling methodology that focuses on the storied experiences of individuals, has become a field of its own for quite some time in the human and social sciences. It is a methodology that orients one towards a narrative way of knowing and includes, but is not limited to, methods such as autobiography, autoethnography, oral history, creative non-fiction, and other methods that incorporate stories as a way to understand and know. The growing body of research literature attests the power of narrative inquiry to deepen our understanding of nuanced human phenomena and sensemaking. With its distinctive nature and significance as a research methodology, narrative inquiry has been instrumental in creating new knowledge concerning the multidimensional aspects of society, culture, human actions, and human experiences.

Narrative inquiry concerns itself with experience as it is articulated through narratives, making narrative inquiry a research approach of choice to explore *how* humans make sense of their lived experiences and, in effect, the world at large. Narrative inquiry is thus a methodology that supports the telling and knowing of our experiences as humans, and, ultimately, it helps us improve and better understand the human condition. The aim of this chapter is to introduce readers to: the usefulness of narrative inquiry to researchers; an overview of its central tenets; its unique elements; its limitations, boundaries, and ethical challenges; its pedagogical implications; and, finally, promising future directions.

A general overview of narrative inquiry

When knowledge gained through a positivist research epistemology is the only kind of knowledge that is seen as legitimate, it becomes severely limited, a fact that many researchers have become increasingly aware of. This is because humans and their problems are "fraught with complexity, uncertainty, uniqueness, instability, ambiguity, and value-conflict" (Kim, 2016, p. 4). This realization has led to a shift in the way many researchers view the practicality of relying solely on what we call scientific research to understand human nature, granting greater recognition of the importance of qualitative research, a paradigm that historically was viewed as less "legitimate" than its more scientific and rigid positivist counterpart.

Narrative inquiry's roots can be traced back to narratology, where early narrative theorists such as Todorov, Roland Barthes, and Gerard Genette employed more structural views of narrative and where analysis was reserved for *grand narratives* (Georgakopoulou, 2006). Structuralist theorists privileged the language system over individual narratives. In other words, the roots of narratology began with inquiry into the way language worked, not on how it created meaning. Narrative scholarship within a structural paradigm captures the following qualities:

> A coherent temporal progression of events that may be reordered for rhetorical purposes and that is typically located in some past time and place. A plotline that encompasses a beginning, a middle, and an end, conveys a particular perspective and is designed for a particular audience who apprehend and shape its meaning.
>
> (Ochs & Capps, 2001, p. 57)

The postmodern and linguistic turn in narrative research was born from the criticisms of structuralist linguistics, which included the gap between theory and practice that begged the question, "so what? — What's the use of all the subcategories for the understanding of texts" (Fludernik, 2005, p. 39)? In addition to the criticisms that were beginning to impact early structuralist narratology, early studies of narrative were influenced by poststructuralism and cultural studies, which became integrated into other disciplines such as philosophy, education, cultural studies, politics, and more.

Finally, philosophy underscores the importance of narrative in how humans come to know. Postmodern philosopher, Lyotard (1979/1984) argues that there is a preeminence of narrative in the formulation of traditional knowledge. It is impossible to seek out an empirical project of inquiry without first indulging in the narrative, or meaning-making, process. When we look at all the knowledge we have gained from scientific knowledge, we should understand that it began from a place of narrative inquiry.

Narrative is everywhere and all at once. Imagine trying to make sense of yourself or the world without narrative — it is impossible because a key component of our existence is to organize and give meaning to experience, and through this process, we create knowledge.

Narrative inquiry's central tenets and elements

According to Bruner (1986), there are two complementary modes of thought which help us to organize experience and construct our realities. These two modes are irreducible to one another, and any effort to rid one in favor of the other will necessarily fail to capture the richness of human experience and thought. The first mode of thought he labels as paradigmatic or logo-scientific, described as an "[attempt] to fulfill the ideal of a formal, mathematical system of description and explanation" (p. 12). In other words, the paradigmatic mode is based on a positivist epistemology — knowledge is obtained through reasoning and logic that can be observed and proven. The paradigmatic mode of knowing has enabled us to make advances in, for instance, logic, mathematics, the natural sciences, or, technology, as it is the kind of thinking that is taught most commonly in our schools (think about how much funding goes into the STEM fields, in contrast to the humanities, for example). The paradigmatic mode of thinking is also the one that is held in greater esteem, even while it depends on the narrative mode to formulate its scientific hypotheses in the first place (Bruner, 1986).

The second mode of thought Bruner called the narrative mode focuses on stories to understand the meaning of human actions and experiences rather than focusing on predictability like the former. In so doing, the narrative mode of knowing provides explanatory knowledge of human experiences through the portrayal of nuances of meaning in stories (Polkinghorne, 1995). The narrative mode is "broader in scope in that it is elaborative rather than reductive. The only criterion for concluding a narrative is when we decide we know enough for now. Its potential for expansion is never exhausted" (Goldin, 2019, p. 513).

The paradigmatic mode can even be employed imaginatively and has led to "good theory, tight analysis, logical proof, sound argument, and empirical discovery guided by reasoned hypothesis" (Bruner, 1986, p. 13). Still, this type of "imagination" is not the same kind of imagination that is required in narrative modes of thinking, or that of the writer or storyteller. It is the narrative mode of thinking that allows us to understand complex nuances and ambiguities that are present in stories of human experiences. Narrative thinking, thus, focuses less on causes and truths and more on *how things appear to be* and *how things come to be* and what meaning humans ultimately take from those experiences. The narrative mode "deals in human or human-like intention and action and the vicissitudes and consequences that mark their course. It strives to put its timeless miracles into the particulars of experience, and to locate the experience in time and place" (Bruner, 1986, p. 13). Hence, the establishment of the narrative mode of knowing has helped justify the use of stories in research, like narrative inquiry, as a legitimate approach to research.

Before diving into the mechanics of narrative inquiry, it would be helpful to first understand the etymology of the word *narrative*. The word *narrative* comes from Latin roots such as *narat-* which roughly translates to "related" and "told," *narrare* ("to tell"), and late Latin *narrativus* ("telling a story"), and are similar to Latin *gnarus* ("knowing"), which is derived from ancient Sanskrit *gna* ("to know") (Kim, 2016). Narrative is a form of knowledge that has two sides: to tell and to know, and it has long been critical to human life. The act of narration is the unique and almost universal aspect of how humans express themselves and how we come to know.

It is also helpful for our purposes within this chapter to clearly delineate the differences between story and narrative. While some narrative researchers use the terms interchangeably, story is a detailed organization of narrative events, which has a beginning, middle, and, eventually, an end. This organization allows for a fuller representation of lived experiences, whereas a narrative can only allude to a partial description of lived experience. A useful metaphor can liken narrative to a rich and boundless patterned quilt; within the quilt are infinite patches with their own borders (their own beginning, middle, and end), and each uniquely designed. These individual patches can, within this metaphor, offer a vague understanding of the richer tapestry to which it contributes, but the entire blanket itself will always present a partial understanding. A patch, however, can be known more fully and provide a more unique account of itself while also resembling the other patches within the quilt because they each are of the same general shape. Thus, narratives enable stories, and stories rely on narratives, and they remain perpetually and intimately intertwined. Another way to think about their differences is this: narratives are driven by context and can be viewed as a larger system through which stories are interpreted, symbolized, and reasoned. Thus, narrative can be described as a *system of stories*, and it is the connections between those stories available to us that influence how we know, how we act, and who we are. *Storytelling* is how we communicate not only how we experience our lives, but who we are; sometimes, but not always, these stories travel and take on a larger effect and encompass a more universal telling of human experience.

Narrative inquiry, then, is built on the tenets which underlie qualitative research — where knowledge concerning human matters is seen through interpretive epistemologies, making room for the complicated nature of the human condition. *Narrative* is a way of how we come to know (Bruner, 2014; Lyotard, 1979), and thus can be an important tool in research. It has become a field in its own right, proliferating within all kinds of disciplines in the social, human, and natural sciences. Narrative as a focal point of research is increasingly seen as a credible way to deeply understand human matters and how we make sense of them.

Narrative inquiry as a unique approach to research

Unlike other research approaches framed within the positivist paradigm, narrative inquiry "offers no automatic starting or finishing points...no overall rules about suitable materials or modes of investigation, or the best level way at which to study stories" (Andrews et al., 2013, p.1). Narrative inquiry is interdisciplinary and has far-reaching usage for a wide variety of disciplines because it grounds itself in a narrative way of knowing and seeks to understand experience through the stories people tell about their lives (Polkinghorne, 1995). Narrative inquiry focuses on understanding *the experiences of others and experience itself*, with central attention to the relationships between tellers and knowers (Clandinin et al., 2018).

"We tell ourselves stories in order to live" is the title of Joan Didion's (2006) collection of nonfiction essays, but it also describes the *essence* of narrative inquiry: that is, it is the study of the stuff of life, of lived experiences. Lived experience is often complex, contradictory, nuanced, and unpredictable, and thus not wholly congruent with the paradigmatic way of knowing which seeks definitive truth, rather than interpretative truth. This is what narrative inquiry can help to explore, understand, and expound upon: what it means to be and know in the world. It makes no claims to objectivity, and instead focuses on what we can learn from one another by engaging with one another in more authentic, local, and human ways.

Narrative inquiry problematizes and interrogates "the nature of dominant curricular stories through which humans have shaped their understanding" (Kim, 2016, p. 19). It makes research relatable and accessible because it is about people and experiences we can envision, while providing deep and nuanced knowledge for a variety of disciplines.

Narrative inquiry may feel "new," but is a practice that is as old as humanity itself (Clandinin, 2006), as humans have always lived and told stories to one another that, once unleashed into the world, help us to create meaning in our lives. It is through the sharing of those stories with one another and in how we enlist other's help in the living of those stories that we not only create meaning, but we also build community. Thus, at its core, narrative inquiry is a relational endeavor.

While narrative inquiry as a practice is not new (it has been used in various other qualitative research methods (autoethnography, oral history, biography, and others to name a few), narrative inquiry as an established research methodology, particularly in the social sciences, is relatively recent (Clandinin, 2006). With this burgeoning methodology, "has come intensified talk about our stories, their function in our lives, and their place in composing our collective affairs" (p. 44). Hence, one might use narrative inquiry if their research is focused on understanding, making meaning from, and improving the human condition. For example, in law, narrative inquiry has been used to explore counter-stories as a way to reveal and challenge injustice and make the legal system more equitable. Counter-stories are the stories told by people, often marginalized, whose experiences challenge commonsense norms, beliefs, and assumptions held by the general public. They are stories that offer alternative ways of knowing while giving voice and power back to the people (Delgado, 1989) and help to broaden the perspectives of those who are a part of and benefit from society's dominant group ideology (Clandinin

& Rosiek, 2006). Within the field of medicine, narrative inquiry has been used to humanize medicine and take a more holistic view of healing, rather than relying on the paradigmatic mode that has proliferated in the field. As Bleakley (2005) wrote, though qualitative research is sometimes seen as soft, contrasted with the hard sciences, "narrative inquiry's soft data can illuminate hard realities" (p. 535). In fact, as early as the 1920s, medical professors complained that students knew a great deal about how diseases progressed, but very little of how to take care of and relate to their patients — stressing the importance of narrative and the humanities, in general (Schwartz et al., 2009). Another field in which narrative inquiry has made an impact is psychology, a discipline that seeks to understand the human mind. Whereas many psychological practitioners are trained in the more clinical mode of psychology, it is the narrative mode by which both patients and their treatment providers create meaning. Narrative is important in psychology because it impacts how clinicians hear their patients, how patients report their lives, how patients are observed, and how research is conducted.

Understanding how narrative is used in other disciplines allows the researcher to adapt unique approaches to experience and phenomena to their own disciplines, and, in turn, altering the nature of those disciplines in the process. This adoption and integration from other disciplines underpins the interdisciplinary nature of narrative inquiry, ultimately creating more enriched and enhanced research practice.

The boundaries, ethics, and reflexivity in narrative inquiry

Narrative inquiry finds differences between those with "'realist,' 'modernist,' 'postmodern,' and constructionist strands" (Riessman & Speedy, 2006, p. 428). Additionally, narrative inquiry projects differ according to their epistemological, ideological, and ontological foundations, differences that at first glance will be less stark than narrative inquiry's differences with other approaches (Clandinin & Rosiek, 2006). It is also helpful to keep in mind that the commonality among all different projects of narrative inquiry is that "narrative inquirers study experience" (Clandinin, 2006, p. 45). Then, how a narrative inquirer defines 'experience' will also inevitably influence the boundaries of the project. For example, Aristotle's dualistic notion of experience where the subjective and the objective are considered separate from one another, necessarily influences the orientation one may take to how people experience their lives. A Feminist and Marxist understanding of experience will view it as locally situated and distorted by ideology and wider cultural and gender norms. A poststructuralist understanding of experience will draw upon the discursive practices that make up our reality, and so on. In short, the boundaries of a narrative inquiry project will be limited to the researcher's perception of experience. While narrative inquirers study the individual's experience, they are also always exploring the wider narratives and stories within which the individual's experience is situated. Through their study of an individual's experience — how they make meaning with the world and the impact the world has mediated that meaning — narrative inquiry helps to not only deepen our understanding of human conditions, but can also enrich and transform them, making a personal story a social story (Clandinin & Rosiek, 2006).

Reflexivity as an ethical necessity

Every researcher must address ethical issues that arise during both the procedural process that occurs before research is conducted and in the space between the researcher and its participants when the research is actively being conducted (Guillemin & Gillam, 2004). While considering the ethics of a research project before it is underway regarding its ability to satisfy the protection of participants' basic rights and from abuse is important, it does not fully address the ethical issues that often arise during the conduction of research. Inherently, to be viewed as and used as a participant in a research study can render obsolete an individual's autonomy and objectify them in one swoop. In other words, if attention is not paid to the inherent ethical tension that is the crux of research itself, it can be easy for participants to be used to an end — simply objects used to generate new knowledge, rather than full beings with rights, autonomy, and dignity.

Measures can and must be taken to address this ethical tension, and the process of narrative inquiry is particularly well-suited to this task. To resolve the ethical problem of objectifying research subjects, the researcher can adopt a more collaborative approach to the design and goals of the research project — in other words, research subjects become research participants who are joined with the researcher in the goals, interpretations, and creation of new knowledge. This can be partially addressed when gaining informed consent (and requires more than just getting some paperwork signed) but does not fully address the harms that can occur *during* the process of conducting qualitative research.

For example, consider an interview with a research subject-participant who becomes audibly distraught while recounting their story to you, the researcher, who is trying to gain data about the experiences of those who struggle with intrusive passive suicidal ideation. Does one continue to move through the interview, or would the researcher pause to check-in and provide some kind of comfort? Even if there may be an obvious right answer, it does not negate the fact that there is an ethical tension between the role of the researcher and the impulses of being an empathetic human being conversing with another human being. Nor does it take away the fact that no matter the choice, there is the potential for wrongdoing or harm to come about from this seemingly easy choice (to stop and comfort the participant). These ethics in practice are the moments that Komesaroff (1995) referred to as microethics. These are those moments that may not feel so much like a dilemma, choosing between two seemingly opposite but equally weighed options, but they still carry ethical importance (Guillemin & Gillam, 2004). The process we suggest to both highlight and explore the microethics of conducting a narrative inquiry research project is reflexivity.

Reflexivity is more than mere reflection; it is a reflection of our reflection, and an othering of the researcher's self in the research process as well as the writing process. Creswell (2013) posits it is impossible to write position-less — we are always writing from a particular stance because we cannot remove ourselves from the equation. Whatever we write reflects our own interpretations of experience that are in turn shaped by our cultural, social, gender, class, and personal backgrounds. Qualitative researchers no longer try to "...play God, writing as disembodied omniscient narrators claiming universal and atemporal general knowledge" (Richardson & St. Pierre, 2005, p. 961). To write in this way is disingenuous, as many postmodern thinkers have deconstructed the meanings behind these texts, arguing that they cannot be understood without considering an authors' concealment of their personal life and how they came to their thinking. Additionally, ethical considerations of qualitative writing, and particularly narrative inquiry, must consider the impact of the writing on participants and the reader. It is also important to consider how participants will interpret the writing of their stories, and whether or not the writing marginalizes or offends them in some way. For readers, the writing also has an impact, and the writer has no real way to control how what they write will be interpreted. Though language is the main tool we have to convey our interpretations of "truth," it is an imperfect tool that is filtered through multiple perspectives and positions. Thus, an ethical requirement of narrative inquiry is the concept of reflexivity wherein the writer can be more intentional about representing in a responsible manner.

Guillemin and Gillam (2004) not only discuss the importance of reflexivity as an ethical tool in qualitative research but also propose that reflexivity be used as a conceptual tool for understanding both the nature of ethics in research and how ethical practice in research can be achieved. A practice of reflexivity that is commonly found in narrative inquiry is a subjectivist, confessional kind of reflexive practice (Foley, 2002), which is a self-critique that pulls apart one's role as a researcher, intermingled with one's subjective human experience *as* a researcher. The researcher steps back to take a critical look at her or his own role in the research process (Guillemin & Gillam, 2004; Mosselson, 2010). Thus, one's fears, doubts, selfish intentions, contradictions, and multiple selves are laid to bare, and the question is always asked: how did one's subjectivity influence or become impacted by the research process?

Creswell (2013) offers the outlines of two parts to guide one's use of reflexivity. The first part requires that the "researcher...talks about his or her experiences with the phenomenon being explored" (p. 216). In this part, the writer would report on past experiences such as work, schooling, biographical history, and so forth. In the second part Creswell (2013) writes about the necessity to then "discuss how these past experiences shaped the researcher's interpretation of the phenomenon" (p. 216). Thus, in the first part the researcher simply relays their experiences with the phenomenon under study, but in the second part they report how those experiences then shaped their findings.

Reflexivity is a tool that one uses throughout a narrative inquiry project to provide a more accurate and authentic account of the research process, thereby helping to achieve rigorous research that upholds the integrity of the researcher, as well as a project's participants. Reflexivity is not just a critical skill needed to add credibility to narrative inquiry, but we argue that it is also a disposition that a narrative researcher must possess. By embodying the principles of reflexivity, we are upholding our commitment to exercise wise and ethical judgment. In other words, to practice reflexivity is to not just view it as something we *do*, but something we *are*.

Limitations of narrative inquiry

Narrative inquiry is a complex, multilayered, and diverse endeavor that is both a phenomenon and method (Clandinin & Connelly, 2000). This makes sense because it is ultimately about the stories of people — how they create, realize, live, and make meaning of their experiences — and people, as we well know, are incredibly complicated and contradictory. A complex research methodology for a complex subject — why, then, would its critical issues be any different?

The issues that are brought up within a narrative inquiry project will depend on many factors: who you are as a researcher, the questions you run into about your participants, the research context, and so on. Perhaps, then, the biggest limitation of narrative inquiry is its seemingly boundlessness — how does a narrative inquirer ground themself, or are we to become more comfortable with the unknown? This is what we argue: that if a researcher is to embark on a narrative inquiry project, then they should understand that it is a field that requires flexibility, open-mindedness, and an understanding that there are always multiple ways to view and understand something; a narrative inquirer should approach the critical issues that may arise during their research as if they were looking through a kaleidoscope — with a slight twist of the instrument, the issue may change in color, change shape, or even disappear altogether, molding into a different shape entirely.

Rashomon effect

One issue that narrative inquirers will doubtlessly run into, as many qualitative researchers do, is the Rashomon effect. The Rashomon effect is a situation wherein multiple people give multiple and contradictory accounts of the same phenomenon. According to Kim (2016), it came from a 1950 Japanese movie, *Rashomon*, directed by famous 20th century director, Akira Kurosawa. The movie follows people who each experienced the murder of a man differently. Each of the four characters give a plausible account of the hows, whys, and whos of the murder, while also contradicting another character's account of the same murder. At the end of the movie, the viewers are left with only questions and no conclusive answers as to who killed the husband, why, and how. Thus, the movie is ultimately about how our experiences of even the same event are subject to personal biases and histories.

Because narrative inquirers largely work with the stories that people tell about their experiences, it inevitably means we may receive conflicting stories from individuals, or stories that we view as self-serving, and stories that are only a partial view of the larger narrative. In narrative inquiry, researchers should go into the project understanding that when dealing with humans and human matters, several things may take place. First, that for every story told, a larger piece of a much larger story may be missing, and we are only ever able to examine one small part of a much bigger narrative. Second, narrative inquiry is conducted within three dimensions of space (Clandinin & Connelly, 2000): "the personal and social (interaction); past, present, and future (continuity); [and] place (situation)" (Clandinin, 2006, p. 47). Thus, narrative inquirers must understand the possibility that depending on where their research was situated along these dimensions (when, where, and situational context), the stories they receive and derive meaning from may vary. And third, the narrative inquiry researcher must take their own subjectivity into account through reflexivity: their personality, values, cultural and religious norms, and so on, as these may affect their findings.

While we cannot expect to account for all the limitations which may occur due to the Rashomon effect, we can think about limitations in terms of different perspectives and how they can enrich the narrative inquiry project.

Backyard research

In an era that is marked by increased demands of productivity, the urge to complete what is called *backyard research* is growing more prevalent among fledgling researchers. It is also important to note that backyard research, a term for research in one's personal environment whether it be the workplace, neighborhood, or affinity group that is a part of one's daily life or lived experiences (Glesne & Peshkin, 1991), is a legitimate form of research. In addition, backyard research is convenient and efficient because relationships are already established. And one does not have to go far to conduct fieldwork and gather data. Not to mention, there is great value in understanding the particular experiences of more localized populations that may previously have not been seen as *research worthy*.

However, it is not without risks. Because the nature of backyard research necessitates already established relationships, the distinction between 'researcher' and 'participant' can become blurry and unclear. Another potential problem can arise from the ethical and political arenas. For example, if a narrative inquirer seeks to understand the work experiences of women in a male-dominated field at a small company, they run the risk of not being able to solicit "real" accounts due to participants worrying about retaliation at their job if they don't provide a glowing review.

Backyard research can provide rich information that may otherwise go uncollected; however, it is also important to understand the confusion over roles and boundaries that can occur, as well as issues around ethics, politics, and confidentiality.

Pedagogical implications of narrative inquiry

As we noted earlier, narrative has been established as a legitimate way of knowing, different from the paradigmatic way of knowing. It is a medium through which we as human beings can understand ourselves and others (Ricoeur, 1991). Therefore, narrative inquiry has further pedagogical implications beyond utilization as a research methodology; it has also impacted how we educate and train educators. In particular, narrative inquiry is used as a curricular and pedagogical strategy in the field of teacher education, and pedagogical means to teach one's reflexive process that should occur in classrooms. A few ways it has been used in this regard is through the encouragement of a reflexive process for teachers to explore and problematize their own teaching and learning; as a strategy for professional development of teachers and administrators (Clark & Medina, 2000; Macintyre Latta & Kim, 2010); and as a tool to interrogate the interconnections between literacy, pedagogy, and culture (see, for example, Conle, 2000; Coulter et al., 2007; Lyons & LaBoskey, 2002).

Clark and Medina (2000), for example, demonstrated how narrative can play a role of pedagogy in shaping pre-service teachers' understanding about literacy and multiculturalism. With secondary education master's students as research participants, Clark and Medina examined the participants' literacy narratives involving reading and writing, conceptualizing narrative and narrative theory as a way of knowing (Bruner, 1986), as we discussed earlier. They stated, "Narrative became an interesting site of praxis — a place to bring our thinking and theorizing about literacy and multiculturalism together with approaches to teaching" (p. 64). In doing so, Clark and Medina further emphasized the role of narrative as a means of exploring different ways of knowing in relation to teaching and learning.

Similarly, Macintyre-Latta and Kim (2010) documented how narrative inquiry could create the space for exploring teacher agency and praxis evidenced in their classroom practices. They interrogated the possibilities of narrative inquiry in developing praxis for educators and discovered how narrative inquiry had contributed to fostering a culture of professional teaching and learning. Hence, narrative inquiry works not only as a meaningful research methodology that explores the lived experience of storytellers but also as a pedagogical medium that fosters professional development.

Possible future directions of narrative inquiry: Posthuman narrative inquiry

Narrative inquiry is both a research approach and a phenomena used to tell and know, and it has largely been isolated to human-centered concerns to improve and better understand the human condition. Critical to these narratives is the understanding that humans have of themselves — how they define 'human' and who is included and who is not within that parameter. The language we use to define 'human' has many implications for how we are in the world and the narratives we create, leaving out many "Others" that might help us further expand how we define ourselves. We envision a new direction for narrative inquiry, and that is for it to consider those "Others" using posthuman philosophy.

Currently, there is a movement in ontological and epistemological framework in the social and human sciences, signaling 'after the human' as a way to decenter "Man" that is considered to be the measure of all things (Kuby, 2017; Snaza & Weaver, 2015). This posthumanist movement includes, but is not limited to, feminist materialism (Barad, 2007), new materialism (Coole & Frost, 2010), and more than human ontologies (Jackson & Mazzei, 2012). In particular, Kuby (2017) writes why there should be a paradigm shift of more than human ontologies. She states, "As educational researchers, it is our responsibility to children, families, and our material world to better understand the realities, knowledges, and relationships being produced daily in the intra-actions of materials (human and non-human) and discourses" (Kuby, 2017, p. 881).

Conceptualizing narrative inquiry with a posthuman philosophy is not only necessary, but it is socially just; after all, numerous atrocities have been committed in the name of humanity and centered around our exclusionary definition of human, such as genocide, colonization, slavery, war, the extermination of entire animal species, and our general treatment of the planet we share. It is this classical rendering of the human subject around which, we believe, oppression is justified and then further reified by the human-centric narratives we privilege within qualitative methodologies. Earlier we wrote that a primary concern of the narrative inquiry researcher should not be to just study the human condition, but to also search for ways we might improve it; a posthuman narrative inquiry is in-line with this goal.

We believe that the current paradigm within narrative inquiry that is human-centric presents a unique opportunity to think differently about the research methodology. It opens space for narrative inquirers to ask: *what if narrative inquiry were made less human-centric and took on a more-than-human, maybe even a posthuman definition of human experience, particularly in relation to language?* It is from this important problematizing of the classical human subject that we hope to suggest that the direction of future narrative inquiry include the narratives and stories of nonhuman, other-than-, or more-than human, by decentering the human and de-privileging the classical human narrative.

Drawing upon posthuman theory, which avoids humanistic ideals to include nonhumans, other-than-humans, and more-than-humans in philosophical discussions (Braidotti, 2013a, b), we challenge narrative inquirers to go beyond the stories of our fellow humans and to decenter ourselves, so that we can further investigate and struggle with what it means to be human in the age of anthropocentrism. It is in this struggle, we believe, that we may engage a new way of thinking and doing narrative inquiry, with the added benefit of expanding our definition of narrative, and who is privileged in the telling of it. Doing this in no way negates the human, but instead creates space for a larger and more encompassing vision for humanity — what happens when we are more intentional with including those non-human actors in the telling and creating of narrative? We hope that in reconceptualizing narrative inquiry through posthumanism, how we tell and know human experiences is made larger and more inclusive.

Posthuman theory problematizes the language we use to define the "human," around which so much of human identity revolves, and it highlights our interdependency on all those other-than-human things we tend to ignore — the mundane, the four-legged, the inanimate, the plant in the corner, the mushrooms that pop up after a rainstorm (Braidotti, 2013a; Snaza & Weaver, 2015). Additionally, a posthuman lens urges researchers to look for ways to abolish hierarchical thinking and falling into rigid binaries supported by the language we use and specific to our classical idea of the human subject. For too long, nonhumans, other-than-humans, and more-than-humans have been relegated to an inconsequential backdrop of animal life; the further an organism seems from our traditional understanding of the human, who is placed conveniently at the center, the less important the organism is labeled and, inevitably, treated.

Despite this knowledge, we know from a wide range of the human and social science fields such as linguistics, biology, botany, astrophysics, and so on, that many of the so-called innate and lesser beings and organisms are capable of sophisticated behaviors, which trouble our notions of what it means to communicate, make decisions, remember, and, specific to this chapter, tell stories (Sheldrake, 2020). This posthuman knowledge becomes an ethical issue to consider that humans are no longer being seen as the center of knowledge and all things, that the hierarchy and privilege of its status also comes into question (Braidotti, 2013b).

Framing posthuman narrative inquiry as a possible future direction, we hope for a more inclusive and affirmative usage of narrative inquiry. In effect, posthuman narrative inquiry can help us challenge our current views on whose stories are privileged or listened to; create a larger and more inclusive human identity; and expand our notions of what constitutes the human experience. It is our recommendation that narrative inquirers embrace and encompass the stories of more-than, less-than, and-other-than human beings, and further trouble our notions of the human subject. Such a direction, we argue, is a calling that narrative inquiry can respond to in the age of anthropocentrism.

Conclusion

Throughout this chapter we have described how narrative inquiry came to be, beginning with understanding the influence of positivism in our shaping of knowledge, learning the difference between the paradigmatic and narrative modes of knowing, and how to define the concepts of narrative and story. We have also briefly outlined the contours of what narrative inquiry as a research methodology looks like, as well as highlighted its unique contributions to many different disciplines, along with its limitations. We leave the reader with possible future directions for how narrative inquiry can be further conceptualized through posthumanism, and we hope to inspire current and future students with a better understanding of the power of narrative — how our stories shape our realities, and how we, in turn, shape one another.

References

Andrews, M., Squire, C., & Tamboukou, M. (2013). *Doing narrative research* (2nd ed.). Sage.

Barad, K. (2007). *Meeting the universe halfway: Quantum physics and the entanglement of matter and meaning.* Duke University Press.

Bleakle, A. (2005). Stories as data, data as stories: Making sense of narrative inquiry in clinical education. *Medical Education, 39*(5), 534–540.

Braidotti, R. (2013a). *The posthuman.* Wiley. Kindle Edition.

Braidotti, R. (2013b). Posthuman humanities. *European Educational Research Journal, 12*(1), 1–19.

Bruner, J. (1986). *Actual minds, possible worlds.* Harvard University Press.

Bruner, J. (2014). Life as narrative. *Social Research, 71*(3), 691–710.

Clandinin, D. J. (2006). Narrative inquiry: A methodology for studying lived experience. *Research Studies in Music Education, 27*(1), 44–54.

Clandinin, D. J., & Connelly, F. M. (2000). *Narrative inquiry: Experience and story in qualitative research.* Jossey-Bass.

Clandinin, D. J., & Rosiek. (2006). Mapping a landscape of narrative inquiry: Borderland spaces and tensions. In D. J. Clandinin (Ed.), *Handbook of narrative inquiry: Mapping a methodology* (pp. 35–75). Sage.

Clandinin, D. J., Caine, V., & Lessard, S. (2018). *The relational ethics of narrative inquiry.* Routledge.

Clark, C. & Medina, C. (2000). How reading and writing literacy narratives affect preservice teachers' understandings of literacy, pedagogy, and multiculturalism. *Journal of Teacher Education, 51*(1), 63–76.

Conle, C. (2000). Narrative inquiry: Research tool and medium for professional development. *European Journal of Teacher Education, 23*(1), 49–63.

Coole, D., & Frost, S. (Eds.) (2010). *New materialisms: Ontology, agency, and politics.* Duke University Press.

Coulter, C., Michael, C., & Poynor, L. (2007). Storytelling as pedagogy: An unexpected outcome of narrative inquiry. *Curriculum Inquiry, 37*(2), 103–122.

Creswell, J. W. (2013). *Qualitative inquiry & research design: Choosing among five approaches.* Sage.

Delgado, R. (1989). Storytelling for oppositionists and others: A plea for narrative. *Michigan Law Review, 87*(8), 2411–2441.

Didion, J. (2006). *We tell ourselves stories in order to live.* Knopf.

Fludernik, M. (2005). Histories of narrative theory (11): From structuralism to the present. In J. Phelan & P. Rabinowitz (Eds.), *A companion to narrative theory* (pp. 36–59). Blackwell.

Foley, D. (2002). Critical ethnography: The reflexive turn. *International Journal of Qualitative Studies in Education, 15*(4), 469–490.

Georgakopoulou, A. (2006). Thinking big with small stories in narrative and identity analysis. *Narrative Inquiry, 16*(1), 122–130.

Glesne, C., & Peshkin, A. (1991). *Becoming qualitative researchers.* Longman.

Goldin, D. (2019). Narrative as a mode of knowing. *Psychoanalytic Inquiry, 39*(7), 512–524.

doi Guillemin, M., & Gillam, L. (2004). Ethics, reflexivity, and 'ethically important moments' in research. *Qualitative Inquiry, 10*(2), 261–280.

Jackson, A.Y., & Mazzei, L.A. (2012). *Thinking with theory in qualitative research: Viewing data across multiple perspectives.* Routledge.

doi Kim, J.H. (2016). *Understanding narrative inquiry: The crafting and analysis of stories as research.* Sage.

Komesaroff, P. (1995). From bioethics to microethics: Ethical debate and clinical medicine. In P. Komesaroff (Ed.), *Troubled bodies: Critical perspectives on postmodernism, medical ethics and the body* (pp. 62–86). Melbourne University Press.

doi Kuby, C. (2017). Why a paradigm shift of 'more than human ontologies' is needed: Putting to work poststructural and posthuman theories in writers' studio. *International Journal of Quaitative Studies in Eduction, 30*(9), 877–896.

Lyons, N., & LaBoskey, V.K. (2002). Why narrative inquiry or exemplars for a shcolarship of teaching? In N. Lyns & V.K. LaBoskey (Eds.), *Narrative inquiry in practice: Advancing the knowledge of teaching* (pp. 11–30). Teachers College Press.

Lyotard, J. (1979/1984). *The postmodern condition: A report on knowledge* (G.M. Bennington & B. Massum Trans.). University of Minnesota Press.

doi Macintyre-Latta, M., & Kim, J. (2010). Narrative inquiry invites professional development: Educators claim the creative space of praxis. *The Journal of Educational Research, 103,* 137–148.

doi Mosselson, J. (2010). Subjectivity and reflexivity: Locating the self in research on dislocation. *International Journal of Qualitative Studies in Education, 23*(4), 479–494.

Ochs, E., & Capps, L. (2001). *Living narrative: Creating lives in everyday storytelling.* Harvard University Press.

Polkinghorne, D. (1995). Narrative configuration as qualitative analysis. In J.A. Hatch & R. Wisniewski (Eds.), *Life history and narrative* (pp. 5–25). Falmer Press.

Richardson, L., & St. Pierre, E.A. (2005). Writing: A method of inquiry. In N.K. Denzin & Y.S. Lincoln (Eds.), *The Sage handbook of qualititve research* (3rd ed., pp. 959–978). Sage.

doi Ricoeur, P. (1991). Narrative identity. *Philosophy Today, 35*(1), 73–81.

Riessman, C.K., & Speedy, J. (2006). Narrative inquiry in social work, counseling, and psychotherapy: A critical review. In D.J. Candinin (Ed.), *Handbook of narrative inquiry: Mapping a methodology* (pp. 426–456). Sage.

doi Schwartz, A., Abramson, J., Wojnowich, I., Accordino, R., Ronan, E., & Rifkin, M. (2009). Evaluating the impact of the humanities in medical education. *The Mount Sinai Journal of Medicine, 76*(4), 372–380.

Sheldrake, M. (2020). *Entangled life: How fungi make our worlds, change our minds, and shape our futures.* Random House.

Snaza, N., & Weaver, J.A. (Eds.). (2015). *Posthumanism and educational research.* Routledge.

Reflectivity and reflexivity and Applied Linguistics Research

CHAPTER 6

Affordances and limitations of autoethnography as a research method in Applied Linguistics

Ana Bocanegra-Valle
University of Cadiz

This chapter explores the affordances and limitations of autoethnography as a research method in Applied Linguistics (AL) and assesses if current literature within the fields of ELT/TESOL and of academic literacies enhances or questions autoethnography as a research method. It first reviews the main approaches to autoethnography and then moves on to consider the ways autoethnographically-oriented studies from major AL publications meet the goals of these approaches. At this stage, the contribution of autoethnography to current AL research is examined through close analysis of 40 studies published in relevant journals and books. In particular, this chapter explores the affordances and limitations of autoethnography as a research method that are revealed in these studies. Lastly, the ethical dilemmas faced by autoethnographers in the studies under review when conducting their research and writing their narratives are also addressed.

Autoethnography has been defined as "an experimental style or genre in applied linguistics" (Yazan et al., 2021, p. 6), an emerging and avant-garde method (Starfield, 2019; Wall, 2006) that either limits or enhances research practice. In the field of Applied Linguistics (AL), autoethnography assists researchers when making use of their own experiences, beliefs and practices to interpret and understand language-related phenomena as part of individual and institutional cultures.

This chapter recognises the diversity of AL and explores what autoethnography as a research method has to offer to AL scholarship; however, it intentionally confines its discussion and analysis to two particular domains within AL, namely, ELT/TESOL and academic literacies. In this exploration, special attention will be paid to the affordances and limitations of autoethnography in these fields. Previous studies (e.g., Adams et al., 2017; Chang, 2008; Ellis et al., 2011; Méndez, 2013) have identified the potentials and limitations of autoethnography as a research

https://doi.org/10.1075/rmal.8.06boc

method; however, and except for Mirhosseini (2018), similar studies within AL are rare. This chapter, therefore, aims to fill this gap.

The chapter is divided into five main sections. The first section provides an overview of the main approaches to autoethnography. The next three sections review the affordances and limitations of autoethnography as a research method through the close analysis of 40 autoethnographically-oriented studies. The last section examines ethical challenges and dilemmas that feature in autoethnography and are depicted in the selected studies. The chapter concludes by considering the limitations of autoethnography and the implications for further AL research.

Main approaches to autoethnography as a research method

Autoethnography is a qualitative method of inquiry that uses the ethnographic approach "to bring cultural interpretation to the autobiographical data of researchers with the intent of understanding self and its connection to others" (Chang, 2008, p. 56). Autoethnographic research varies depending on the emphasis placed on the personal experience ("auto"), the cultural experience ("ethno") or the research process ("graphy"), and also on "the nature of the issue, the context, and researcher tendencies" (Mirhosseini, 2018, p. 80). Accordingly, there are three main approaches to autoethnography: evocative, analytical, and collaborative.

Evocative (also "heartfelt" or "emotional") autoethnography favours emotional self-reflexivity to produce meaningful and accessible texts based on personal experience. It addresses personal issues and circumstances usually shrouded in silence and aims at evoking emotional responses from readers (Adams et al., 2017; Ellis, 2007; Ellis et al., 2011). Evocative autoethnography has been criticised on the grounds of personal subjectivity and lack of theorisation.

Analytical (also "analytic" or "realistic") autoethnography goes beyond the self to involve others in the research and is characterised by: theoretical analysis, analytic reflexivity, researcher's narrative visibility, dialogue with informants beyond the self, and full researcher positionality as a member in the social group or setting under investigation (Anderson, 2006).

In collaborative autoethnography (CAE) a team of researchers works together collaboratively and cooperatively, sharing their personal experiences and pooling their stories as data to find commonalities and differences (Chang et al., 2013). In comparison with the two approaches above, CAE has been acknowledged to be a powerful method of team building that lends itself to greater rigour (Lapadat, 2017).

Analysis of autoethnographically-oriented studies

What are the affordances and limitations of autoethnography as a research method? How are they portrayed in existing journal articles and book chapters within AL? To what extent do AL studies meet the goals of the main approaches to autoethnography? What does autoethnography as a research method offer to current scholarship in AL?

In order to answer these questions, I examined autoethnography-inspired articles published until spring 2022 in 24 relevant journals in AL. Regarding the search process, I first searched the term "ethnography" in article titles, abstracts, keywords, and main text, and found 2,596 articles. Then, the search was narrowed down to the term "autoethnography" in the same query fields. This also narrowed down the number of journals and articles (to 10 and 44, respectively). I had a closer look at those 44 apparently autoethnographically-oriented articles and eventually excluded those that did not use autoethnography as a methodological approach and did not fall within the scope of ELT/TESOL and academic literacies. Search queries were limited to these subfields for two main reasons: firstly, to match personal research interests (see Guillén-Galve & Bocanegra-Valle, 2021); and, secondly, because autoethnography has been found to be a common approach for the study of teachers and other social entities pertinent to the teaching context (Loo, 2017). This selection yielded the first 20 articles shown in Table 1. Three more studies were added from other AL journals that had unexpectedly become visible in the first search queries (see "Other articles" in Table 1). Lastly, some recent AL books containing chapters with a clear autoethnographic focus were added to the corpus with a view to enhancing the discussion (see "Book chapters" in Table 1).

Regarding the analysis procedure, I analysed the final group of 40 studies (comprising 23 articles and 17 book chapters) thoroughly and filled in a table with these items: research goals, context, writing genre, autoethnographic approach, and data-collection materials. I completed this basic information with notes and verbatim extracts on the challenges, weaknesses, fears, strengths and opportunities that were reported by the authors when conducting their research. The discussion that follows is based on the insights gained from the analysis of this group of 40 academic studies.

Table 1. Autoethnographically-Oriented studies under review

Publication		Selected studies
Journals	Applied Linguistics	1. Phipps (2012)
	Journal of Second Language Writing	2. Sánchez-Martín & Seloni (2019)
	Language Teaching	3. Wijayatilake (2012)
	Language Teaching Research	4. Busteed (2022)
		5. Hooper (2022)
		6. Liu, Yuan, & Wang (2021)
	Linguistics and Education	7. Fallas-Escobar & Pentón Herrera (2022)
	Modern Language Journal	8. McGregor & Fernández (2019)
	RELC Journal	9. Banegas & del Pozo Beamud (2022)
		10. Liu (2020)
		11. Rose & Montakantiwong (2018)
		12. Sondari (2021)
	System	13. Back et al. (2021)
		14. Miyahara & Fukao (2022)
		15. Song (2022)
	TESOL Journal	16. Solano-Campos (2014)
		17. Yazan (2019)
		18. Zacharias (2019)
	TESOL Quarterly	19. Atkinson & Sohn (2013)
		20. Canagarajah (2012)
Other articles		21. Ai (2016)
		22. Catalano, Shende, & Suh (2018)
		23. Kim & Saenkhum (2019)
Book chapters		24. Burgess (2021)
		25. Carciu (2021)
		26. Darvin (2021)
		27. Deroo (2021)
		28. Deveci (2021)
		29. Fazel (2021)
		30. Gormley (2021)
		31. Habibie, Swayer & Norris (2021)
		32. Herrando-Rodrigo (2021)
		33. Kohls (2021)
		34. McCulloch (2021)
		35. Mochizuki (2021)
		36. Mur-Dueñas (2019)
		37. Olmos-Lopez (2021)
		38. Shahriari (2021)
		39. Shaw (2021)
		40. Van Viegen (2021)

Affordances of autoethnography as a research method

It is difficult to solely showcase the advantages offered by autoethnography because, as is the case with all research methods, some strengths might also entail some kind of limitation. What follows is, therefore, a discussion of the potential of autoethnography in light of the analysis of the studies under review.

Autoethnography as a researcher-centered approach

Autoethnography places the researcher in the centre of the research process in an effort to understand the self in connection to others — thus, autoethnographers are insiders in their own research contexts (Duncan, 2004). It is the author's voice that is disclosed to find a place within individual and collective identity, and by exploring internal and external conditions, the depth of the research is enhanced (Mirhosseini, 2018) and researchers sensitise themselves to the topic of investigation (Méndez, 2013).

The self permeates through the 40 studies reviewed, but some of them take a step further to highlight the benefits of drawing on autoethnography for introspection, self-reflection, and self-study, and, therefore, claim their "authorial power" to tell their own stories with their own voice (Yazan et al., 2021, p. 4). By way of example, Fallas-Escobar and Pentón Herrera (2022) explain that they did not take the self as the topic of research but as the site for research, and endeavoured to ensure that their voices were explicit in their narrative. In the same vein, Darvin (2021) adopted his own research profile in academic social platforms as both subject of and tool for his self-reflective account. Ai (2016), Burgess (2021), Carciu (2021), Fazel (2021), Liu et al. (2021), Miyahara and Fukao (2022), Mur-Dueñas (2019), Sánchez-Martín and Seloni (2019), Shaw (2021), Solano-Campos (2014), Sondari (2021), Song (2022) and Van Viegen (2021) are other studies in which the investigation of the self in relation to a cultural site is particularly prominent.

Autoethnography as a driver for change

An important assumption held by autoethnographers is that reality is created by the changing perceptions and beliefs of the viewers and moves along with them (Duncan, 2004) to represent the researchers' right to tell their truth (Méndez, 2013). In an effort to adopt a critical orientation to societal injustices and asymmetrical power relations, autoethnography frequently presents intimate but transgressive accounts (Lapadat, 2017) that challenge the mainstream — this also entails a limitation, which is discussed in the next section. Such critical orientation allows the researchers' personal (often marginalised and minoritised) voices to be heard in their narratives.

In the group of studies reviewed, there are some examples of critical autoethnography that report stories of struggle and conflict, as well as experiences of marginalisation at the intersection of language, gender, ethnicity or nationality, to offer an understanding of authors' complex realities as linguists in their roles of teachers, researchers or academics. Studies like Back et al. (2021), Canagarajah (2012), Sondari (2021), Van Viegen (2021), and Yazan (2019) are overtly reported as critical autoethnographies.

Some studies share the autoethnographers' internal struggles with their teacher identity and the efforts to address reflection for action (Rose & Montakantiwong, 2018) and to cover the need for agency (Canagarajah, 2012; Hooper, 2022; McGregor & Fernández, 2019; Sánchez-Martín & Seloni, 2019; Sondari, 2021; Song, 2022). In line with some chapters in Yazan et al. (2021), there are emotionally charged narratives of transnationals when crossing physical and cultural borders who endeavour to explore complex personal and social issues from the inside and decentre the centre (Ai, 2016; Banegas & del Pozo Beamud, 2022; Canagarajah, 2012; Sánchez-Martín & Seloni, 2019; Shahriari, 2021; Solano-Campos, 2014; Zacharias, 2019). Other diverse issues are also addressed, like those of solidarity, when we are cognizant of how language was used in the process of avoiding the deportation of the authors' daughter (Phipps, 2012), building self-confidence (Deveci, 2021) or documenting raciolinguistic struggles and fighting back against experiences of oppression within institutional settings (Fallas-Escobar & Pentón Herrera, 2022).

Autoethnography as a provider for rich and easily-accessible data

Autoethnographers enact data-collection instruments, data and text authorship (Tullis, 2013) and autoethnographies facilitate the collection of data that could not be otherwise gathered. Because the narratives give access to the researchers' internal and social worlds, autoethnographers provide rich data (Méndez, 2013). Also, because the source and research site are the researchers themselves, the primary data is easily accessible and, thus, autoethnography becomes a researcher-friendly method (Chang, 2008).

As attested by the group of studies under review, rich data can be enhanced in three ways: (i) with the parallel exploration of other participants' similar experiences (Back et al., 2021; Banegas & del Pozo Beamud, 2022; Sánchez-Martín & Seloni, 2019; Wijayatilake, 2012; Zacharias, 2019); (ii) when the temporal dimensions of past, present and future merge in the narrative (Burgess, 2021; Carciu, 2021; Fazel, 2021; Phipps, 2012; Liu, 2020; Solano-Campos, 2014); and (iii) when, as Ellis et al. (2011) explain, common values and beliefs are explored and this helps insiders (cultural members) and outsiders (cultural strangers) in reaching a better understanding of the ethnographer's culture (Atkinson & Sohn, 2013; Busteed, 2022; Gormley, 2021; Liu et al., 2021; McGregor & Fernández, 2019; Rose & Montakantiwong, 2018).

Autoethnography as a method for professional development

In the fields of ELT/TESOL/academic literacies, autoethnography has demonstrated to be beneficial for other teachers and researchers because it portrays similar experiences and raises awareness of the complex issues faced by English teaching professionals in different parts of the world (Loo, 2017).

A common thread in most of the articles reviewed is that autoethnography is an effective tool for promoting professional development and supporting research engagement through reflexivity and self-exploration. This value has become particularly evident in the case of duoethnographies (Banegas & del Pozo Beamud, 2022; Fallas-Escobar & Pentón Herrera, 2022; Kim & Saenkhum, 2019; Rose & Montakantiwong, 2018; Sánchez-Martín & Seloni, 2019) and CAEs (Back et al., 2021; Catalano et al., 2018; Habibie et al., 2021; Miyahara & Fukao, 2022) because authors have explored together their growth as teachers or academic writers and have negotiated identities in an exercise of joint reflective practice and dialogic interaction.

Teachers report their professional careers from the early stages (as students or early-career writers) to the present (as language teachers, teacher trainers, or academics) in an effort to reinterpret their personal experiences, gain insight, and reconstruct their professional identities as enacted by the self within the surrounding cultures (Ai, 2016; Carciu, 2021; Liu, 2020; Mur-Dueñas, 2019; Olmos-Lopez, 2021; Song, 2022). Another option is to present a set of narratives selected from different contexts that describe isolated personal moments to construct dialogues with others and show how teacher identity is gradually built as a network of social interactions (Zacharias, 2019). Also, by going back in time authors bring their personal lived experiences in relation to institutional cultures and create new avenues for personal and professional growth — what Canagarajah (2012) and Fazel (2021) respectively refer to as a "journey of professionalization" (p. 258) or "socialization" (p. 189).

In these authors' career progression, making use of autoethnography as a research method has meant crossing physical borders and ideological boundaries (Ai, 2016; Banegas & del Pozo Beamud, 2022; Shahriari, 2021; Solano-Campos, 2014; Zacharias, 2019), challenging established research evaluation and funding regimes (Fallas-Escobar & Pentón Herrera, 2022; McCulloch, 2021; Van Viegen, 2021), attaining career progression (Burgess, 2021; Wijayatilake, 2012; Hooper, 2022; Liu,

2020), self-monitoring (Carciu, 2021), becoming a scholarly writer (Mochizuki, 2021), engaging in transdisciplinary becoming (Sánchez-Martín & Seloni, 2019), constructing identity (Darvin, 2021; Herrando-Rodrigo, 2021; Kim & Saenkhum, 2019; Sondari, 2021; Yazan, 2019), adapting to new teaching modes (Back et al., 2021; Catalano et al., 2018; Liu et al., 2021; Rose & Montakantiwong, 2018; Song, 2022), understanding participation in online scholarly communities (Darvin, 2021) and interviews in research (McGregor & Fernández, 2019; Miyahara & Fukao, 2022), managing peer reviewing processes (Shaw, 2021), developing writing strategies for publication (Fazel, 2021; Mur-Dueñas, 2019; Olmos-Lopez, 2021), and exploring scholarly publication practices (Habibie et al., 2021) and trajectories (Darvin, 2021; Gormley, 2021; Herrando-Rodrigo, 2021). As these studies reveal, by gaining sensitivity about the self and the surrounding context, teachers, and researchers will be able to open new windows for social inclusion within the profession.

Autoethnography as a therapeutic and emancipatory practice

Autoethnography is a valuable form of inquiry because it informs and educates readers (Ellis et al., 2011; Méndez, 2013), while at the same time it humanizes research (Adams et al., 2017). Autoethnography is therapeutic for authors, who write to make sense of themselves and their experiences, and face stigmas (Lapadat, 2017), but it is also therapeutic for readers, who validate the narrative which they share and feel identified with (Ellis et al., 2011). Also, while reflecting and empathising with the narratives, the author's personal self-exploration is encouraged, and readers become emancipated (Méndez, 2013) and are given a voice (Ellis et al., 2011).

Many authors in the studies under review report a comforting and restorative feeling while writing their texts. Emotional commitment, honesty, and willingness to reflect on painful events are essential to get advantage of the researchers' insider position (Wijayatilake, 2012) as well as to engage with others (Kohls, 2021). Autoethnographies have allowed researchers to access sensitive and private thoughts in pursuing verisimilitude in their social context (Liu et al., 2021); in bringing out their own vulnerabilities that are not spoken in academic circles (Sánchez-Martín & Seloni, 2019; Song, 2022); in asking difficult questions of the selves and writing as a form of self-care researcher (Kohls, 2021); in maturing and growing confidence in one's identity as a member of a community of practice (Herrando-Rodrigo, 2021); in offsetting external and internal loads against external and internal power for increased engagement in academia (Deveci, 2021); or in speaking freely about raciolinguistic inequality and marginalization (Fallas-Escobar & Pentón Herrera, 2022).

Interestingly, a number of authors express their emancipation in relation to nativeness and nativespeakerism, which is a recurrent theme in many narratives. For non-native English teachers and writers, attaining native-like proficiency was key for their social acceptance in the teaching profession and academia and, most importantly, for the construction of teaching identities and community memberships (Canagarajah, 2012; Mochizuki, 2021; Shahriari, 2021; Solano-Campos, 2014; Sondari, 2021; Yazan, 2019; Zacharias, 2019). Likewise, native scholars are aware of the "unearned privilege of facing virtually no linguistic barriers to publishing in an international context" (McCulloch, 2021, p. 267), which helps to embed the self with culture and context.

Wider outreach of autoethnographically-oriented research

Autoethnography has been acknowledged "to create texts that are accessible to larger audiences, primarily audiences outside academic settings" (Adams et al., 2017, p. 4), fostered by the Internet that has created a global platform that supports fascination with personal narratives (Lapadat, 2017). This is an asset for autoethnographers, because their narratives can also reach and engage non-academic audiences. Moreover, because autoethnographies are written in a more personal style that do not always match the established writing conventions in academia, these personal stories become more accessible to diverse readers (this also entails some limitations, which are discussed in the next section). Banegas and del Pozo Beamud (2022) expect that the conversations they engaged in be useful for those teacher educators who do not often do research or write for publication. In the same vein, Back et al. (2021) expect to provide teacher candidates who are not typically engaged in academic research with the process of praxis and opportunities for solidarity. In the field of academic writing, Shahriari (2021) wishes to connect with emerging scholars; and Gormley (2021) hopes that his "embedment of isolated experiences" (p. 259) inspires other scholars to look at discursive and non-discursive realities of writing.

Likewise, the emotional strength of the narrative and the description of everyday moments that are not often captured in academic journal articles help to disclose cultural contexts that would otherwise be hidden by traditional research paradigms (Loo, 2017). This contributes to making these studies more valuable to different readers despite not sharing identical social-cultural contexts or not having lived similar moments. The autoethnographer's introspection brings to the foreground snapshots of their lives which would have remained hidden should autoethnography not have been the method of inquiry. Such lived moments may be evoked with feelings of nostalgia, happiness, or displeasure; they may also be humorous, encouraging or moralising. But they provide the narrative with a literary, evocative tone that makes texts more accessible to non-academic audiences and early-career scholars (see e.g., Burgess, 2021; Canagarajah, 2012; Deroo, 2021; or Kohls, 2021).

Limitations of autoethnography as a research method

The discussion in the next subsections reveals that autoethnography challenges established research methods and practices in many ways and this might explain why autoethnographically-oriented studies are scarce in extant AL literature. Ethics also poses some other limitations which are addressed in a separate section.

The structure of autoethnographically-oriented texts

Authoethnographies exhibit a varied rhetorical structure that steers clear of the canonical article with an Introduction-Methods-Results-Discussion (IMRD) structure of an empirical paper in standard academic writing conventions. This rhetorical variability poses problems in academic journals when empirical articles are submitted for peer review and researchers are expected to strengthen the "graphy" component over the "auto" and "ethno". As Duncan (2004) puts it, in autoethnographic texts "the boundaries of scholarship are merged with artistic expression as a way of challenging the limitations of what is normally accepted as knowledge in academic contexts" (pp. 36–37) — see for example the opening lines of Canagarajah (2012).

   Among the studies reviewed, personal accounts or self-narratives (e.g., Ai, 2016; Mur-Dueñas, 2019; Rose & Montakantiwong, 2018; Song, 2022) are the most frequent genre; however, there are poetic commentaries (Phipps, 2012), self-studies (Liu et al., 2021), epiphanies (Burgess, 2021; Olmos-Lopez, 2021), dialogues (Habibie et al., 2021), exploratory work (Gormley, 2021), or short stories (Canagarajah, 2012). These vary from first-person (e.g., Busteed, 2022; Canagarajah, 2012; Deroo, 2021; Hooper, 2022; Liu, 2020; Song, 2022) to third-person narratives that place the focus on one of the author's (Atkinson & Sohn, 2013; Solano-Campos, 2014) or other participants' autoethnographies (Yazan, 2019). Although rare, it may also be the case that the text is written from a third-person perspective to show that the narratives presented are the authors' own interpretations of their lived experiences as well as to illustrate the way authors inhabit the simultaneous roles of researchers and participants (Kim & Saenkhum, 2019). The use of a simulated third-person may also be an ethical strategy to grant distance and protect the self (Tullis, 2013; see also Chapter 2 and next section on the ethics of autoethnography).

On the grounds of analytic autoethnography: (i) some texts are organised according to research questions so that the study looks like a traditional IMRD research article (Busteed, 2022; Liu et al., 2021; Sánchez-Martín & Seloni, 2019); (ii) a thematic analysis is applied to showcase and analyse prominent themes (Darvin, 2021; Miyahara & Fukao, 2022; Rose & Montakantiwong, 2018; Sondari, 2021; Yazan, 2019; Zacharias, 2019); or (iii) qualitative data analysis software is used to explore emerging themes (Solano-Campos, 2014).

There are cases in which a number of independent narratives are put together to demonstrate a progression of events within the text (Herrando-Rodrigo, 2021; Wijayatilake, 2012; Zacharias, 2019), whereas others recount the whole story from beginning to end (Burgess, 2021; Canagarajah, 2012; Fazel, 2021; Phipps, 2012; Shahriari, 2021; Solano-Campos, 2014). In the cases of duoethnographies (Banegas & del Pozo Beamud, 2022; Fallas-Escobar & Pentón Herrera, 2022; Kim & Saenkhum, 2019; Rose & Montakantiwong, 2018; Sánchez-Martín & Seloni, 2019) or CAEs (Back et al., 2021; Habibie et al., 2021; McGregor & Fernández, 2019; Miyahara & Fukao, 2022), a number of autoethnographic accounts are drawn together to show common and differing motivations and outcomes.

Autoethnography and canonical research

Autoethnography as a research method questions the dominant scientific paradigm (Wall, 2006) and has been reported to be weak and trivial on the grounds of scientific rigour, analysis, accuracy, systematicity, bias, or weakness of fieldwork and writing standards (Delamont, 2009; Ellis et al., 2011; Mirhosseini, 2018). Moreover, because the self is the primary subject and object of study, it has also been criticized for being problematic, self-indulgent, sensationalist, introspective, and individualized (Holt, 2003), narrowing down the potential pool of participants and limiting research in its scope and conclusions (Lapadat, 2017; Méndez, 2013). Also, the criteria of reliability, validity, and generalizability that apply in qualitative research need to be revisited so that they are also useful for autoethnographers wishing to reach the expected quality in their studies (Loo, 2017). To efficiently address this, Ellis et al. (2011) suggest accepting the narrator's credibility and story verisimilitude. They also suggest aiming at "generalizability", not by gathering large random samples of respondents, as would be the case in traditional social scientific research but, instead, by moving from respondents to readers, who can validate the autoethnography by comparing their lives to the personal story that is presented.

Autoethnographers are concerned that by writing narrative texts which evoke direct emotional responses, they are building "unorthodox modes of knowledge construction" (Habibie et al., 2021, p.304) and placing their research outside canonical scholarship on a publication journey covered with hurdles. Examples are diverse in this group of studies: Phipps (2012) explains that even though her research had been rejected several times, she felt she could not make sense of her case "through the discursive limits of normative academic prose" (p.597). Miyahara and Fukao (2022) wrote their article as a research report to "engage in a more typical academic discourse" (p.8). Mochizuki (2021) reported framing her narrative with theories and concepts to make it more academic. For Atkinson and Sohn (2013) autoethnography was the only option left once traditional approaches had been discredited for their purpose.

From the studies reviewed it appears that by conducting analytic rather than evocative autoethnography research might be uncritically accepted by current scholarship; therefore, authors highlight the analytic character of their autoethnography in an effort to place their narrative within canonical research paradigms (Burgess, 2021; Deveci, 2021; Gormley, 2021; Herrando-Rodrigo, 2021; Kim & Saenkhum, 2019; Mur-Dueñas, 2019; Shahriari, 2021; Sondari, 2021). It stands out that no evocative autoethnography has been overtly claimed by chapter authors despite some examples being present in the studies under review (e.g., Ai, 2016; Kohls, 2021; Liu, 2020; Phipps, 2012; Song, 2022; Solano-Campos, 2014). An interesting explanation is that of Canagarajah (2012), who justified his decision of conducting an analytic autoethnography because the journal lacks a long tradition of publishing narratives and, hence, he felt that a more evocative text would not have been welcome.

Memory as a data-collection instrument

Reliance on researchers' memory and recall has been reported to be a major limitation of autoethnography as a research method. Firstly, memory is prone to failure because we cannot recall events exactly as they occurred (Ellis et al., 2011); and, secondly, memory is censoring (Chang, 2008), which prevents it from providing a reliable access to "truth" (Canagarajah, 2012). Given that autoethnography requires researchers to recall key moments that transformed their lives (or "epiphanies", following Denzin, 2013), and that some of those moments may be traumatic and harrowing, researchers will need to make an effort to bring those painful moments to light and avoid involuntary censoring. Trauma has been portrayed as a major ethnical concern in the literature (e.g., Chang et al., 2013; Ellis, 2007; Lapadat, 2017; Roth, 2009; Tullis, 2013) and will be illustrated in the last section of this chapter. By writing their traumatic stories, autoethnographers explore emotional trauma, overcome their own vulnerabilities and make sense of unresolved emotions at the same they help readers elicit similar feelings, relieve past traumas, and reduce a sense of isolation.

The 40 studies under review contain instances of narratives in which autoethnography has helped researchers to (i) explore traumatic personal periods; (ii) use their insider position to gain awareness; and (iii) accept, if possible improve, the situation. We can read about internal struggles in the construction of a professional identity (Fazel, 2021; Hooper, 2022; Shahriari, 2021; Solano-Campos, 2014; Yazan, 2019; Zacharias, 2019); emotional experiences (Liu et al., 2021; Phipps, 2012); hidden feelings and suppressed emotions (Canagarajah, 2012; Liu et al., 2021); discussions within the family (McGregor & Fernández, 2019); episodes of domestic violence (Van Viegen, 2021); conflicts within the institution (Wijayatilake, 2012); job insecurity (McCulloch, 2021); disability and illness (Kohls, 2021); vulnerabilities (Sánchez-Martín & Seloni, 2019; Song, 2022); inequalities and marginalization (Fallas-Escobar & Pentón Herrera, 2022; Sondari, 2021); feelings of uncertainty and anxiety (Back et al., 2021; Gormley, 2021); or feelings of fear and guilt (Deveci, 2021; Song, 2022). To what extent can readers be sure that these accounts are free from omissions or changes? To what extent do they represent objective accounts of the "truth"?

To trigger memory and compensate for gaps or oversights, authors triangulate internal data (memory and recall) with external data like instruments and materials (e.g., Banegas & del Pozo Beamud, 2022; Carciu, 2021; Deroo, 2021; Fallas-Escobar & Pentón Herrera, 2022; Shaw, 2021; Solano-Campos, 2014; Sondari, 2021; Song, 2022; Zacharias, 2019) and use diverse research instruments and materials collected over time (many of them present in canonical research) to add to their retrospective accounts. In the studies reviewed, these instruments and materials range from a number of written artefacts (e.g., journal/blog entries, personal journals, research diaries, research paper drafts, reviewers' comments, teaching notes, teaching materials, emails and personal communications, academic social networking sites, photographs, school applications or tenure narratives) to visual and non-written instruments (e.g., informal conversations, recorded Zoom conversations, concept maps, diagrams, collaborative discussions, or interviews). For authors like Banegas and del Pozo Beamud (2022) triangulation helps to reduce distortion and avoid subjective interpretations. For others, however, an autoethnographic account gains credibility or rigour when the dimensions of temporality (backward and forward), sociality (inward and outward), and space (within and across situations) prevail in the narrative and, hence, avoid triangulation and explicitly refuse to collect external data (e.g., Liu, 2020).

A method for experienced researchers

Reflective and dialogic approaches such as autoethnography, duoethnography and CAE have been reported to be underrepresented among AL early-career and novice scholars' publications (Habibie & Burgess, 2021). By the same token, autoethnography has been claimed to be a difficult method for novice researchers (Keles, 2022; Méndez, 2013; Starfield, 2019), probably because autoethnographic texts are not frequent in AL academic publications (hence, they are not familiar with the genre), the added difficulty to publication options (which challenges standard academic writing and often makes AL journals resistant to publishing personal narratives), or probably because early-career researchers are not ready to either self-disclose or simply cannot afford to put their career development at stake if they challenge disciplinary orthodoxies. It has also been acknowledged that junior researchers engaged in autoethnographic writing benefit from mentorship and guidance (Tullis, 2013).

These concerns have been attested in part of the studies reviewed (Habibie et al., 2021; Shahriari, 2021). The effort of more established scholars in bringing junior researchers into self-reflection and self-observation proves to be an outcome of mentoring practices (Atkinson & Sohn, 2013; Fallas-Escobar & Pentón Herrera, 2022; Sánchez-Martín & Seloni, 2019), apprenticeship (Deroo, 2021), and collaborative work between less and more experienced researchers (Back et al., 2021; Catalano et al., 2018; Yazan, 2019) — these types of interpersonal relations are not exempt from power imbalances between the authors.

Ethics and autoethnographically-oriented research

Autoethnography is an ethical practice (Ellis, 2007; Méndez, 2013; Roth, 2009) and an ethical approach to inquiry (Lapadat, 2017) in which, as is the case in any other type of research (Guillemin & Gillam, 2004), decisions need to be made before conducting the study, during the process of data collection and analysis, and while reporting the data for eventual publication (De Costa, 2014). Current literature has addressed the multifarious ethical challenges faced by autoethnographic research from a broad perspective (e.g., Lapadat, 2017; Tullis, 2013). A key finding is that autoethnographers face ethical challenges that mainly arise from "relational ethics" because while writing about personal experiences they implicate others in the work (Ellis, 2007; Ellis et al., 2011) who are portrayed as visible or invisible participants (Chang, 2008).

Doing autoethnography means "taking ethics seriously" (Tullis, 2013, p. 257); however, only seven of the 40 studies under review explicitly address ethical-related issues. This finding may suggest that autoethnographers should aim at writing more ethically-driven narratives and showcasing "ethically important moments" (Guillemin & Gillam, 2004, p. 261) from their research. In the discussion that follows, I explore ethical concerns through a macroethical and microethical lens (De Costa, 2014; Kubanyiova, 2008) to show that in the studies under the review, and hence in the fields of ELT/TESOL/academic literacies, these concerns often pertain to institutional and relational ethics as well as to the protection and vulnerability of both participants and researchers.

The macroethics of autoethnographically-oriented research

Macroethics, or "procedural ethics" (Guillemin & Guillam, 2004, p. 262), covers the need to seek approval from ethics committees or institutional review boards (IRBs), meet standardised procedures and comply with professional codes of conduct when carrying out a piece of research in which human beings are involved. In the studies under review, authors typically show adherence to the general procedural aspects of research ethics established in institutional research ethics guidelines in two ways: (i) by highlighting that recruitment and confidentiality procedures together with data-collection instruments have been sanctioned by their respective IRBs (Hooper, 2022; McGregor & Fernández, 2019); or (ii) by justifying that IRB approval is not necessary because the researchers are also the participants in the study (Catalano et al., 2018).

The microethics of autoethnographically-oriented research

Microethics, or "ethics in practice" (Guillemin & Guillam, 2004, p. 262), involves those everyday ethical issues that unexpectedly arise in a particular context while conducting the research. Five studies (Fallas-Escobar & Pentón Herrera, 2022; Liu et al., 2021; McGregor & Fernández, 2019; Miyahara & Fukao, 2022; Phipps, 2012) address specific ethical dilemmas that emerged before or during the research or amidst the writing process but in varying degrees of depth. These dilemmas, which show the complex dynamics between researchers and participants (Guillemin & Guillam, 2004), are often interrelated and concern the protection of the self and others, vulnerability of participants and researchers, and relational ethics.

Autoethnographers need to consider privacy and confidentiality concerns in all aspects of the study (Starfield, 2019). In the studies under review, pseudonyms are used to protect participants' identities; however, there is no reference to informed consent and we cannot know if individuals are participating voluntarily. Likewise, the anonymity of the relational others that are implicated in the narratives is difficult to protect when very precise biographical or personal details are given — for example Phipps' (2012) daughter, Solano-Campos' (2014) father, or Deroo's (2021) supervisor and peers.

Liu et al. (2021) explicitly address an issue within the scope of relational ethics when the first author briefly reports how she experienced greater closeness to her students and mutual caring during the pandemic despite physical distance. The building of interpersonal ties and friendship during the research has been reported to entail ethical issues which may affect the research process and product (Ellis et al., 2011). Likewise, Liu concedes "mixed affects" in the relationship with her students during online teaching in that her private life was occasionally affected by her students' continued text messaging. In this narrative, the need to protect the self becomes evident and by disclosing this personal story of private feelings in the form of a permanent record, the researcher is exposed and becomes a vulnerable subject (Lapadat, 2017). A rather different example is Phipps' (2012) poetic commentary which narrates how the author used "linguistic hospitality" to stop the detention and deportation of her daughter. In this case, it is the need to protect the intimate other (that is, her vulnerable daughter) what is at stake.

Fallas-Escobar and Pentón Herrera (2022) remain vigilant of their ethical stances and try to protect their research by ensuring that they do not "reify, trivialize, vilify or romanticize each other's stories" (p. 3). In a similar vein, and for an ethically appropriate CAE, Miyahara and Fukao (2022) recommend sharing content equally amongst all researchers involved in the study and conducting participation on a completely voluntary basis. The procedure in these two studies connects with the "do no harm" ethical principle and ensures an equal distribution of risks and benefits between the researchers (Tullis, 2013). In comparison with other types of autoethnography, CAE has been claimed to be in a better position to face the ethical challenges of the method — for example, by defining roles and setting boundaries for each participant (Chang et al., 2013) and by addressing guidelines for respectful engagement (Lapadat, 2017).

On a final note, McGregor and Fernández (2019) is a case in point to illustrate microethical challenges and dilemmas in the field. The interviewee participant, Mayden, is depicted along the narrative as "a queer, gender nonconforming (pronouns: they/them), African American student" (p. 237), and one of nine students participating in the summer study abroad programme delivered by the first author in Leipzig. Even though Mayden is a pseudonym in the text, on the grounds of relational ethics, the details provided will very likely make the participant and the relational others recognise themselves in the narrative (Ellis, 2007; Lapadat, 2017). We learn about Mayden's gender-related struggles and mental health concerns which eventually made them depart the programme after many discussions with their family and faculty leader. But we also learn that the first author experienced "very negative emotions" (p. 239) and that her own participation in the interviews affected her as a researcher. An ethical action in this autoethnography is that the first author reviewed her notes and listened to the interviews together with Mayden so as to follow up, refine and enhance final data. Interestingly enough, both participant and researcher's stance changed between the first and the second interview. The reported events in this study help to illustrate how to do autoethnography ethically (Ellis, 2007; Lapadat, 2017; Tullis, 2013), namely: (i) not only the participant, whose struggles are exposed, but also the researcher, who may be affected in unforeseen ways, become vulnerable subjects; (ii) the researcher's positionality evolves with a view to minimising harm; (iii) the implication of the participant in the analysis of the interview data has a double effect that prevents deception: participation is informed and voluntary at the same time it affords "member checking" (Tullis, 2013) for accuracy and agreement.

Concluding remarks

In this chapter I have tried to show that autoethnography as a research method has much to offer to current scholarship in AL. Autoethnographic research entails affordances and limitations; however, constraints can be turned into opportunities, and, consequently, AL researchers can use this method to their best advantage. Firstly, applied linguists can write autoethnographies to make sense of under-researched topics representing conceptual challenges (like issues of identity, personal growth, or social inclusion) that cannot be merely analysed and discussed in terms of qualitative or quantitative results. Secondly, autoethnography as a research method is an enacting tool that can help applied linguists to engage in transformational interactions with academia because their personal voices can challenge canonical scholarship from the inside. Lastly, autoethnographically-oriented research can reach and engage non-academic or non-specialist audiences with an interest in language, thereby contributing to disseminating AL-related knowledge and increasing research and researchers' visibility.

Researchers write their autoethnographic texts under different labels ("autobiography", "autobiographical ethnography", "ethnographic autobiography", "evocative narrative", "evocative written account", "life history", "lived experience", "memoir", "personal experience story", "personal letters", "personal essay", "personal narrative", "self-reflective account", or "reflexive ethnography"), and the existence of this array of terms has certainly impinged on the final selection of studies that have been examined in this chapter. While writing it, I became aware of the existence of articles that were not captured in my search despite having been published in the journals reviewed. An example is Canagarajah (1996), which had not popped up in my search process because the text does not contain the term "autoethnography". By reading other authors' discussions (e.g., Keles, 2022; Loo, 2017) I also became aware of other ethnographically-oriented studies in the field of ELT/TESOL that were published in journals that had not been included in my search and which might have provided additional insights (e.g., Holt, 2003). I may have also missed book chapters which passed unnoticed when reviewing the literature; and I have not considered edited book collections which I could not access fully at the time of writing (e.g., Habibie & Hultgren, 2022; Yazan et al., 2021). Nevertheless, I hope that these gaps can be filled with further research in the near future.

Autoethnography is a research method that is gradually gaining prominence in academic publications and across disciplines (Adams et al., 2017). This is evident in the selected studies reviewed in this chapter, all of them published during the past decade and many of them very recently. If we agree that, firstly, Canagarajah's (1996) discussion on the difficulties faced by periphery scholars when writing for publication is the earliest autoethnography in AL; and, secondly, that, as attested in this study, the number of researchers who have embraced this method has flourished in the last decade, it can be concluded that autoethnography is still an emerging, but yet promising, method in the fields of ELT/TESOL/academic literacies that helps to enhance research practices.

By exploring the affordances, limitations, and ethics of autoethnography as a research method, I have examined a number of personal narratives that have made me reflect upon the strengths, weaknesses, and opportunities of autoethnography for my own research. I have not written an autoethnography myself, but writing this chapter has certainly been therapeutic and educational for me: I have looked into others and sympathised with their life histories, which have been a source of critical reflection of my own lived experiences as academic and researcher. It is, precisely, in this reality where the richness of autoethnography lies (Méndez, 2013).

References

Adams, T. E., Ellis, C., & Holman Jones, S. (2017). Autoethnography. In C. S. Davis & R. F. Potter (Eds.), *The international encyclopedia of communication research methods* (pp. 1–11). John Wiley & Sons.

Ai, B. (2016). Experiencing different identity prototypes in learning and teaching English: A Chinese learner's autoethnography. *Changing English: Studies in Culture and Education*, 23(3), 280–291.

Anderson, L. (2006). Analytic autoethnography. *Journal of Contemporary Ethnography*, 35(4), 373–395.

Atkinson, D., & Sohn, J. (2013). Culture from the bottom up. *TESOL Quarterly*, 47(4), 669–693.

Back, M., Golembeski, K., Gutiérrez, A., Macko, T., Miller, S., & Pelletier, D. Lanie Pelletier. (2021). "We were told that the content we delivered was not as important:" Disconnect and disparities in world language student teaching during COVID-19. *System, 103*, 102679.

Banegas, D. L., & del Pozo Beamud, M. (2022). Content and language integrated learning: A duoethnographic study about CLIL pre-service teacher education in Argentina and Spain. *RELC Journal, 53*(1), 151–164.

Burgess, S. (2021). Learning to be a non-native speaker: A retrospective autoethnographic account of an early-career researcher's publishing trajectory. In P. Habibie & S. Burgess (Eds.), *Scholarly publication trajectories of early-career scholars. Insider perspectives* (pp. 113–129). Palgrave Macmillan.

Busteed, S. (2022). Communication and the student experience in the time of Covid-19: An autoethnography. *Language Teaching Research*, 1–19.

Canagarajah, A. S. (1996). "Nondiscursive" requirements in academic publishing, material resources of periphery scholars, and the politics of knowledge production. *Written Communication, 13*(4), 435–472.

Canagarajah, A. S. (2012). Teacher development in a global profession: An autoethnography. *TESOL Quarterly, 46*(2), 258–279.

Carciu, O. M. (2021). Juggling early-career demands: Research publication productivity, strategies, practices. In P. Habibie & S. Burgess (Eds.), *Scholarly publication trajectories of early-career scholars. Insider perspectives* (pp. 23–40). Palgrave Macmillan.

Catalano, T., Shende, M., & Suh, E. K. (2018). Developing multilingual pedagogies and research through language study and reflection. *International Journal of Multilingualism, 15*(1), 1–18.

Chang, H. (2008). *Autoethnography as method*. Routledge.

Chang, H., Ngunjiri, F., & Hernandez, K. A. C. (2013). *Collaborative autoethnography*. Routledge.

Darvin, R. (2021). The digitally-mediated scholar: Online identities and investment in the discursive practices of an academic community. In P. Habibie & S. Burgess (Eds.), *Scholarly publication trajectories of early-career scholars. Insider perspectives* (pp. 169–188). Palgrave Macmillan.

De Costa, P. I. (2014). Making ethical decisions in an ethnographic study. *TESOL Quarterly, 48*(2), 413–422.

Delamont, S. (2009). The only honest thing: Autoethnography, reflexivity and small crises in fieldwork. *Ethnography and Education, 4*, 51–63.

Denzin, N. K. (2013). *Interpretive autoethnography*. Sage.

Deroo, M. R. (2021). Writing with, learning from, and paying forward mentorship from early-career scholars: My scholarly formation into academic writing. In P. Habibie & S. Burgess (Eds.), *Scholarly publication trajectories of early-career scholars. Insider perspectives* (pp. 59–75). Palgrave Macmillan.

Deveci, T. (2021). A scholar's efforts to increase margin: Reflection on a journey of academic enculturation. In P. Habibie & S. Burgess (Eds.), *Scholarly publication trajectories of early-career scholars. Insider perspectives* (pp. 281–298). Palgrave Macmillan.

Duncan, M. (2004). Autoethnography: Critical appreciation of an emerging art. *International Journal of Qualitative Methods, 3*(4), 28–39.

Ellis, C. (2007). Telling secrets, revealing lives. Relational ethics in research with intimate others. *Qualitative Inquiry, 13*(1), 3–29.

Ellis, C., Adams, T. E., & Bochner, A. P. (2011). Autoethnography: An overview. *Forum: Qualitative Social Research, 12*(1), Art. 10. https://www.jstor.org/stable/23032294

Fallas-Escobar, C., & Pentón Herrera, L. J. (2022). Examining raciolinguistic struggles in institutional settings: A duoethnography. *Linguistics and Education, 67*, 101012.

Fazel, I. (2021). Socialization into scholarly publication as a multilingual, early-career scholar. In P. Habibie & S. Burgess (Eds.), *Scholarly publication trajectories of early-career scholars. Insider perspectives* (pp. 189–205). Palgrave Macmillan.

Gormley, K. (2021). An account of bifurcated senses and spaces in the pursuit of early-career academic publications. In P. Habibie & S. Burgess (Eds.), *Scholarly publication trajectories of early-career scholars. Insider perspectives* (pp. 244–261). Palgrave Macmillan.

Guillemin, M., & Gillam, L. (2004). Ethics, reflexivity, and "ethically important moments" in research. *Qualitative Inquiry, 10*(2), 261–280.

Guillén-Galve, I., & Bocanegra-Valle, A. (Eds.). (2021). *Ethnographies of academic writing research. Theory, methods, and interpretation.* John Benjamins.

Habibie, P., & Burgess, S. (2021). Scholarly publication, early-career scholars, and reflectivity. In P. Habibie & S. Burgess (Eds.), *Scholarly publication trajectories of early-career scholars. Insider perspectives* (pp. 1–19). Palgrave Macmillan.

Habibie, P., & Hultgren, A. K. (2022). *The inner world of gatekeeping in scholarly publication.* Palgrave Macmillan.

Habibie, P., Sawyer, R. D., & Norris, J. (2021). Thinking beyond ourselves. Career reflections on the Trojan horse of hegemonic discourses (2021). In P. Habibie & S. Burgess (Eds.), *Scholarly publication trajectories of early-career scholars. Insider perspectives* (pp. 299–320). Palgrave Macmillan.

Herrando-Rodrigo, I. (2021). A question of balance: The scholarly publication trajectory of a dual profile language professional. In P. Habibie & S. Burgess (Eds.), *Scholarly publication trajectories of early-career scholars. Insider perspectives* (pp. 225–242). Palgrave Macmillan.

Holt, N. L. (2003). Representation, legitimation, and autoethnography: An autoethnographic writing story. *International Journal of Qualitative Methods, 2*(1), 18–28.

Hooper, D. (2022). Action logs as meditational means for teacher development. *Language Teaching Research, 26*(5), 1034–1046.

Keles, U. (2022). Autoethnography as a recent methodology in applied linguistics: A methodological review. *The Qualitative Report, 27*(2), 448–474.

Kim, S. H., & Saenkhum, T. (2019). Professional identity (re)construction of L2 writing scholars. *L2 Journal, 11*(2), 18–34. https://escholarship.org/uc/item/4j82s0ng.

Kohls, R. (2021). "Will you ever write about this?": Diagnosis, self-care, and writing for publication. In P. Habibie & S. Burgess (Eds.), *Scholarly publication trajectories of early-career scholars. Insider perspectives* (pp. 133–149). Palgrave Macmillan.

Kubanyiova, M. (2008). Rethinking research ethics in contemporary applied linguistics: The tension between macroethical and microethical perspectives in situated research. *Modern Language Journal, 92*, 503–518.

Lapadat, J. C. (2017). Ethics in autoethnography and collaborative autoethnography. *Qualitative Inquiry, 23*(8), 589–603.

Liu, S., Yuan, R., & Wang, C. (2021). 'Let emotion ring': An autoethnographic self-study of an EFL instructor in Wuhan during COVID-19. *Language Teaching Research*, 1–21.

Liu, W. (2020). teaching methodology as a lived experience: An autoethnography from China. *RELC Journal*, 53(1), 14 pp.

Loo, D. B. (2017). Trust the researcher? Autoethnography as a tool to study English teaching professionals. *Selected Proceedings of the International Conference DRAL 3/19th ESEA* (pp. 45–58). Retrieved on 7 October 2024 from https://sola.kmutt.ac.th/dral2017/proceedings/3-Papers/45-58_Trust%20the%20researcher_Daron%20Loo.pdf

McCulloch, S. (2021). Establishing a track record in an age of precarity. In P. Habibie & S. Burgess (Eds.), *Scholarly publication trajectories of early-career scholars. Insider perspectives* (pp. 263–280). Palgrave Macmillan.

McGregor, J., & Fernández, J. (2019). Theorizing qualitative interviews: Two autoethnographic reconstructions. *The Modern Language Journal*, 103(1), 227–247.

Méndez, M. (2013). Autoethnography as a research method: Advantages, limitations and criticisms. *Colombian Applied Linguistics Journal*, 15(2), 279–287.

Mirhosseini, S. A. (2018). An invitation to the less-treaded path of autoethnography in TESOL research. *TESOL Journal*, 9(1), 76–92.

Miyahara, M., & Fukao, A. (2022). Exploring the use of collaborative autoethnography as a tool for facilitating the development of researcher reflexivity. *System*, 105, 1–9.

Mochizuki, N. (2021). Becoming a scholarly writer for publication: An autoethnography of boundary crossing, linguistic identity, and revising. P. Habibie & S. Burgess (Eds.), *Scholarly publication trajectories of early-career scholars. Insider perspectives* (pp. 207–224). Palgrave Macmillan.

Mur-Dueñas, P. (2019). The experience of NNES outer circle novice scholar in scholarly publication. In P. Habibie & K. Hyland (Eds.), *Novice writers and scholarly publication* (pp. 97–116). Palgrave Macmillan.

Olmos-Lopez, P. (2021). Walking the early-career researcher path in an adoptive culture. In P. Habibie & S. Burgess (Eds.), *Scholarly publication trajectories of early career scholars. Insider perspectives* (pp. 151–167). Palgrave Macmillan.

Phipps, A. (2012). Voicing solidarity: Linguistic hospitality and poststructuralism in the real world. *Applied Linguistics*, 33(5), 582–602. https://doi.org.bibezproxy.uca.es/10.1093/applin/ams054.

Rose, H., & Montakantiwong, A. (2018). A tale of two teachers: A duoethnography of the realistic and idealistic successes and failures of teaching English as an international language. *RELC Journal*, 49(1), 88–101.

Roth, W.-M. (2009). Auto/ethnography and the question of ethics. *Forum: Qualitative Social Research*, 10(1), Art. 38.

Sánchez-Martín, C., & Seloni, L. (2019). Transdisciplinary becoming as a gendered activity: A reflexive study of dissertation mentoring. *Journal of Second Language Writing*, 43, 24–35.

Shahriari, H. (2021). Pulling yourself up by the bootstraps: An insider's perspective on learning how to publish in the Iranian higher education context. In P. Habibie & S. Burgess (Eds.), *Scholarly publication trajectories of early-career scholars. Insider perspectives* (pp. 95–111). Palgrave Macmillan.

Shaw, O. (2021). Misguided allegiances, misjudged weaknesses, and mixed messages in peer review. In P. Habibie & S. Burgess (Eds.), *Scholarly publication trajectories of early-career scholars. Insider perspectives* (pp. 77–93). Palgrave macmillan.

Solano-Campos, A. (2014). The making of an international educator: Transnationalism and nonnativeness in English teaching and learning. *TESOL Journal, 5*(3), 412–443.

Sondari, P.S. (2021). Reflecting on the intersection of critical pedagogy, identities, and spaces: An Indonesian doctoral students' autoethnography. *RELC Journal*, 1–14.

Song, J. (2022). The emotional landscape of online teaching: An autoethnographic exploration of vulnerability and emotional reflexivity. *System, 106*, 1–10.

Starfield, S. (2019). Autoethnography and critical ethnography. In J. McKinley & R. Heath (Eds.), *The Routledge handbook of research methods in Applied Linguistics* (pp. 165–175). Routledge.

Tullis, J.A. (2013). Self and others. Ethics in autoethnographic research. In S. Holman Jones, T. E. Adams, & C. Ellis (Eds.), *Handbook of autoethnography* (pp. 244–261). Routledge.

Van Viegen, S. (2021). Writing belonging with critical autoethnography. In P. Habibie & S. Burgess (Eds.), *Scholarly publication trajectories of early-career scholars. Insider perspectives* (pp. 41–58). Palgrave Macmillan.

Wall, S. (2006). An autoethnography on learning about autoethnography. *International Journal of Qualitative Methods, 5*(2), 146–160.

Wijayatilake, C. (2012). An autoethnographic exploration of my professional experiences as teacher trainer and principal at two international schools in Sri Lanka. *Language Teaching, 45*(3), 403–405.

Yazan, B. (2019). Identities and ideologies in a language teacher candidate's autoethnography: Making meaning of storied experience. *TESOL Journal, 10*(4), 1–21.

Yazan, B., Canagarajah, S., & Jain, R. (Eds.) (2021). *Autoethnographies in ELT. Transnational identities, pedagogies, and practices.* Routledge.

Zacharias, N.T. (2019). The ghost of nativespeakerism: The case of teacher classroom introductions in transnational contexts. *TESOL Journal, 10*(4), 1–14.

CHAPTER 7

The role of duoethnography in critical ELT research

Reflexivity, ideology critique, and praxis

Robert J. Lowe
Ochanomizu University

Duoethnography is an approach to research often associated with critical projects; that is, with research which is focused on issues of discrimination, prejudice, and social justice. In recent years, such research has often been aligned theoretically with post structuralism, which resists theory building, and instead aims to question and deconstruct dominant power relations. However, there has been a recent move in critical ELT research towards forms of critique associated with Marxism, critical realism, and critical theory. Building on this structural (re)turn, this chapter explores the role duoethnography could play in a research program oriented around the post-Marxist critical theory of the early Frankfurt School. Drawing on a conception of critical theory as a form of self-reflexive social science focused on ideology critique and emancipatory praxis, this chapter explores how the dialogic nature of duoethnography could be reconstituted as an engine for theoretical development and consciousness raising. It is suggested that through processes of immanent critique, duoethnography could be used to evaluate the internal coherence of claims within a critical program of research in ELT, as well as identifying starting points for ideology critique. Finally, the accessibility of duoethnographic work is presented as a possible route for transforming research into praxis.

Introduction

Critical research in English language teaching (ELT) is generally understood as research which is politically engaged, and focused on making progressive change within the field. In the past, the work of many researchers has focused primarily on issues of identity and discrimination, and has been carried out from a post-structural theoretical perspective. However, in recent years there has been some movement among critical researchers away from pure poststructuralism, and back

https://doi.org/10.1075/rmal.8.07low

towards approaches which include elements of neo-Marxism and critical theory. For researchers moving in this direction, it is instructive to consider how research approaches such as duoethnography, which within ELT research has been connected primarily with poststructuralism, could be integrated into this new research program. In this chapter, I will first describe the uses of duoethnography in ELT to date and explore the current landscape of critical ELT. Next, I will outline a research framework which takes a more structural approach to critique, based on the early critical theory of the Frankfurt School. Finally, I will discuss three ways in which duoethnography may be able to contribute to this conception of critical research in the form of reflexivity through immanent critique, through the critique of ideology, and as a tool mediating between research and practice.

Duoethnography in ELT

Duoethnography is a qualitative research method in which the focus is on researchers in dialogue. Through an exploration and comparison of their personal life histories, duoethnographers aim to view a particular phenomenon from a new vantage point, a process facilitated by dialogue with a research partner whose life experiences diverge from their own. Duoethnographers draw on and contrast their life histories to co-construct new understandings surrounding topics which have had an influence on their lives, and this co-construction is reflected in the playscript-like, dialogic presentation of the data that is commonly employed. Duoethnography draws on both autoethnography and narrative inquiry, and, despite reluctance from journals and reviewers, the method has started to gain acceptance as a legitimate mode of inquiry. Within ELT, the first duoethnography (Lowe & Kiczkowiak, 2016) followed fast on the heels of the first autoethnography (Canagarajah, 2012), and both shared a common focus on issues of discrimination surrounding language, culture, and identity in language teaching. This critical edge has remained a common feature of duoethnography in ELT, echoing the suggestion from the method's progenitors that it may be used to promote social justice and effect progressive social change (Norris & Sawyer, 2012; Sawyer & Norris, 2013). Indeed, Stanley (2019) suggests that autoethnographic work in ELT should be oriented towards social justice, and be focused on redressing social imbalances through giving voice to "people and ideas that might otherwise be voiceless" (p. 57).

The personal and deconstructive elements central to duoethnography belie the form of criticality with which it is generally associated in ELT research; one which draws on post structural and postcolonial theory, challenges inequitable social hierarchies, questions the politics of representation of self and other in text, and attempts to move away from the extractive and exploitative nature of much social and ethnographic research (see Tuhiwai Smith, 2021). Within ELT, many published duoethnographies have followed this critical spirit, focusing on issues related to multilingual identities (Ahmed & Morgan, 2021; Hammine & Rudolph, 2022; Rose & Montakantiwong, 2018), native-speakerism (Hooper & Iijima, 2019), race (Duran & Tanita Saenkhum, 2022) and the intersections between these (Lawrence & Nagashima, 2020). The method is fast becoming an established form of research in ELT which is characterized as *critical*.

Critical ELT research

Critical research in ELT has generally taken one of two major approaches. The first of these is related to theory we could loosely term 'neo-Marxism,' which is, as Pennycook (2021) observes, interested in ideology critique and redistribution (p. 24). One well-known area of ELT literature in this vein is concerned with *linguistic imperialism*, as conceptualised by Phillipson (1992). According to this theory, ELT functions as a form of soft power, spreading Western cultural and linguistic hegemony around the world through the dominance of Western organisations in ELT, such as the British Council. Although Phillipson's original text is three decades old, more recent work by Phillipson (2017), Widin (2010), and O'Regan (2021) has demonstrated the ongoing relevance of this thesis. O'Regan, in his recent book on global Englishes and political economy (O'Regan, 2021), has suggested that English acted as a 'free rider' on the back of global capitalism, and that as such, economic interests dictate which forms of the language are deemed acceptable for carrying out global business. Because of this, liberatory theories and movements in ELT (such as English as a Lingua Franca, translingualism, and advocacy for so-called 'non-native speaker'[1] teachers) face almost insurmountable opposition in their quest to move ELT in a less linguistically and culturally chauvinistic direction. Another major focus of critical research in this vein is native-speakerism (though not all would agree with such a characterization). This refers to the idea that Western so-called 'native speakers' represent the idealized English models and institutions of the West, and are thus given preferential treatment in hiring and employment (Holliday, 2006; Lowe, 2020).

A second approach to critical work in ELT has been more poststructural in nature, and has focused on the development of local knowledge and the identity

---

1. Following Holliday (2005), I place the terms 'native speaker' and 'non-native speaker' in inverted commas to identify them as cultural constructions, applied largely on the basis of non-linguistic factors such as race, nationality, and accent.

formation of teachers and students. In contrast to neo-Marxist work, poststructuralism is suspicious of "system-building in any form" (Morgan, 2007, p.1035), and seeks to challenge inequalities through deconstructing dominant perspectives, investigating how identity is historically negotiated and constructed (Hammine & Rudolph, 2022), and troubling the binaries and boundaries that neatly separate people into different, hierarchically organized groups (Norton & Morgan, 2023). The goal of this work in ELT has been to help students encounter and accept more varieties of the language, encourage the full use of students' multilingual resources, and create equitable classrooms in which students and teachers are free to express all facets of their identity. Influential work has been carried out from this point of view on issues related to culture (Kubota, 1999), race (Motha, 2014; Golombek & Jordan, 2005; Kubota & Lin, 2009), sexuality and gender identity (Nelson, 1999; 2009; Knisely & Paiz, 2021; Lawrence & Nagashima, 2021; Moore, 2021), and speakerhood (Holliday, 2005, 2014).

Until recently, this poststructural theoretical base has tended to predominate, with issues of identity central to most critical projects. However, many writers have begun to reconsider this approach, and to reengage with types of critical scholarship informed by Marxism, critical theory, and critical realism (Block, 2022; Bouchard, 2022; Pennycook, 2021; Simpson, 2018; 2022). Researchers such as Block (2022) and Pennycook (2021) have discussed their shift away from a poststructuralist perspective, and towards one in which more modernist ideas are reconciled with poststructuralism. There has also been an increase in recent work which connects discussions of identity and marginalization to the structural influence of global capitalism (see Gerald, 2022; Ramjattan, 2019) and to embodied forms of capital (e.g., Jenkins, 2019). Such approaches are perhaps more fully adequate to the task of analysing the serious global challenges of the last decade, including accelerating global inequality, climate change, and the connections of these to language and discourse. As such, my goal in this chapter is to discuss how duoethnography, which in ELT has generally been associated with poststructuralism (see Lawrence & Lowe, 2020), may be reconciled with a more structuralist form of critical social theory, to which I will now turn.

Critical theory

Critical theory, in the sense understood here, is a product of work conducted from the 1930s onwards by the scholars at the Institute for Social Research, known colloquially as the 'Frankfurt School'. These included the longtime director of the institute Max Horkheimer, and prominent figures such as Theodor Adorno, Leo Löwenthal, and Herbert Marcuse. The Institute for Social Research was originally founded with the aim of conducting sociological research through a Marxist lens

(Jay, 1973), and critical theory was conceptualized by Horkheimer as being a sociology which was oriented towards human emancipation from reified social structures,[2] and based on a program of ideology critique (Held, 1980). Expanding the scope of research from the economic base of society to the cultural superstructure, these theorists sought to investigate how dominant social beliefs and values which were antithetical to social progress (otherwise known as ideology) were inculcated in the population (Abromeit, 2011). Drawing on the work of Marx and Engels (1846/1988), ideology is understood here not as *any* set of political beliefs, but rather as sets of beliefs which misrepresent the dominant social structure as natural, immutable, and beneficial, and thus stand as a barrier to the progressive transformation of society. For Horkheimer, one of the main goals of critical theory was to expose the false nature of these beliefs, and thus create possibilities for people to move towards a society which would satisfy their needs (Held, 1980). The false nature of ideology could be revealed through contrasting claims about society with its actuality. By finding internal contradictions between the cognitions people hold about society and their experience of living within it, the beliefs are shown to have an ideological character. This process of seeking out internal contradictions is known as *immanent critique* (Antonio, 1981). By negating these internal contradictions, the possibility is created for the current society to be transcended in favour of a new, qualitatively different social order. The overall aim of the early Frankfurt School's program of research was to contribute to the emancipation of mankind from relations of domination (Horkheimer, 1937/1972a; b).

Naturally, the researcher also cannot imagine themselves free from ideological presuppositions. For the Frankfurt theorists, what Horkheimer termed 'traditional theory' is either unaware of, or disregards, the way it is shaped by historical, social, and economic conditions, and in turn plays a role in the perpetuation of the social order. Critical theory, on the other hand, was conceptualized as research conducted in a way mindful of the historical preconditions that have influenced its development, and of the role it plays in both challenging and reinforcing society (Best, Bonefeld, & O'Kane, 2018). As McCarthy (1993) puts it, critical theory takes "the reflexivity of social research" as one of its topics of investigation, and reflects "on the contexts of its own genesis and application" (p.136). With the understanding that the theorist is in no sense exempt from ideological limitations on thought and imagination, they must evaluate their own claims

---

2. The foundation of critical theory is under constant dispute. Personally, I ground this in the concept of alienation, conceived of by Marx (1844/1992; see also Fromm, 1961; Musto, 2021; Ollman, 1976), and reconceptualized by Jaeggi (2014) as the ability to engage in the free authorship of one's life through the self-directed appropriation of the material world. I believe the goal of critical research should be to help people live unalienated lives.

with as much rigor as they do all others (Freyenhagen, 2018). Accordingly, another key element of critical theory is that it must be constantly self-critical and self-correcting, using the same versatile tool of immanent critique. In this respect, the idea of critical theory stands in a tradition of Western Marxism which can be traced to seminal texts such as György Lukács' *History and Class Consciousness* (1923/1971) and Karl Korsch's *Marxism and Philosophy* (1923/1971). These books critiqued the kind of orthodox (or 'vulgar') Marxism which had attempted to transform Marxist theory into a mechanistic science. In sympathy with these ideas (though not necessarily directly influenced by them — see Abromeit, 2011), it was evident to the Frankfurt theorists that it was necessary to apply the dialectical method of Marx to the history of Marxism itself, and thus to constantly reevaluate critical social theory in a way both mindful of altered historical conditions, and of whether its goals were realized in its outcomes. In critical theory then, all claims and prescriptions about society must also be subjected to continual immanent critique; that is, they must be evaluated on their own terms regarding whether they are contributing to their goal of human emancipation, lest they themselves become unwitting handmaidens to social and economic oppression.

The research methods of the early Frankfurt School featured a variety of empirical approaches to data collection. Horkheimer suggested a program of research which was interdisciplinary, and which combined empirical science with philosophy and social theory (Horkheimer, 1931/1993, 1939/1972). Descriptions of society and suggestions for change were intended to arise from a productive dialogue between theory and data, a tradition carried forward by writers such as Adorno (1964/2019).

In sum then, critical theory is understood here as a program of empirical research which is oriented towards freeing humans from relations of economic and social domination. It aims to do this through the uncovering of ideology, and through a constant process of reflexive, immanent critique both of society, and of its own claims. While there is increasing interest in applying critical theory to ELT-related research (see Bori, 2018; Lowe, 2022; 2023; MacDonald & O'Regan, 2013; O'Regan, 2014; Pennycook, 2001; 2021), I believe it is necessary for critical researchers in the field of language teaching to more firmly reengage with this foundational strand of critical thought.

What role does duoethnography play?

As already noted, there has been a shift among critical ELT researchers to reconcile poststructuralist with more modernist forms of critique, and it is my goal here to identify points of resonance between duoethnography and early Frankfurt School critical theory. On the surface, research approaches such as duoethnography may appear to be somewhat at odds with critical theory. Although the two approaches are often connected or conflated in the popular imagination, Frankfurt School critical theory has traditionally stood strongly in opposition to postmodernism and poststructuralism. As McCarthy (1993) writes, "unlike contemporary deconstructionists" Horkheimer did not understand the reflexivity of critical theory to entail "prohibiting all but 'local' knowledge. Rather, he seeks to locate both traditional and critical research within a broad account of contemporary society" (p. 136).

However, while duoethnography shares with poststructuralism the goal of deconstructing grand narratives (Norris & Sawyer, 2012), it has also taken up the challenge of connecting biography with oppressive social structures, and thereby of questioning, challenging, and negating them. For example, Sawyer and Liggett (2012) used the method to explore how their socialization into particular dominant cultural values allowed colonialist elements to seep into their teaching practice. Through dialogue, these elements were uncovered and interrogated, and both participant-researchers were able to consider ways to "construct new learning spaces for our students and ourselves that can create new ways of perceiving and working together" (p. 647). Thus, while duoethnographic work in ELT has generally been conducted from a poststructuralist perspective, I here wish to build on this foundation of structuralist critique, and to outline some of the ways in which duoethnography may contribute to a research program specifically inspired by the neo-Marxist critical theory of the early Frankfurt School.

In the following sections, I will lay out three key roles that I believe duoethnography could play in such a research program. As explained earlier, two key elements of critical theory are the critique of ideology, and an ongoing, reflexive, critique of society and of its own claims, both of which can be conducted through immanent critique. These are two areas in which duoethnography could contribute to critical research. Following this, I will outline how duoethnography could mediate between research and practice, and act as a spur to critical consciousness among educators.

Reflexivity and critique of the claims of critical ELT

Critical theory (of the type considered here) is intended to help researchers come to an understanding of how social structure influences ideology, and how ideology maintains social structure. However, the conclusions of this inquiry are not intended to be static and final. As already noted, one key feature of critical theory is that it must be constantly self-reflexive, and this ongoing internal critique is an integral part of the approach. For early critical theorists such as Horkheimer, what distinguished the Western Marxism of Frankfurt School from the Eastern orthodoxy was the need for constant, dialectical, immanent critique of claims made by the theory. These theorists had seen how orthodox Marxism had become increasingly bureaucratic and mechanistic, and in countries in which it was in power freedom for the individual became increasingly elusive, and oppression was justified in the interest of the state. In formulating critical theory, Horkheimer stressed the importance of ongoing, dialectical, immanent critique of the claims made by the theory, and any recommendations which may follow from them.

It is first in this reflexive capacity that duoethnography may contribute to the program of critical research in ELT outlined earlier. In duoethnography, researchers contrast their life histories in order to reveal points of difference and similarity, which may lead them to new perspectives on an issue. In other words, by examining their experiences in contrast with another's, they gain a new vantage point from which to view the phenomenon, thus allowing them to form a new perspective. In dialectical terms, the researchers are able to find contradictions between the two experiences, thus enabling them to develop a new understanding in which these contradictions are reconciled.

Let's consider an example. Within critical ELT research, the topic of native-speakerism is one which has recently gained a great deal of attention. Native-speakerism refers to an ideology in which so-called 'native speaker' teachers, understood as embodiments of desirable inner-circle forms of the language, and as representatives of powerful ELT organisations, are given preferential treatment and assumed to have superior linguistic and pedagogical skill to their 'non-native speaker' counterparts. This leads to a situation in which so-called 'non-native speakers' are discriminated against, non-Western education systems are dismissed as incompetent, and students are chauvinistically Othered for their supposed cultural deficiencies. This is a serious issue of inequality in the field of ELT, and it is an inequality based on structural issues connected to the closeness of certain forms of English with dominant political and economic powers.

In response to this, teachers, researchers, and advocacy groups have begun to push back against these narratives. One approach taken in this has been to suggest that the fact 'non-native speakers' have gone through the process of learning English means they are superior to most 'native speakers' in their knowledge about the language, particularly in terms of grammar. This has led some authors to claim that, in fact, 'non-native speaker' teachers are the most suitable teachers of the language (e.g., Yoo, 2014), having gone through the learning process themselves, holding a strong level of language awareness, and thus being in a position to explain things to their students and to understand and empathise with their students' struggles. At first glance, these seem like reasonable conclusions. However, when we look at the policies which have resulted from this, they do not appear to have redressed the balance in a desirable way. Rather than freeing teachers from assumptions about their abilities and limitations, this has rather had the effect of creating new professional boundaries that simply reflect this new understanding. For example, 'native speakers' are frequently hired to teach speaking courses, while 'non-native speakers' are hired to teach writing courses, disregarding their actual teaching specialisms or interests (Lowe, 2020). In other words, rather than freeing people, this approach simply swaps one set of limitations for another.

Duoethnography could play a key role in highlighting these contradictions, through examining such claims and beliefs as they manifest in the lives of individuals. For example, in a duoethnograhy by Lowe and Kiczkowiak (2016), the authors discussed the notion that 'non-native speakers' are inherently more empathetic with their students than 'native speakers', having gone through the language learning process themselves, and thus being able to understand their students' struggles. Kiczkowiak, the 'non-native speaker' author, suggested that for him, the opposite was in fact true. He became a language teacher because he was an unusually good language learner, who rarely encountered difficulties in assimilating new linguistic input. As such, he found it very difficult to empathise with the struggles faced by his students, and found himself getting frustrated and unable to understand why they were having difficulties. On the other hand, Lowe, the 'native speaker' author, was not an exceptional language learner, and had invested significant time and effort into his learning of Japanese, without gaining a high level of fluency. As a result, he was much more able to appreciate the difficulties of his students, and was able to empathise with their struggles. This highlighted a contradiction which would suggest a need to rethink previously reached conclusions, having come to realise their problematic nature. In this way, duoethnography adds a reflexive, dialectical element to critical work, acting as an engine which moves theory forward by uncovering, or at least hinting at, its contradictions and inadequacies.

Ideology critique

As already mentioned, within critical theory one major concern is ideology critique. That is, researchers are focused on uncovering widely held beliefs which may prevent progressive social change. It should be remembered that to be characterised as ideological, these beliefs must be in some sense false; they add legitimacy to the social order, while masking the abuses taking place within it. This of course raises the question of how a belief or a political commitment can be identified as in some sense 'false.' This is certainly a difficult question. In suggesting someone holds a false belief, do we not deny them their agency? Do we not unfairly valorize our beliefs over and above theirs? How can we distinguish between those beliefs that are true and those that are not? This is a longstanding difficulty for theorists who espouse ideology critique. For critical theorists such as those of the early Frankfurt School, this is accomplished through *immanent critique* (Held, 1980) a form of internal, dialectical critique in which a belief is tested on the basis of its internal consistency. Does the belief lead to its intended outcomes, or does it negate its own premises? A belief which leads to results contrary to those desired reveals its ideological character.

Duoethnography could be a starting point for investigating ideology. In duoethnography, there is a focus on difference between the researchers. Difference is necessary for new understandings of a phenomena to arise (Norris & Sawyer, 2012), as it is through the contrast of experiences that contradictions are revealed. Thus, by placing researchers with different beliefs in dialogue, it may be possible to begin to find difficulties and internal contradictions in each other's ideas, and thus point towards potentially ideological belief structures. This would not be the end of the investigation, but rather a starting point. Such an inquiry would raise questions which could then be investigated in more detail through ongoing interdisciplinary work. Through this kind of ongoing investigation, it may be possible to identify ideological beliefs, and move past them, thus opening up a space for organization of the field in such a way as to satisfy the needs of learners and teachers.

In ELT, we may consider the ways in which language learning is advertised as, and thought to be, a method of self-realisation. For example, Bailey (2006) examines how language school advertisements in Japan promote English as a path for women to develop a new selfhood associated with personal freedom and individual development. However, as De Costa et al. (2016) write, under neoliberal capitalism "learners (...) are pressed to mold themselves into neoliberal subjects who brand themselves for better positions and maximize their potential on the global stage" (p.696). In other words, despite often being packaged as a form of self-realisation, language learning is in reality a heavily prescribed process. The necessity of language learning itself, and the form of language to be learned, are often impressed from the outside onto the subject, rather than being chosen willingly. Given this, language learning appears less a form of self-realisation, and more a response to circumstances beyond one's control, influenced by external powers that one may not even be aware of. This internal contradiction suggests an ideological character to these beliefs. Through duoethnographic exploration, it may be possible for both language learners and teachers to become aware of ideological beliefs such as these, and thus begin on the journey of investigating and uncovering these ideological assumptions.

One example of this kind of process (though not labelled as such in the text) can be found in a trioethnography by Hooper et al. (2020) on their experiences of teaching English in the *eikaiwa* (English conversation) school sector in Japan. In the second part of their dialogue, they focus on the issue of teacher roles, and Hooper appears to be perturbed by a statement by Yamazawa that she has "always felt that foreign teachers were like mascots" (p.39). This leads to Hooper making the following statement (Hooper et al., 2020, p.40):

> Hooper: (...) this links up with one point from our previous conversations that I wanted to bring up. One of you guys said that you didn't know if NESTs actually knew how to be strict and that was why they had this playful presence in class. To be honest, this made me feel quite uncomfortable (...). This statement bothered me because it assumes that NESTs lack professional authority because of an inherent deficiency rather than because of tensions stemming from institutional or social demands. During my time in *eikaiwa*, I witnessed many times where teachers were reprimanded or even fired for 'being too serious', 'not smiling enough' or because their classes weren't 'fun'. These were not lax backpackers, but rather experienced and passionate teachers who were pressured by the school to conform to a stereotype of what NESTs should be (...)

Here, Hooper pinpoints an area that is ripe for ideological exploration. Through discussions with his research partners, he noticed a discourse which suggested that the lack of seriousness associated with 'native speaker' teachers is attributable to something inherent in the teachers. Pushing back on this, he suggested that this is actually due to "institutional or social demands," which were enforced on these teachers with strict punishments. In this section of the dialogue, the three researchers notice and address a severe breach between ideas and reality, opening a space for further exploration, and for the dismantling of ideological beliefs. This is an example of how the contrast of experiences in a duoethnography could provide starting points for ideology critique.

Contributing to praxis

A final element which duoethnography can contribute to the program of critical research laid out here is the potential it has for raising awareness of ideology, and thus of developing critical consciousness among ELT practitioners. This is due to its unique presentational format.

One of the major features of duoethnography identified by Norris and Sawyer (2012) is its accessibility to practitioners and non-academics, who may not regularly engage with academic work. The dialogic, playscript-like format in which most duoethnography is presented makes it an ideal method for communicating ideas to a wider audience beyond the ivory tower. There is an often-discussed gap between research and practice in ELT, with teachers expressing frustration that academic articles are not only written in an impenetrable way, but are also sealed behind paywalls, and thus inaccessible to practitioners (Borg, 2009). Duoethnography, through its dialogic, playscript-like presentation, circumvents at least one of these issues, existing in a format which is both accessible, and, if done well, enjoyable to read. This is key for the notion of ideology critique, especially if such a notion is intended to have reverberations beyond the academic echo chamber. The purpose of conducting research into ideology is to expose those beliefs which hold back emancipatory change; to problematize them and put into question their 'common sense' status. Thus, this kind of research opens up a space for people to reconsider and question strongly held beliefs, and thus potentially reconfigure their situation in such a way as to align with those new understandings.

Through reading duoethnographies, teachers may be inspired to see not only the conflicts which arise between the two participant-researchers, but also to consider how the phenomena under discussion in the dialogue may have impacted their own lives, and thus to reevaluate their beliefs on this basis. Duoethnography could thus be an important communicative tool for research to make its way to teachers, alert them to potential contradictions between their beliefs and their situation, and thus cause them to question things such as 'English-only' policies in schools (Menken & Sánchez, 2019), the testing regimes that guide so much of language learning (Jordan & Long, 2022), and the cultural values expressed in language teaching materials (Copley, 2018). Here duoethnography may act as an important tool of mediation between researchers and practitioners, and as a spur to teachers making actual change in their classrooms and institutions.

As an example, Fallas-Escobar and Pentón Ferrera (2022) engaged in a duoethnographic discussion of their institutionalised raciolinguistic struggles. They define these as "racialized individuals' ongoing and everyday experiences of having their subjectivities and professional/educational opportunities constrained by institutional listening subject positions that conflate racialized bodies with linguistic deficiency" (p. 2). One major theme which emerged from this discussion was the prevalence of spaces within their institutions which were maintained either tacitly or explicitly as monolingual, and in which English was primarily spoken, despite the multilingual skills of both the teachers and students. Despite the presence of bilingual Spanish and English speakers, English was reserved for institutional functions, while Spanish was relegated to more casual or informal interactions, thus setting up an implicit hierarchy of languages, and of the speakers who embody those languages. Through reading a study such as this, it is possible that teachers may become aware of the ideological assumptions that cause them to privilege one language over another in their workplaces or other institutional settings, and thus unintentionally reinforce these problematic hierarchies.

The model of critical theory outlined in this paper is fundamentally orientated towards achieving emancipatory change, and yet much research in this mold has been accused of losing sight of this goal, and instead retreating into dense and impracticable theory. Duoethnography could be a key way for critical research to contribute not only to theory but also to praxis, by communicating ideas to teachers and acting as a model of dialectical thought. This should not be understood as theorists trying to 'brainwash' teachers with their political ideas, but rather, as Freire (1974/2005) says with regard to critical pedagogy, to help teachers "perceive themselves in a dialectical relationship with their social reality" (p. 30). Rather than attempting to tell teachers what to think and what not to think, this kind of approach could play the role of putting teachers into an active state of constant reevaluation of their profession and practice, and inspire them to push for changes that would benefit both themselves and their students.

Limitations and concerns

In this section I will attempt to outline and address some concerns that may be raised about the ideas put forward in this chapter.

One concern that may be raised is that the proposed role for duoethnography outlined here relegates it to an ancillary position in theory building; a supplement to and check on other empirical and theoretical work, that does not by itself offer new insights or data. I would contest this on two grounds. Firstly, the form of critical research outlined in this chapter is inherently interdisciplinary and dialectical in nature. All empirical work is taken as acting as a supplement and check on all other work, with none being awarded primacy. The insights gained from all relevant fields of inquiry complement and inform one other, and the same would be true of duoethnographic work conducted within this framework. Thus, duoethnographies would be no less ancillary than any other empirical work conducted. Secondly, the fact that duoethnographies could act as an engine for the uncovering and eventual overcoming of internal contradictions suggests the method would in fact hold a position of particular importance, warranted by its uniquely dialogic and reflective elements.

Ethical issues

Ethical concerns may also be raised regarding duoethnography in the form presented in this chapter. While duoethnography, much like autoethnography, is sometimes seen as circumventing many ethical issues related to participants -as there are no specific human subjects taking part other than the researcher-participants (Chang, 2008), it is not the case that no such ethical issues exist. Firstly, there are concerns about power imbalances between researchers, and the attendant need for trust in dialogue (Norris & Sawyer, 2012). Further, the fact that duoethnographers are specifically involved in an investigation of their own, named, life histories means that other characters appearing in accounts of those life histories may be vulnerable to identification and suffer damage to their reputation or standing (Fox & Gaspers, 2020). Accordingly, Ellis (2007) suggests that in any form of self-ethnography, it is necessary for researchers to consider the 'relational ethics' between themselves and any significant figures in their lives that they may discuss. They must make sure to treat anyone appearing in their accounts with sensitivity and respect. This is particularly true for critical work, in which sensitive issues related to personal identities are discussed, and situations of oppression and marginalization are foregrounded. This is not a concern unique to the use of duoethnography outlined here, but it is one that must be taken into account by all researchers seeking to conduct duoethnographic work. As with other forms of qualitative inquiry, a number of procedures exist to avoid this issue, including anonymization, creative rewriting, and the alteration of identifying details (Davis, 1995). Researchers may also be required to seek consent from those who feature in the recounted episodes.

Conclusion

In this chapter, I have considered some of the ways in which a method of research such as duoethnography, which within ELT is strongly associated with poststructuralism, could be incorporated into a program of critical ELT research inspired by the early critical theory of Max Horkheimer and the Frankfurt School. I have suggested that duoethnography could play three key roles in such a program.

Firstly, it can be used to introduce ongoing reflexivity into the process of theory construction, so that researchers are constantly aware of the possible contradictions between their recommendations and the outcomes these may have on the field. This would allow theory to be continually updated and reconsidered, so as to realise the ultimate goal of human flourishing. Secondly, it could be used as a way of identifying areas for ideological critique. By examining beliefs through the contrasting of personal experiences, researchers may become alert to contradictions and problems within belief structures, thus revealing a potential ideological character contained within them. Such an investigation would perhaps not be sufficient to make any strong claims about ideology, but it has the potential to reveal cracks in the wall; weaknesses that further studies could explore more deeply. Finally, the dialogic and accessible format of duoethnography could make it an ideal tool for communicating research findings to practitioners, and also act as a model of reflexive thought, which could lead to the development of critical consciousness on the part of teachers.

It is important to note that these three applications do not require a change in the underlying method of duoethnography. My goal here has not been to fundamentally reconfigure duoethnography for a new purpose, but rather to examine how duoethnography, respected for what it is and the insights it can offer, may contribute to a research program that might, on the surface, appear not to fully align with what is often taken to be its underlying theoretical basis in poststructuralism. Much as in the recent work of Block (2022) and Pennycook (2021), the aim of this chapter has been to find some reconciliation between the poststructuralist work represented by duoethnography, and the more modernist forms of critical social theory which are gaining currency in ELT. The deconstructive and reflexive character of duoethnography can help to open up questions for further exploration, and can also act as the conscience of a critical approach, constantly testing and problematizing claims, and thus acting as an engine of further research and theoretical sophistication. Within ELT, this can allow us to explore in detail the relationship between the structure of the industry as informed by neoliberal global capitalism and the power of nation states, and the individual lives of teachers and learners, always keeping the one in mind as we contemplate the other. Finally, through its potential to mediate between researchers and teachers, duoethography can help critical theory achieve praxis, by making the findings relevant to practitioners, and spurring critical thought and engagement. Through this, we may create a research program which can contribute to the freedom of teachers, learners, and users of the language to live, develop, and express themselves in ways unconstrained by political, economic, or ideological barriers.

Acknowledgements

I would like to thank Daniel Hooper and Marc Jones for their comments on early drafts of this chapter.

References

Abromeit, J. (2011). *Max Horkheimer and the foundations of the Frankfurt School.* Cambridge University Press.

Adorno, T.W. (2019). *Philosophical elements of a theory of society.* Polity. (Original work published 1964).

Ahmed, A., & Morgan, B. (2021). Postmemory and multilingual identities in English language teaching: A duoethnography, *The Language Learning Journal, 49*(4), 483–498.

Antonio, R. (1981). Immanent critique as the core of critical theory: Its origins and developments in Hegel, Marx and contemporary thought. *The British Journal of Sociology, 32*(3), 330–345.

Bailey, K. (2006). Marketing the eikaiwa wonderland: Ideology, akogare, and gender alterity in English conversation school advertising in Japan. *Environment and Planning D: Society and Space, 24*, 105–130.

Best, B., Bonefeld, W., & O'Kane, C. (2018). Introduction: Key texts and contributions to a critical theory of society. In B. Best, W. Bonefeld, & C. O'Kane (Eds.), *The Sage handbook of Frankfurt School critical theory* (pp.1–16). Sage.

Block, D. (2022). *Issues and challenges in identity research.* Routledge.

Borg, S. (2009). English language teachers' conceptions of research. *Applied Linguistics, 30*(3), 358–388.

Bori, P. (2018). *Language textbooks in the era of neoliberalism.* Routledge.

Bouchard, J. (2022). Critical applied linguistics. *JALT Journal, 44*(1), 153–169.

Canagarajah, A.S. (2012). Teacher development in a global profession: An autoethnography. *TESOL Quarterly, 46*(2), 258–279.

Chang, H. (2008). *Autoethnography as method.* Routledge.

Copley, K. (2018). Neoliberalism and ELT coursebook content. *Critical Inquiry in Language Studies, 15*(1), 43–62.

Davis, K.A. (1995). Qualitative theory and methods in applied linguistics research. *TESOL Quarterly, 29*(3), 427–453.

De Costa, P., Park, J., & Wee, L. (2016). Language learning as linguistic entrepreneurship: Implications for language education. *The Asia-Pacific Education Researcher, 25*, 695–702.

Duran, C.S., & Saenkhum, T. (2022). *"Because she's not a native speaker of English, she doesn't have the knowledge": Positioning NNES scholars in U.S. higher education,* Race Ethnicity and Education.

Ellis, C. (2007). Telling secrets, revealing lives: Relational ethics in research with intimate others. *Qualitative Inquiry, 13*(1), 3–29.

Fallas Escobar, C., & Pentón Herrera, L.J. (2022). Examining raciolinguistic struggles in institutional settings: A duoethnography. *Linguistics and Education 67*, 101012.

doi Fox, J., & Gasper, R. (2020). The choice to disclose (or not) mental health ill-health in UK higher education institutions: A duoethnography by two female academics. *Journal of Organizational Ethnography*, 9(3), 295–309.

Freire, P. (2005). Education for critical consciousness. *Continuum*. (Original work published 1974).

Freyenhagen, F. (2018). *Critical Theory: Self-reflexive theorizing and struggles for emancipation.* Oxford Research Encyclopedia of Politics. Retrieved 18 May 2023 from https://oxfordre .com/politics/view/10.1093/acrefore/9780190228637.001.0001/acrefore-9780190228637-e-195

Fromm, E. (1961). *Marx's concept of man.* Frederick Ungar Publishing.

Gerald, J.P.B. (2022). *Antisocial language teaching: English and the pervasive pathology of whiteness.* Multilingual Matters.

doi Golombek, P., & Jordan, S.R. (2005). Becoming "Black lambs" not "parrots": A poststructuralist orientation to intelligibility and identity. *TESOL Quarterly*, 39(3), 513–533.

doi Hammine, M., & Rudolph, N. (2022). Perceiving and problematizing 'invisibility' in English language education and criticality: A duoethnographic dialogue. *Asian Englishes*, 25(3), 311–325.

doi Held, D. (1980). *Introduction to critical theory: Horkheimer to Habermas.* University of California Press.

Holliday, A. (2005). *The struggle to teach English as an international language.* Oxford University Press.

doi Holliday, A. (2006). Native-speakerism. *ELT Journal*, 60(4), 385–387.

Holliday, A. (2014). Researching English and culture and similar topics in ELT. *The English Foreign Language Journal*, 5(1), 1–15.

Hooper, D., & Iijima, A. (2019). Examining the "invisible wall" of native-speakerism in Japanese ELT: A duoethnography of teacher experience. *Asian Journal of English Language Teaching*, 28, 1–27.

doi Hooper, D., Oka, M., & Yamazawa, A. (2020). Not all eikaiwas (or instructors) are created equal: A trioethnography of 'native speaker' and 'non-native speaker' perspectives on English conversation schools in Japan. In R.J. Lowe & L. Lawrence (Eds.), *Duoethnography in English language teaching: Research, reflection, and classroom application* (pp. 29–49). Multilingual Matters.

doi Horkheimer, M. (1993). The present situation of social philosophy and the tasks of an institute for social research. In M. Horkheimer, *Between philosophy and social science: Selected early writings* (pp.1–14). Continuum. (Original work published 1931).

Horkheimer, M. (1972a). Traditional and critical theory. In M. Horkheimer, *Critical theory: Selected essays.* (pp.188–243). Continuum. (Original work published 1937).

Horkheimer, M. (1972b). Postscript. In M. Horkheimer, *Critical theory: Selected essays.* (pp.244–252). Continuum. (Original work published 1937).

Horkheimer, M. (1972). The social function of philosophy. In M. Horkheimer, *Critical theory: Selected essays.* (pp.253–272). Continuum. (Original work published 1939).

Jaeggi, R. (2014). *Alienation.* Colombia University Press.

Jay, M. (1973). *The dialectical imagination: A history of the Frankfurt School and the Institute for Social Research.* University of California Press.

Jenkins, S. (2019). Examining the (im)mobility of African American Muslim TESOL teachers in Saudi Arabia. *Transitions: Journal of Transient Migration*, 3(2), 157–175.

Jordan, G., & Long, M. (2022). *English language teaching now and how it could be.* Cambridge Scholars.

Knisely, K., & Paiz, J. M. (2021). Bringing trans, non-binary, and queer understandings to bear in language education. *Critical Multilingualism Studies*, 9(1), 23–45.

Korsch, K. (1971). *Marxism and philosophy.* Verso. (Original work published 1923).

Kubota, R. (1999). Japanese culture constructed by discourses: Implications for applied linguistic research and English language teaching. *TESOL Quarterly*, 33(1), 9–35.

Kubota, R., & Lin, A. (Eds.). (2009). *Race, culture, and identities in second language education: Exploring critically engaged practice.* Routledge.

Lawrence, L., & Lowe, R. J. (2020). An introduction to duoethnography. In R. J. Lowe & L. Lawrence (Eds.), *Duoethnography in English language teaching: Research, reflection, and classroom application.* (pp.1–26). Multilingual Matters.

Lawrence, L., & Nagashima, Y. (2020). The intersectionality of gender, sexuality, race, and native-speakerness: Investigating ELT teacher identity through duoethnography. *Journal of Language, Identity & Education*, 19(1), 42–55.

Lawrence, L., & Nagashima, Y. (2021). Exploring LGBTQ+ pedagogy in Japanese university classrooms. *ELT Journal*, 75(2), 152–161,

Lowe, R. J. (2020). *Uncovering ideology in English language teaching: Identifying the 'native speaker' frame.* Springer.

Lowe, R. J. (2022). Native-speakerism among Japanese teacher trainees: Ideology, framing, and counter-framing. *JALT Journal*, 44(2), 235–259.

Lowe, R. J. (2023). Frames, ideologies, and the construction of professional identities among non-Japanese EFL teachers in Japan. In M. Mielick, R. Kubota, & L. Lawrence (Eds.), *Discourses of identity: Language learning and teaching perspectives in Japan.* (pp.301–319) Palgrave millan

Lowe, R. J., & Kiczkowiak, M. (2016). Native-speakerism and the complexity of personal experience: A duoethnographic study. *Cogent Education*, 3(1), 1264171.

Lukács, G. (1971). *History and class consciousness.* The MIT Press. (Original work published 1923).

MacDonald, M. N., & O'Regan, J. P. (2013). The ethics of intercultural communication, *Educational Philosophy and Theory*, 45(10), 1005–1017.

Marx, K. (1992). Economic and philosophical manuscripts. In K. Marx, Early writings. (pp. 279–400). Penguin. (Original work published 1844).

Marx, K. & Engels, F. (1988). *The German ideology.* Prometheus. (Original work published 1846).

McCarthy, T. (1993). The idea of a critical theory and its relation to philosophy. In S. Benhabib, W. Bonß, & J. McCole (Eds.), *On Max Horkheimer: New perspectives* (pp.127–152). The MIT Press.

Menken, K., & Sánchez, M. T. (2019). Translanguaging in English-only schools: From pedagogy to stance in the disruption of monolingual policies and practices. *TESOL Quarterly*, 53(3),741–767.

Moore, A. (2021). A plea to stop debating and erasing queer lives in ELT. *ELT Journal*, 75(3), 362–365.

doi Morgan, B. (2007). Poststructuralism and applied linguistics: Complementary approaches to identity and culture in ELT. In J. Cummins & C. Davison (Eds), *International handbook of English language teaching (Vol. 2, pp. 949–968).* Springer.

Motha, S. (2014). *Race and empire in English language teaching.* Teachers College Press

doi Musto, M. (2021). Alienation redux: Marxian perspectives. In M. Musto (Ed.), *Karl Marx's writings on alienation.* (pp. 3–48). Palgrave Macmillan.

doi Nelson, C. (1999). Sexual identities in ESL: Queer theory and classroom inquiry. *TESOL Quarterly,* 33(3), 371–391.

Nelson, C. (2009). *Sexual identities in English language education: Classroom conversations.* Routledge.

Norris, J., & Sawyer, R. (2012). Toward a dialogic methodology. In J. Norris, R. Sawyer, & D. E. Lund (Eds.). *Duoethnography: Dialogic methods for social, health, and educational research* (pp. 9–40). Left Coast Press.

doi Norton, B., & Morgan, B. (2023). Poststructuralism. In C. A. Chapelle (Ed.), *The encyclopedia of applied linguistics.*

doi O'Regan, J. P. (2014). English as a lingua franca: An immanent critique. *Applied Linguistics,* 35(5), 533–552.

doi O'Regan, J. (2021). *Global English and political economy.* Routledge.

Ollman, B. (1976). *Alienation: Marx's conception of man in capitalist society (2nd ed.).* Cambridge University Press.

doi Pennycook, A. (2001). *Critical applied linguistics: A critical introduction (1st ed.).* Routledge.

doi Pennycook, A. (2021). *Critical applied linguistics: A critical (re)introduction (2nd ed.).* Routledge.

Phillipson, R. (1992). *Linguistic imperialism.* Oxford University Press.

doi Phillipson, R. (2017). Myths and realities of 'global' English. *Language Policy* 16, 313–331.

doi Ramjattan, V. A. (2019). Racializing the problem of and solution to foreign accent in business. *Applied Linguistics Review,* 13(4) 527–544.

doi Rose, H., & Montakantiwong, A. (2018). A tale of two teachers: A duoethnography of the realistic and idealistic successes and failures of teaching English as an international language. *RELC Journal,* 49(1), 88–101.

doi Sawyer, R. D., & Liggett, T. (2012). Shifting positionalities: A critical discussion of a duoethnographic inquiry of a personal curriculum of post/colonialism. *International Journal of Qualitative Methods,* 11(5), 628–651.

Sawyer, R. D., & Norris, J. (2013). *Duoethnography.* Oxford University Press.

doi Simpson, W. (2018). Neoliberal fetishism: The language learner as homo œconomicus. *Language and Intercultural Communication,* 18(5), 507–519.

doi Simpson, W. (2022). *Capital, commodity, and English language teaching.* Routledge.

doi Stanley, P. (2019). Autoethnography and ethnography in English language teaching. In A. Gao (Ed.), *Second handbook of English language teaching* (pp. 1071–1090). Springer.

doi Tuhiwai Smith, L. (2021). *Decolonizing methodologies: Research and indigenous people (3rd ed.).* Bloomsbury.

doi Widin, J. (2010). *Illegitimate practices: Global English language education.* Multilingual Matters.

doi Yoo, I. W. (2014). Nonnative teachers in the expanding circle and the ownership of English, *Applied Linguistics,* 35(1), 82–86.

CHAPTER 8

Currere
A Research method to deconstruct previous experiences in Applied Linguistics Research

Maria Garcia & Jessica Masterson
Washington State University

In this chapter we discuss how *currere* can support research in Applied Linguistics (AL). We examine studies where *currere* or a similar approach has been used as a research method in Applied Linguistics. Citing these studies, we discuss how they can be used as examples for future *currere*-based AL research. Following that discussion, we also provide guidance about considerations that researchers should be aware of before choosing *currere* as their research approach. This discussion will help guide AL researchers in using currere in the different stages of a *currere*-based AL research project. Lastly, we address affordances, limitations, and ethical considerations of using *currere* in AL research, especially within studies that examine power dynamics used within language. Additionally, we provide guidance on how to use *currere* in studies where there is a larger group of participants.

Introduction

Applied linguistics (AL), like many other fields of research, has expanded its focus in response to global trends and considerations, and in the process has warranted the use of new research methodologies. *Currere* as a research approach provides a critical perspective on previous educational life experiences that researchers have encountered personally. Recursively engaging the four steps of *currere* (the regressive, the progressive, the analytical, and the synthetic), inquirers begin to access recessed memories and knowledge and imagine new possibilities for themselves in a more socially just future.

Throughout this chapter, we discuss how *currere* can support research in Applied Linguistics. *Currere*-based research in the field of AL is limited, so we draw on adjacent studies where *currere* has been used as the method in linguistics research or where a similar approach to *currere* has been used in AL research.

https://doi.org/10.1075/rmal.8.08gar

We also discuss some considerations for researchers before choosing *currere* as their method. Lastly, we address some of the affordances, limitations, and ethical considerations of using *currere* in AL research. This is especially critical as AL researchers continue to increase efforts in addressing issues related to social justice, such as identifying power dynamics used within language.

Theory and practice in applied linguistics

In the U.S., where both authors are based, AL research has continued to examine topics aligned with sociolinguistics and social justice, adding to the increased awareness and urgency surrounding social justice issues in the United States (and elsewhere). Across the world, AL research has included sociocultural understandings of language, including topics such as language policy, language ideology, and multilingualism (Lei & Liu, 2019). With an increase in societal awareness of issues related to social justice, AL research is generating new opportunities and expanding into new methods — such as that provided by *currere* — to advance AL research further to address issues of power and inequity within sociolinguistic contexts.

Pavlenko (2007) notes that traditional approaches to AL can run the risk of reducing linguistic form to content, ironically, overlooking the myriad complexities of language used to convey narrative accounts. While some AL research positions participants as little more than note-takers and reporters of their own experience, Pavlenko (2007) suggests that "[t]his treatment disregards the interpretive nature of storytelling, that is the fact that the act of narration unalterably transforms its subject, and any further interpretation interprets the telling and not the event in question" (p.168).

Currere also has the potential to contribute to another important topic of AL research — the link between language and practice: that is, while participants and subjects may position themselves in certain ways through speech, we know little about how this speech actually relates to how these same individuals choose to live their lives. Indeed, all humans, as innate storytellers, "use language to interpret experiences and position themselves as particular kinds of people" (Pavlenko, 2007, pp.166–167). As such, scholars have suggested the need for blending AL approaches with ethnographic and/or case study observations in order to increase research rigor and validity (Everett, 2018; Rogers & Wetzel, 2013; Shaw et al., 2008).

Taken together, the well-established focus in AL research toward issues of equity and social justice — one that necessarily highlights and interrogates lived experiences — is well-aligned with the method of *currere*, as discussed in the following sections.

Currere and (critical) applied linguistics

As a research method, *currere* provides a guided way to further social-justice-centered interdisciplinary AL research. *Currere,* as defined by Baszile (2017), is a

> method of autobiographical or biographical inquiry that suggests that the re-searcher re-remembers lived educational experiences and moves them through four moments or stages of critical self-reflection and contemplation, giving shape to an internal dialogue where the researcher develops future desires for a more socially just world. (p. vi)

The deeply emic, subjective, and creatively generative dynamic of *currere* offer exceptional potential for research in Applied Linguistics.

AL emerged as a fundamentally interdisciplinary field in the 1980s as part of a growing interest among linguistics researchers in oral communication who sought a "methodological convergence" among such previously-disparate fields as critical discourse analysis, sociolinguistics, social psychology, education, anthropology, and history (Catalano & Waugh, 2020). Though many AL definitions exist, for the purposes of this chapter we employ Peniro and Cyntas's (2019) explanation: "Applied linguistics is an interdisciplinary field that identifies, investigates, and offers solutions to language-related real-life problems" (p. 1). Further, we find that *critical Applied Linguistics* (Pennycook, 1990) — which applies an approach rooted in asking the most urgent, critical questions of the discourse we employ in our everyday, power-laden interactions — is most suitable for a methodological pairing with *currere*. As critical Applied Linguistics (CAL) addresses issues of inequality rooted in language, inherent in the employment of this research approach is a commitment to fighting inequality (Catalano & Waugh, 2020). More specifically, CAL links

> micro-relations of Applied Linguistics to macro-relations of social and political power. In this vein, it empowers applied linguists in the sense that it enables them to make the connection between discourse, language learning, language teaching, language use, and the social and political contexts in which these processes take place. (Catalano & Waugh, 2020, p. 249)

Given these explicit aims, we argue that *currere* has much to offer CAL, particularly in its rootedness in everyday experiences and its lean toward social justice goals.

As a field that is primarily concerned with real-life issues as revealed and addressed through language, we see a natural connection between critical Applied Linguistics research and *currere*, which helps researchers excavate and understand the patterns and themes in lived experiences in order to make informed decisions for a more just world.

While CAL can provide a lens through which to examine such experiences, *currere* provides a much-needed theoretical grounding that can meaningfully anchor data analysis and reporting (Pavlenko, 2007). Further, while certain forms of CAL research, namely corpus analyses, have been criticized as insufficiently rigorous on their own (Fairclough, 2015), *currere* as a form of praxis can assist these methods with identifying and challenging "the role of power and status in language" (Peniro & Cyntas, 2019, p.7).

Finally, though critical researchers within AL in recent years have made important moves to address the myriad and intersecting functions of race, gender, social class, and sexuality in Applied Linguistics, far less work has been done to unpack the experiences of racism, homo/transphobia, sexism, and classism among AL researchers and students (Kubota, 2020). *Currere*, which critically centers these experiences and stories, can serve as a complement to CAL. To this end, Pavlenko (2007) identified three directions in narrative-driven CAL research:

a.   cognitive approaches that treat autobiographies as meaning-making systems and thus as evidence of how people understand things;

b.   textual approaches that see them as a creative interplay of a variety of voices and discourses, and thus as evidence of larger social and cultural influences on human cognition and self-presentation...; and

c.   discursive approaches that view them as interaction-oriented productions, and thus as evidence of the co-constructed nature of our life storytelling. (p.171)

When paired with the theoretical depth and approach of *currere*, we see endlessly fruitful approaches to CAL research. In the following sections, we articulate possible pathways to incorporate *currere* into AL research.

Applying currere in AL research

A *currere* is undertaken with a researcher's considerations of the following four stages: the analytical, the synthetical, the regressive, and the progressive, with each stage taking on an analytical lens toward the researcher's previous experiences (Pinar, 2013). Pinar (2013) emphasizes that the importance of examining the intersections of one's lived and educational experiences supports the case for using *currere* as a method in AL research to explore educational experiences.

Although these stages might suggest a somewhat rigid research approach, these stages are fluid, and those who have conducted a *currere* suggest that researchers weave in and out of stages in a nonlinear matter as they deconstruct their educational experiences or the experiences of potential research participants (Sawyer, 2022).

Fluidity in currere research

These four stages provide a structure for researchers to use *currere* as a research approach in Applied Linguistics, but they also give freedom for them to interact with each stage as they see fit for their lived educational experiences or those of the participants in their study. In some cases, this means that researchers or participants will interact with two stages at once as they navigate through their *currere* and may also revisit previous stages in order to come to their conclusions. This fluidity allows the researcher or participants to uncover new information about the experiences they are analyzing by interacting with each stage as they see fit. This is explicitly mentioned in a *currere* about high school experience completed by Sawyer (2022), who models this fluidity in describing his process of using art and photography during the analytic phase:

> I laid the photos out on the desk and let them talk to me. I arranged them one way and then another way, with different stories emerging from changing juxtapositions. With random juxtapositions, the photos broke their narrative contexts and told new stories in the spaces that lay between them.   (p. 7)

Engaging in *currere's* nonlinear process, AL researchers may access an alternative method that embraces a less restrictive take on data collection, thereby expanding the scope of AL research. For example, Edwards (2021) conducted a *currere* in order to uncover the relationship between writing voice and identity in a small group of Chinese first-year international college students. She used *currere* as an analytical framework to begin to understand how international students made sense of their narratives of learning to write in academic English as non-native speakers of English. She explored "how English language learners learn, relate, and identify differently over time and space as they experience different roles, contexts, and interactions" (Abstract section). To assist with story clarification and accuracy, Edwards (2021) obtained information about the students from observation notes, emails, and coursework from their first-year composition classes. Similar to how Sawyer (2022) used a series of photographs and yearbook captions to construct a *currere*, Edwards used a mix of data sources to help the students (and herself) restory their educational experiences, their analytical thought process of those experiences, and their hopes for the future of their writing voice and identity.

Various *curreres* in the *Currere Exchange Journal* have showcased an additional layer of fluidity that *currere* as a research method can offer for AL research, especially in terms of representation and expression of knowledge. Many of those who have submitted to this journal have chosen various ways to express their previous educational experiences and their *currere* in the form of poetry, comics, or more academic papers, all of which provide insight to the central animating dynamic of *currere*. This approach recenters inquiry away from normative find-ings to more open, emergent, and dynamic findings.

As exemplified in Sawyer's (2022) and Edward's (2021) *currere's,* fluidity in the data collection process supports researchers in coming to conclusions which can offer a broader understanding of questions that researchers seek to answer. The innovative ways in which a *currere* can be presented add an additional layer of fluidity that can enhance and broaden future AL research studies.

The openness of currere

Currere may be conducted on new topics or even or previously researched topics. As researchers learn more about a topic with new experiences and research, they might see fit to revisit a previous *currere* to form new conclusions. This is espe-cially valuable to AL, where the use of language is examined from various perspec-tives, including temporal contexts. Furthermore, with perceptions of language as well as its use changing and evolving in society, researchers benefit from a dynamic method that is open to these changes. Furthermore engaging in nonlin-ear ways to present and represent story (and narrative), researchers open the pos-sibilities for new insights and understandings.

Along with providing four stages for the inquiry, *currere* also seeks to guide the researcher in exploring specific questions. These include, for example, "What has been my educational experience? How have and how will these experiences shape who I have been and who I hope to be as a student, educator, scholar, activist, advo-cate?" (Baszile, 2017, p. vii). While these questions provide a flexible framework in contrast to a more defined methodological structure in AL research, it is important to note that lived responses to these questions vary from researcher to researcher and, as mentioned previously, the conclusions that researchers make at the end of *currere* are subject to change leading to a possibility of conducting another *cur-rere*-based study in AL research. The possibility of variation in responses to *cur-rere's* essential questions highlights the subjective aspects that *currere* research can bring to AL research.

Currere as an AL method

As AL research topics have continued to address themes rooted in sociocultural understandings such as language policy and multilingualism, using *currere* as a research approach to explore such sociocultural understandings aligns well with the goals of AL research. *Currere* encourages researchers to focus an analyti-cal lens onto their past educational experiences while also encouraging them to consider the significance of those experiences in relation to a more socially just future. *Currere* also reminds researchers to take into account the situated historical, cultural, social and political contexts of their lived educational experiences or the experiences of others when making conclusions that aim to change the current education system (Baszile, 2017; Lei & Liu, 2019). Moreover, successful *curreres* uncover biases that the researcher might have had and might have also perpetuated in research, as well as in educational spaces: "As a form of contemplative inquiry, then, *currere* can help us identify subconscious thoughts and patterns of thinking that explain our actions, and with this awareness, we can work to decolonize both our thinking and our actions" (Baszile, 2017, p. viii). Part of "diving deeply" into sociocultural understandings is making sense of unconscious biases that might have infiltrated our ways of thinking. As research in AL continues to move toward subjective and socio-cultural issues, *currere* can help researchers to "re-member" and critically reflect on previous educational experiences. This process in turn helps researchers to turn solutions into practice in both schools and future research projects as they pertain to language ideology and educational policy.

Moreover, the four steps of *currere* can also provide additional contexts to themes and phenomena identified in previous AL research, expanding their narrative base. These narratives can serve as a form of counternarrative, providing additional subjective perspectives and knowledge that may have been overlooked. Discussing how consciousness may be expanded by engaging in *currere*, Pinar (2013) references Bhabha (1994) to emphasize how *currere* can be used to open a third space, furthering knowledge and producing "cultural translations" within non-binary-based ways of thinking and offering decolonial pathways within AL research. For example, Edwards (2021) showed in her *currere* about English language learners that more inclusive higher education learning environments can contribute in positive ways to the linguistic and cultural identities of multilingual college students. In a recent *currere* on translanguage, Sondari (et al., 2023) explored Southeast Asian Ph.D. students' perceptions of different "Englishes" in their university experience in the United States.

Similarities and contrasts between currere and duoethnography

While limited *currere*-based research in AL currently exists, Werbińska's's (2020) elucidation of duoethnography and its relationship to *currere* is instructive. Duoethnography and *currere* share many similarities. For example, duoethnography and *currere* both provide an analytical space for participants to ponder, deconstruct, and reconceptualize their relationship to past experiences and stories (Werbińska, 2020). However, they also differ. The most overt difference between duoethnography and *currere* is that duoethnography takes a more dialogic approach to deconstructing previously lived experiences by having two people with juxtaposing stories of the same phenomenon reconceptualize their perspectives and ideas (Werbińska, 2020). *Currere*, on the other hand, is primarily an individual process (although there have been collaborative *curreres*) in which the researcher dialogues with other participants as part of the inquiry.

Werbińska (2020) writes that data sources that duoethnographers can draw from to support their studies include various types of artifacts such as photographs, report cards, class assignments, textbooks, journal entries. Such artifacts have also supported *currere*-based research. For example, Edwards' (2021) included email correspondence, writing samples, and class assignments in her *currere*. Within *currere*, the dialogue between artifacts may generate unexpected turns in the inquiry. This may be seen with how Sawyer (2022) contrasted formal yearbooks photos with informal personal photos to construct an in-depth *currere* about previous high school experiences from a queer perspective. In *currere*, the analysis of language-based artifacts may generate stories that flourish into unexpected perspectives and possibilities, as well as show how they may represent and manifest systems of power and privilege.

Affordances to *Currere* within AL

As life-history curriculum with which people engage in "an embodied deconstruction of the past to reconstruct the future though wide-awake study in the present" (Sawyer, 2017, p.90), *currere* (Pinar et al., 1995) ideally provides a reflexive and deeply emic lens for research in Applied Linguistics. As primarily a language-based method, *currere* allows researchers to study the layered meanings of language within their actual use, creating the context, at least ideally, for a language-based reflexivity. The outcomes of such a dynamic may be found, for example, in the implications of Safari and Rashidi'sRashidi (2015) study, for example, in which they advocate for greater connections between life history and the more formal ESL curriculum in their native Iran. In their *currere*-informed research study with Iranian teachers of English, they sought to provide new understandings about how English-language education in Iran could shift to a more transformative approach to teaching and learning. In their study, they had thirteen participants first take "how to" conduct *currere* workshops, then had conversational interviews with these participants to better sensitize them in conducting their own *curreres*. From this study, Safari and Rashidi (2015) were able to identify various themes, such as disconnects between teachers' updated knowledge and the needs of the educational system, requirements around development of critical thinking skills, and lack of motivation from educators to update knowledge. These perceptions can ignite conversations about areas of improvement in English education among educators, administrators, and politicians for linguistic education in Iran and across other countries. Their study illustrates the interest in *currere* among language researchers examining native speakerism (e.g., Tan and Chang, Chapter 12 in this book), second language development, and even the narrative and rhetorical structure of how the inquiry itself is presented (e.g., Sawyer, 2017).

Perhaps the strongest affordance of the use of *currere* as a research method is that it allows researchers to represent themselves. As they tell their own story — and represent themselves in all steps of the inquiry — they are then positioned to gain a deeper understanding how they make and remake meaning and perceptions of experience. This self-representation allows them to explore aspects of their identity which are often missing from more conventional studies on language acquisition.

Part of this exploration is structured by the four steps of *currere*, encouraging researchers to go back and more deeply look at their histories surrounding their socialization into and use of language. The two transtemporal steps of *currere* scaffold and move the inquiry to new territory; while the two trans-conceptual steps expand the conceptualization of experience, allowing the researcher to view self from multiple viewpoints. And while there are social and political aspects to this examination, both Wang (Chapter 4 this book) and Pinar et al. (1995) have suggested that there are also unconscious manifestations and latent meanings to language.

And, as researchers using *currere* have the opportunity to tell and perceive their own story in new ways, this process also supports a form of personal and professional liberation, as Tan and Chang (Chapter 12, this book) experienced in their *currere* of learning English as a second language in their native China. These reconceptualizations may lead to new understandings and insights for the inquirer, facilitating reflexivity. They also present the reader with new strategies of resistance within situations, as they read about new counter-narratives.

Another affordance is *currere's* flexible use with other research methods. As seen in Edwards" (2021) study, *currere* may be paired with additional methods and research tools. For example, as seen in the previously mentioned study of Iranian teachers by Safari and Rashidi (2015), *currere* may be used with other methodological tools to aid in data collection, such as collaborative dialogue procedures and lengthy semi-structured interviews to ensure the accuracy of and to honor the participants' experiences. Sondari et al., (2023), who explored questions pertaining to participants' relationships between the formal and personal curriculums related to language learning and how these relationships then impacted their perceptions of "Englishes," also used a range of qualitative methodologies to enhance participants' dialogue surrounding their perceptions of past, present, and especially future educational practices related to linguistics. *Currere* served as a tool in their study to help participants envision new directions for communicative and instructional practices within linguistics education. The dialogic and collaborative aspects of the method — such as participants engaging in a group dialogue surrounding their narratives, working together to answer questions about their previous experiences, and reading other narratives from within the group — their public sharing of narrative understandings served as a means of ensuring accuracy in the narrative-creation process. These studies by Sondari and Phetchroj (2023) and Safari and Rashidi (2015) also show the versatility of *currere* in qualitative AL research. This versatility ranges, for example, from small group and individual *curreres* to a larger group and more collaborative studies.

Currere also lends itself to multiple forms of presentation. It may be expressed in many different ways that allow the researcher to convey the narrative that they are trying to share. Typically, *curreres* can be written in the form of a paper or essay. An example of this more traditional approach can be seen in Edwards (2021) in which the researcher chooses to restory each of the participants' *curreres* in a structured written format. However, as demonstrated in some of the submissions in the *Currere Exchange Journal, curreres* can be written or demonstrated in various formats, such as poetry, as shown in Grubb's (2022) *currere* on teaching.

While these studies highlight the affordances of *currere* as a methodological tool in AL research, there are some limitations to the use of *currere* as method in AL research.

Limitations in using *currere* in applied linguistics research

Although *currere* offers many affordances for Applied Linguistics research, there are also limitations, or at least complications, for researchers to contemplate. As with other forms of qualitative research, ethical issues arise in relational forms of research (Kubanyiova, 2008). Even though *currere* is an autobiographical research approach, researchers who have used it have been aware of complexities of how they present their narratives and construct their representations of others (often as part of their own story).

Considerations of presentation and representation become especially important when using *currere* as a form of data collection in a mixed-methods study. Sensitive issues for a researcher to consider include, for example, participants' histories of racism, discrimination, and oppression. For this reason, researchers need to be aware of the sensitive nature of each *currere*, especially when guiding participants to conduct *curreres* on their own experiences. Participants' previous educational experiences may be extremely personal and even traumatic and involve the revisiting of traumatic situations.

For example and as mentioned, Safari and Rashidi (2015) took extra time and care when asking a large group of participants to conduct their own *currere* about their teaching experiences in Iran. As part of the process, they had conversational interviews first with their 13 participants. Each session lasted about one hour and forty-five minutes to ensure that participants had enough time to articulate their teaching experiences and reflect on them critically. As this example illustrates, a need exists for researchers to work with participants before the *currere* process to ensure that they and the researcher can agree on what the participant is comfortable sharing. Especially within mixed-method studies, the analysis and presentation of participants' stories should be handled with sensitivity so that the researcher remains open to the unique and situated nature of their participants' conceptualizations and experiences. When guiding other participants to conduct their own *curreres*, researchers may wish to consider how they themselves are positioned in the process and how they have facilitated their participants' ownership of their own stories.

It is especially important for researchers to be transparent with potential participants about the types of stories that they wish participants to deconstruct and agree to the degree that these stories will be shared with others. It is also helpful for researchers to evaluate their own goals and intentions in conducting a *currere*, especially one in which there is an implicit or explicit promise to benefit a traumatized community. It is especially important for researchers to address this ethical concern when considering working with historically and contemporarily marginalized groups.

Additionally, when writing a *currere*, the writer should attempt to hold a high level of reflection and introspection about the past, present, and future. "I" statements are central to *currere*, especially when the researcher foregrounds the critical nature of the research. For example, Sawyer (2022), in his *currere* on queer narrative theory, examined how past-and-present lived experiences affected him in social and political ways. For Sawyer and other researchers critically engaging in transtemporal reflection, deep personal connections and associations can forge personal reconceptualizations in support of a more socially just future. However, to avoid solipsism, it is important to keep the reflection focused on the self as the site, though, not the topic, of the inquiry. Rather than just recalling previous experiences, those who use *currere* need to ensure that they are also deconstructing those experiences to facilitate understanding for a more socially just future.

Another consideration is the actual form of the presentation, as the form should further enhance the narrative grounded in the study's meanings. Discussing *currere*, Baszile (2017) noted that those working with this method have to be careful not to frame representations by using a traditional Eurocentric form of autobiography, suggesting that such a structure may emphasize heroic terms. To foreground the importance of intentionality in questions of representation and presentation, it may be useful for a researcher who chooses to represent their currere in the form of a poem or a collection of images share their presentation rationale with the reader.

As with much qualitative research, *currere* is focused on unique and situated experience, thus researchers cannot make generalizable claims from their study to larger populations. However, researchers can identify themes in their *currere* data with which to help researchers, their participants, and readers of the study draw their own conclusions and apply meanings from the study to their own settings.

Conclusion

As a research method *currere* highlights the value of subjectivity in research, shedding light on the question of why phenomena unfold as they do. It provides another part to a story once told largely through numerical data. As discussed earlier, the nature in which *currere* takes place provides a methodological example of how fluidity in the research process can provide those who use *currere* with more contingent endings and open-ended conclusions. Although there are many affordances that *currere* can bring to AL research, there are also various limitations and ethical considerations for researchers as they engage in *currere* for themselves and encourage others to use it. As with much qualitative research, these concerns involve issues of representation, trust within relational forms of data collection, and understanding the boundaries of informed consent.

Even though there are currently few studies that use *currere* as a research approach in AL, we hope this chapter will provide researchers in AL with a perspective on how *currere* can be incorporated into the field, increasing its scope.

References

Baszile, D. (2017). On the virtues of currere. *The Currere Exchange Journal, 1*(1), vi–ix. Retrieved on 7 October 2024 from https://www.currereexchange.com/uploads/9/5/8/7/9587563/2taliaferrobaszillecejv1i1.pdf

Bhabha, H. (1994). *The location of culture*. Routledge.

Catalano, T., & Waugh, L. R. (2020). *Discourse analysis, critical discourse studies and beyond.* Springer.

Edwards, J. F. (2021). "My voice is me": Using currere to explore international students' constructions of voice and identity in a new language and culture (Unpublished doctoral dissertation). Miami University.

Everett, S. (2018). "Untold stories": Cultivating consequential writing with a Black male student through a critical approach to metaphor. *Research in the Teaching of English*, 53(1), 34–57.

Fairclough, N. (2015). *Language and power*. Routledge.

Grubb, S. J. (2022). A reflection on teaching. *The Currere Exchange Journal*, 6(1), 1–1.

Kubanyiova, M. (2008). Rethinking research ethics in contemporary applied linguistics: The tension between macroethical and microethical perspectives in situated research. *The Modern Language Journal*, 92(4), 503–518.

Kubota, R. (2020). Confronting epistemological racism, decolonizing scholarly knowledge: Race and gender in applied linguistics. *Applied Linguistics*, 41(5), 712–732.

Lei, L., & Liu, D. (2019). Research trends in applied linguistics from 2005 to 2016: A bibliometric analysis and its implications. *Applied Linguistics*, 40(3), 540–561.

Pavlenko, A. (2007). Autobiographic narratives as data in applied linguistics. *Applied Linguistics*, 28(2), 163–188.

Peniro, R., & Cyntas, J. (2019). Applied linguistics theory and application. *Linguistics and Culture Review*, 3(1), 1–13.

Pennycook, A. (1990). Towards a critical applied linguistics for the 1990s. *Issues in Applied Linguistics*, 1(1), 8–28.

Pinar, W. F. (2013). The reconceptualization of curriculum studies. In D. J. Finders & S. J. Thornton (Eds.), *The curriculum studies reader* (2nd ed., pp. 153–161). Routledge.

Pinar, W. F., Reynolds, W. M., Slattery, P., & Taubman, P. M. (1995). *Understanding curriculum: An introduction to the study of historical and contemporary curriculum discourse*. Peter Lang.

Rogers, R., & Wetzel, M. M. (2013). Studying agency in literacy teacher education: A layered approach to positive discourse analysis. *Critical Inquiry in Language Studies*, 10(1), 62–92.

Safari, P., & Rashidi, N. (2015). Teacher education beyond transmission: Challenges and opportunities for Iranian teachers of English. *Issues in Educational Research*, 25(2), 187–203.

Sawyer, R. D. (2017). Tracing dimensions of aesthetic currere: Critical transactions between person, place, and art. *Currere Exchange Journal*, 1(1), 89–100. https://www.currere exchange.com/uploads/9/5/8/7/9587563/14sawyercejv1i1.pdf

Sawyer, R. D. (2022). Queer narrative theory and currere: Thoughts toward queering currere as a method of queer (curricular) self-study. *JCT (Online)*, 37(1), 23–38.

Shaw, D. M., Barry, A., & Mahlios, M. (2008). Preservice teachers' metaphors of teaching in relation to literacy beliefs. *Teachers and Teaching*, 14(1), 35–50.

Sondari, P. S., & Phetchroj, Y. (2023). Traversing perceptions toward Englishes: A *currere*-informed duoethnography of Southeast Asian PhD students studying in the US. *Linguistics and Education*, 77, 101192.

Werbińska, D. (2020). Duoethnography in applied linguistics qualitative research. *Neofilolog*, 54(2), 269–283.

CHAPTER 9

Narrative inquiry in Applied Linguistics Research

The pleasures and perils

Hanako Okada
Sophia University, Tokyo

Everyone loves a good story, including an increasing number of scholars in Applied Linguistics. A well-told story holds our attention, conveys messages that might otherwise be lost in conventional research reports' dense, dry prose, and connects readers to experiences in their own lives. Novice and experienced scholars alike who are deeply interested in people's lives may find that some Applied Linguistics literature misses what they are most drawn to. Its distanced and impersonal stance somehow does not feel right when we wish to learn about people's lives. The fact that stories are so (deceptively) easy to tell and compelling to read and listen to thus holds great appeal, particularly for novice scholars who are interested in doing research on people's lives and experiences with languages, such as learning and teaching second and foreign languages. However, they may not fully comprehend the perils, as well as the pleasures, of conducting and writing up narrative inquiry. In this chapter, I begin with a brief background and history of narrative inquiry in applied linguistics. I follow by addressing the pleasures and perils, as well as the ethical concerns involved in conducting and writing narrative inquiry, with the goal of making a case for the value of carefully done narrative inquiry in Applied Linguistics research.

Introduction

Narrative inquiry is a flexible and interdisciplinary approach to eliciting and examining accounts of personal experiences and making meaning from them (Clandinin, 2007; Kramp, 2004; Riessman, 2008). It has found a growing place in Applied Linguistics research, especially as the 'social turn' (Block, 2003) called for a more social, contextual, holistic, and ecological research orientation from a predominantly cognitive one.

https://doi.org/10.1075/rmal.8.090ka

Even so, some literature in Applied Linguistics still takes a distanced and impersonal stance — one that somehow does not feel right when we wish to learn about the richness of people's lives. On the contrary, a well-told story holds our attention, adds details about people and their lives that might be missing in these research reports, and connects readers to experiences in their own lives. The fact that stories are so (deceptively) easy to tell and compelling to read and listen to thus holds great appeal, particularly for novice scholars interested in researching people's lives and experiences with languages. The pleasures of conducting and writing up narrative inquiry are many; however, the perils must also be acknowledged.

In this chapter, I begin by providing a brief background and history of narrative inquiry in applied linguistics, focusing on language learning and teaching research, and discussing its contributions. I follow by addressing the pleasures and perils involved in conducting and writing narrative inquiry, as well as the ethical concerns that may emerge. I close by making a case for the value of carefully done narrative inquiry in Applied Linguistics research.

A brief background and history

What is narrative inquiry?

Although the term narrative inquiry can be elusive and ubiquitous, in a nutshell, narrative inquiry refers to a broad, interdisciplinary approach that aims to understand how people make sense of their life experiences through stories — it is *a way of knowing*. The form of stories includes orally told stories, interviews, letters, diaries, memoirs, and autobiographies. Narratives are understood as "the primary form by which human experience is made meaningful" (Polkinghorne, 1988, p.1). In addition to making experiences meaningful, they also "preserve our memories, prompt our reflections, connect us with our past and present, … assist us to envision our future" (Kramp, 2004, p.107), and enable us "to see the world through the eyes of others" (Riley & Hawe, 2004, p.226).

The roots of contemporary narrative inquiry can be seen in the early Chicago School sociologists who collected life histories and personal documents as a source of data in the 1920s and 30s and the mid-20th century anthropologists and oral historians who recorded and analyzed narratives (Holstein & Gubrium, 2012; Riessman, 2008).[1] The use of narratives in the social sciences subsided due to the doubts and constraints of the 'scientific' and experimental research approaches.

---

1. Narrative inquiry includes different strands such as 'realist,' 'postmodern,' and 'constructionist,' and scholars disagree on its precise origin and definition (Riessman & Speedy, 2007).

However, narrative inquiry returned to the fore in the late 1980s and early 1990s with the 'narrative turn' in the human and social sciences associated with post-modernism — positivistic assumptions and quantifications were insufficient to capture the complexities of subjective human experience (Pinnegar & Daynes, 2007). The launch of the *Journal of Narrative and Life History* (more commonly known as the flagship journal *Narrative Inquiry*),[2] "a multi-disciplinary journal for work on and with narrative in different disciplines, establishing narrative inquiry as a trans-disciplinary new field" (*Journal of Narrative and Life History*, n.d.), in 1991 marked such a return and a renewed appreciation towards narrative inquiry.

Narrative inquiry in applied linguistics

It was not until the early 21st century that narrative inquiry found its place in the field of Applied Linguistics — particularly in the domain of Second Language Acquisition (SLA). Although there were some early language learning studies that included narratives such as diary studies and longitudinal ethnographic case studies (e.g., Bailey, 1980; Schmidt & Frota, 1986; Schumann & Schumann, 1977), until much of the 1980s, SLA research primarily focused on cognitive-based language acquisition theories and took on a logical-positivistic perspective to gain hard data and replicable findings (Catford, 1998; Lazaraton, 1995).

In the late 1980s and 1990s, with influences from the social sciences, researchers gained increasing interest in the social and cultural aspects of language acquisition and use and turned to postmodernism as an epistemological and theoretical orientation (Davis, 2013). With such interests, researchers questioned the cognitive bias that viewed language learners and users solely as isolated 'information processing devices' and argued for their treatment also as 'real people', situated and embedded in context (e.g., Firth & Wagner, 1997; Lantolf & Pavlenko, 2001). This questioning led to a lively 'cognitive-social' debate, and although met with resistance by mainstream SLA researchers, it was instrumental for the aforementioned 'social turn' in SLA (Block, 2003) to take place.

The social turn brought forth an increase in qualitative research approaches, particularly case studies to examine language learning, teaching, and use of individuals *within* social contexts (e.g., Norton, 2000, 2001), as well as work on discourse and sociolinguistics of narrative (e.g., Bamberg, 2013; De Fina & Georgakopoulou, 2012, 2020).[3] To take language learning studies as an example, they were no longer

---

2. The journal was renamed *Narrative Inquiry* in 1998 when the publisher changed from Lawrence Erlbaum to John Benjamins (*Journal of Narrative and Life History*, n.d.).

solely about the learners' development of second language (L2) linguistic competence. They were also about the development of individual learners' and teachers'
identities, sociocultural relationships, and ideologies, and how such development
was affected by sociopolitical positionings, such as race, class, gender, and unequal
power relations (e.g., Canagarajah, 1993; Norton Peirce, 1995). To borrow the words
of Prior (2019),

> An outcome of these developments has been an expanded focus from the *experi-
> mental* to the *experiential* side of human language and life and how it shapes and
> is shaped by diverse ways of communicating, knowing, doing, being, becoming,
> belonging, desiring, and feeling. (p. 517)

Narrative inquiry found its place in Applied Linguistics because its focus on *lived*
experiences (cf. Ochs & Capps, 2001; Freeman, 2004) suited such orientation, and
its accessibility appealed to researchers who were weary of positivistic approaches
and also to a broader audience such as language teachers (Benson, 2018).

Within Applied Linguistics, narrative inquiry was often used as an umbrella
term for research focusing on the stories of experiences with languages, such as language learning and teaching, including diary studies, case studies, ethnographies,
and autobiographies (Barkhuizen, 2014; Benson, 2014). Notable contributions of
narrative work include research on language learner identity and subjectivity (e.g.,
Benson et al., 2013; Block, 2006; Kanno, 2003), as the process of narrating stories
functions as a coherence-making device for participants (and the researchers) to
bring together their sociocultural, emotional, and embodied experiences as well
as their 'different selves' and to negotiate and construct meaning from them (Dyer
& Keller-Cohen, 2000; Kanno, 2003). Experiences told as a story hold our attention, convey messages that might otherwise be lost in conventional research reports'
dense, dry prose, and connect readers to experiences in their own lives. Importantly, narratives infuse research participants and researchers themselves with *life*
(Freeman, 2004; Kramp, 2004). We can see some of this life in other notable contributions of narrative work in applied linguistics, such as language teachers' narratives of their teaching and professional development experiences (e.g., Barkhuizen,
2017; Johnson & Golombek, 2002), language learners' motivation (e.g., Norton
Peirce, 1995, Shoaib & Dörnyei, 2005), multilingualism, particularly work that mov-
ingly documents the complexities of living, working, and learning in more than
one language (e.g., Kouritzin, 2000b; Pavlenko, 2001, 2003), and autobiographical
reflections of applied linguists and second language education scholars (e.g.,

---

3. Given the depth and breadth of narrative inquiry, the focus of this volume, and the scope of
this chapter, I limit my focus mainly on studies related to language learning and teaching, and
not on narrative-oriented sociolinguistics research.

Casanave & Li, 2008; Habibie & Burgess, 2021), each of them capturing emotional dimensions (Prior, 2016). These narrative tales have given us vivid insights into people's lives, both social and academic, including marginalized groups whose voices tend not to be heard in the academy, and have allowed scholars to make a strong case for the value of narrative inquiry (cf. Canagarajah, 1996).

As mentioned above, narrative inquiry is still a comparatively recent development within Applied Linguistics — the publication date of the first articles that explicitly discuss narrative inquiry and narrative studies as a research approach in Applied Linguistics (Bell, 2002; Pavlenko, 2002) was as late as 2002. However, there is now a substantial body of literature focusing on narrative inquiry as a research approach, notably, but not limited to work by Gary Barkhuizen, including books (e.g., Barkhuizen, 2013; Barkhuizen et al., 2013); chapters in research methods handbooks (e.g., Barkhuizen, 2019; Benson, 2018; Murray, 2009), and journal special issues (e.g., Barkhuizen, 2011; Consoli & Barkhuizen, 2021). Such literature suggests the prominence of research focusing on *lived* experiences (cf. Ochs & Capps, 2001; Freeman, 2004) in Applied Linguistics. As pleasurable as it may be to focus on and research such experiences, whether it be others' or one's own, there are also challenges and potential risks involved. In the following two sections, I address such pleasures and perils involved in conducting and writing up narrative inquiry in Applied Linguistics.

Pleasures

The pleasures of narrative inquiry and narrative writing abound for both researchers and participants. They include the pleasures of attending to the stories told or written by multicultural informants, watching insights develop in the processes of narrating, and in constructing narrative reports in open and engaging ways. Here are further thoughts on some of the pleasures.

Listening to and documenting stories

First, it is pleasurable to listen to and document stories of people's lives. This pleasure may be particularly salient in Applied Linguistics, where participants (as well as researchers) share diverse multicultural experiences. Unlike in many other research approaches, the relationship between storytellers and listeners potentially creates a "more personal, collaborative, and interactive relationship" (Ellis & Bochner, 2000, p. 744). Such interactive relationships are not only pleasurable for all but allow for rich, emotional, and subjective stories — the kind that Bochner et al. (1998) call *evocative narratives* — to emerge. These stories project complexities and inner subtleties hidden in 'scientific' research approaches.

Constructing stories

Second, pleasure derives from researchers' constructing coherent stories from the spurts or fragments told by the teller. Stories are sometimes told monologically but may often be told discontinuously and partially, mirroring the way life itself is experienced. In discussing identity narratives, Kanno (2003) described them as "fragments of stories that do not fit perfectly together... like fragments of an ancient tapestry that an archaeologist is trying to piece together" (p.132). Researchers can find pleasure in putting the 'tapestry' together, creatively weaving the different fragments of talk and writing into a work of art. The finished, more coherent story may also bring pleasure to the narrator, as one of the goals of telling stories is to produce continuity (Ellis & Bochner, 2000). Seeing continuity and coherence in representations of their lives is particularly valuable for those who have experienced difficulties, enabling them to make sense of life's complexities and confusions. Such merit is salient in Applied Linguistics research, where many research participants have gone through challenging transitions and discontinuities, such as migrating to a country with an entirely different culture and language, often involving loss of social, cultural, economic, and linguistic capitals (cf. Bourdieu, 1986). I do not know of better or more pleasurable ways in Applied Linguistics to help others (and ourselves) adjust to new linguistic and cultural experiences and contribute to scholarship simultaneously.

New awareness of self

Third, storytellers may develop a new awareness of themselves. In the process of narrating, tellers may, for the first time, put the meanings and emotions of otherwise fragmented experiences into words (Bochner, 2002; Polkinghorne, 1988). Such opportunities provide pleasure by enabling tellers to

> unite the selves of our [their] past with those of the present, and even with the projected selves of the future..., bringing together in a coherent fashion differing versions, each narrative providing the authors with a deeper sense of understanding.
> (Dyer & Keller-Cohen, 2000, p.285)

By reflecting on and revising their stories, tellers may also be able to (re)construct their identities (Dyer & Keller-Cohen, 2000; Ellis & Bochner, 2000), thus coming to a new awareness of self. This kind of awareness can be eye-opening and reviving, especially when tellers feel lost, insecure, or marginalized, as many language learners and immigrants do (cf. Norton, 2000). Applied Linguistics research that helps others achieve self-awareness thus promotes an ethic of care and respect for participants.

Empowerment and agency

Fourth, constructing narratives is pleasurable because it promotes the empowerment and agency of both tellers and researchers. Narrative inquiry reconfigures
traditional research relationships, and the narrators are considered as not just
research subjects but unique individuals with authority to share their meaningful
stories (Kramp, 2004; Polkinghorne, 1995). This aspect may be particularly valuable for those who are not fully competent in the language being used (Kouritzin,
2000a), a common scenario in Applied Linguistics research. Narrative inquiry is
thus *empowering research* (Cameron et al.,1992), in which (a) individuals are not
objects, (b) their agendas are addressed by the researcher, and (c) their knowledge
is that worth sharing. Cameron et al. (1992) call for research that values interactions between researchers and the researched, thus enabling the researched to
exercise agency over the representations of their lives.

Researchers, too, find pleasure in the agentive role they play in co-constructing
narratives with others (De Fina, 2009; Ochs & Capps, 2001) and weaving their
own stories into their work. Co-constructed narratives are "powerfully shaped...
by the relationship between the storyteller and the interlocutor" (Pavlenko, 2002,
p. 214). As long as researchers attend sensitively to their own power-infused positions in the relationship between themselves and participants, their indispensable
role as collaborators brings pleasure because it helps voices that may otherwise
stay silenced be heard. Ideally, multicultural researcher-collaborators engage in
this co-construction with an openness and honesty that empowers researchers and
participants alike.

Reflectivity and reflexivity

Fifth, overlapping with 'New Awareness of Self' and 'Empowerment and Agency'
discussed above, narrative inquiry allows researchers and tellers to be reflective
and reflexive. Telling and listening to stories involve reflection — we engage in and
think about the story being told, regardless of our status. Such experiences provide opportunities for the researchers and the tellers to perform reflective practices — "the process of learning through and from experience towards gaining
new insights of self and/or practice" (Finlay, 2008, p.1). Furthermore, they also
enable the researcher and the teller to be reflexive — to go through "a more
immediate and dynamic process that involves continuing *self*-awareness" (p.6).
Such processes are pleasurable and meaningful for the researcher as they promote
enhanced and constantly renewing critical awareness of self as part of the context
and social phenomenon being examined. As such, reflexivity fosters researchers'

growth, promotes analytical rigor, and establishes integrity in narrative inquiry (cf. Finlay, 2006; Richardson & St. Pierre, 2018).

Engaging and accessible writing

Finally, in the writing of storied data in narrative analysis, it is pleasurable to include descriptive and literary details that capture the particulars of scenes and experiences, providing readers with a vivid reading experience of engaging and accessible writing. Although such writing is difficult to do well and requires that writers resist the temptation to display 'sophisticated' esoteric and arcane language, it is more compelling, direct, and accessible than conventional research reports (Barone, 1992; Canagarajah, 1996; Richardson & St. Pierre, 2018). Such writing can appeal to a wide audience in Applied Linguistics and beyond – a further pleasure for the researcher. Take Kanno's (2003) longitudinal study about the languages and identities of Japanese adolescents who lived in Canada but returned to Japan for university as an example of this pleasure (as well as all other 'pleasures' addressed in this chapter). In this study, the data from each of her four participants are presented as stories. Put together with Kanno's clear and accessible writing, the storied form helps the audience to read her book like a compelling novel about the lives of four young people who are "betwixt two worlds" (Kanno, 2003, p.ii). The story chapters not only enable the readers to feel like they have known these young people as well as Kanno did, but also comprehend her study's scholarly and pedagogical implications even without a background in Applied Linguistics research and theory. In this regard, unlike most Applied Linguistics research, narrative research reaches out to teachers and other practitioners, bridging the theory-practice divide (see Kramsch [2015] for a discussion on theory and practice and the gap between researchers and practitioners in Applied Linguistics).

In short, the pleasures of narrative inquiry derive from many sources, from the joys of listening to, telling, and co-constructing stories about language learning, teaching, and using to forming ethical relationships with people from diverse language and sociocultural backgrounds. The pleasures of writing with openness and honesty and of producing writing that is engaging and accessible likewise await researchers who commit to carefully done narrative inquiry. Lest "narrative inquiry may appear to be seductively simple" (Kramp, 2004, p.113); I next describe some of the perils that also await us.

Perils

Narrative inquiry cannot be considered conventional research (Hendry, 2007), so openness to nontraditional approaches is needed for it to continue developing in Applied Linguistics. The perils are many, particularly given the aforementioned elusiveness of the term. Also, our love for stories, together with the compelling nature of a well-told story about multilingual-multicultural participants, may lead us to lose a critical eye once we are drawn into fascinating worlds that differ from our own. Indeed, herein lies much of the power of well-done narrative research. But perils lurk, as they do with much social science research. Here are just a few.

Pretensions to truth and authenticity

Perhaps the central peril is dealing with the issue of 'truth.' From the perspectives of those with realist or positivist epistemologies, the trustworthiness of narrative as data may be questionable due to the following: First, stories and interpretations of their meanings change according to time and evolving circumstances (Mishler, 2006). Second, stories are reconstructed from memory, narrated in one way to the researcher and differently to another listener (Mishler, 1986), and told selectively with details changed for public presentation (Goffman, 1959). Stories are thus "assembled to meet situated interpretive demands" (Gubrium & Holstein, 1998, p. 166). Third, although time in narratives is temporal, it is not necessarily linear, being deeply connected to the plot rather than to chronology (Ricoeur, 1988). As such, from a skeptical perspective, stories do not provide "privileged access to personal experience" (Atkinson, 1997, p. 325). However, as Denzin (2000) points out, "we have no direct access to experience.... We can only study experience through its representations, through the ways stories are told" (p. xi). Furthermore, "narratives are reflections *on* — not *of* — the world as it is known" (p. xiii). Thus, the narrative truth reflected in stories and factual or historical truth of what really happened are fundamentally different. However, it may be perilous to convince the value of such representations and reflections to critics and skeptics of narrative inquiry and other interpretivist Applied Linguistics research approaches (cf. Bouchard, 2021).

Another perilous issue concerning truth is that of deception. While participants may possibly not tell the truth, the same applies to participants of other types of research, such as survey research. However, "For some reason, stories and storytellers as research participants are often viewed with a suspicious eye" (Barkhuizen, 2022, p. 10).

Fuzzy and ubiquitous nature of stories, narratives, and narrative inquiry

Second, as Barkhuizen (2013) points out, "Narrative and narrative research are notoriously hard to define" (p. 2) as definitions and what 'counts' as narrative vary according to disciplines and even within disciplines. The fact that stories and narratives are used interchangeably despite their analytical difference (Frank, 2000) adds further confusion. Even within the field of Applied Linguistics, we see different variations in narrative research, such as 'analysis of narratives' involving thematic analysis and 'narrative analysis,' which is configuring or restorying data (Benson, 2018; Polkinghorne, 1995). Another significant variation is 'big stories,' focusing on the content of the stories, and 'small stories,' with a discourse analytic approach focusing on meanings in contexts of interactions derived from everyday social exchanges. There is also a difference between biographical and autobiographical research, with differing roles of the researchers (Barkhuizen et al., 2013). There are also various alternative forms of narratives, such as multimodal digital narratives (Kalaja & Melo-Pfeifer, 2019). To further complicate the problem, there are studies that claim to be narrative research but with no stories involved, and some researchers do not explain what they mean by narrative (Consoli & Barkhuizen, 2021). Thus, it is perilous, especially for those new to narrative research, to fully comprehend the wide variety and relationships between narrative research within Applied Linguistics. However, such understanding (as well as a critical eye) is crucial for researchers interested in conducting narrative inquiry.

Stand-alone stories

Third, it is perilous to think that we do not need to go beyond the telling of a story in a research report — that the story somehow can stand on its own and that analytic rigor is not required (Atkinson & Delamont, 2006; Bell, 2002; Pavlenko, 2007). Perhaps this idea distinguishes narrative as research from narrative as literature or a narrative from a story (Frank, 2000). As Bell (2002) points out, narrative inquiry is "More than just telling stories" (p. 207). Researchers must make methodological and analytical procedures explicit and show how they have drawn from an appropriate theory.

Pavlenko (2007) warns that work using content and thematic analysis, the most common analytical approach, often lacks a theoretical framework. In the absence of a theoretical premise, it is "unclear where conceptual categories come from and how they relate to each other" (p. 166), and overreliance on thematization risks obvious conclusions. In addition to having a clear theoretical framework, to enhance analytical rigor, Pavlenko (2007) urges researchers to analyze content together with context and form, given their interdependent nature. Similarly, Riessman (2008) suggests combining content and structural analysis to enhance the quality of analysis.

Stories told in L2

Fourth, in several domains of Applied Linguistics research, participants often respond to researchers in their L2. We cannot assume that a story told to us in a teller's L2 is being conveyed in the way the participant intends. For one, the researcher may not know enough about the participant's L2 or cultural background to fill gaps in understanding with linguistic and cultural knowledge (Kouritzin, 2000b). Also, stories told in the L2 may differ emotionally from stories told in the language in which events were experienced. Pavlenko (2007, p.174) asks: "Did the language of the story correspond to the language in which the events in question took place? If not, is it possible that the discrepancy influenced the telling, for instance, by lowering the level of affect and the amount of detail?" Finally, it is still common for Applied Linguistics research to take place between L2-speaker participants and first language (L1)-speaker researchers, with the inevitable power and status differences between them (see 'Ethical concerns' section below). Together with language differences, such differences no doubt greatly influence the stories we hear and tell.

Transcripts as 'real' data

Fifth, there is danger in seeing transcripts as 'real' data when they are only representations of data (e.g., recordings). But even "recordings are not the same as the social interaction they record" (Hammersley, 2003, p.759). Transcripts are thus not facts but "discursive constructions" (Pavlenko, 2007, p.168). Moreover, in narrative research (and in any interview research), transcriptions of audio or video-recorded interviews are not straightforward representations of events or speech, unaffected by interpretations and choices made in the process of transcribing (Temple, 1997). Accurate transcribing is difficult and time-consuming, particularly in the transcriber's L2 or foreign language. Many researchers go too quickly from recordings to transcripts rather than listening repetitively to what was said. Applied linguists thus need to decide how to represent a participant's narrative (as normal prose? full of details of how the talk was spoken?), keeping in mind that the transcripts are textual constructions in all cases. The issues of representation and interpretation in transcripts are complicated further when participants narrate in a language other than the researchers' L1, usually obligating researchers and interpreters to translate the data into their L1 and 'cross borders' with their stories (Birbili, 2000; Pavlenko, 2007; Smith et al., 2008). Among other issues concerning translation (see Temple & Young, 2004), the same words will be translated differently, with different nuances of meaning, by different translators. Even if participants and researchers are all working in their L1, researchers inevitably "'translate' the experiences of others"—that is, they bring their own intellectual autobiographies to any research project (Temple, 1997, p. 609).

Time-consuming and labor-intensive research approach

Finally, a conducting well-done narrative inquiry is time-consuming and labor-intensive. Bell (2011) mentions that for most narrative researchers, six months is the *minimum* period to negotiate participation and to collect some data; other studies may last longer. This period excludes the vast amount of time spent transcribing, organizing, interpreting, analyzing the data, and writing up the study. In addition, more time is often needed to construct the study and gather data, as it is challenging in narrative inquiry to pose clear research questions at the beginning of a project (Clandinin & Connelly, 2000).

Presenting the finished work is another issue. A book-length project is often required to do justice to the rich stories while maintaining the rigor of scholarly research. However, peer-reviewed journal articles are the commonly expected venue for publication in Applied Linguistics (American Association for Applied Linguistics, 2019). Pruning or condensing the study to meet the length requirements of journal articles and conference presentations without losing the richness of the stories can be immensely challenging, requiring careful crafting (Murray, 2009).

Conducting narrative inquiry can also be emotional labor. While the beauty of narrative inquiry is in the honest and compelling stories the participants tell, the stories may be unexpectedly vexing and traumatic (Okada, 2019), impacting not only the narrator, but also the researcher. Upon establishing rapport, researchers may feel compelled or positioned to share their own experiences, which may not be easy to do (Prior, 2016). The close personal involvement and honesty in telling the stories make both the participants and the researchers vulnerable (De Costa et al., 2021). These perils may seem overwhelming, but they are not. They pertain to all the research we do and need to be dealt with openly in our research processes and writing.

Ethical concerns

Although neither a pleasure nor a peril, ethical concerns must be addressed due to their critical importance in narrative inquiry. Ethical tensions in narrative inquiry are common, particularly because it "assumes 'personal involvement' [between the researcher and the participant] as the very condition" (Kramp, 2004, p. 114). Thus, narrative researchers must be especially sensitive and careful about their interactions and relationships with their participants and how to represent them and their stories. Researchers, thereby, need to go beyond just fulfilling macroethical principles such as those addressed by the institutional review board and be considerate of context-dependent, microethical scenarios (Kubanyiova, 2008) that may arise in the processes of storytelling.

Some common ethical tensions in narrative inquiry include the aforementioned unequal power relations between the researcher and the researched (that is often further complexified by issues such as gender, race, and language), negotiating entry and exit to a research relationship (Bell, 2011), and guaranteeing participants' anonymity without obscuring their life stories. A notable challenge in narrative inquiry and other interpretive qualitative research in Applied Linguistics includes the issue of representation, reflexivity, and positionality (Bold, 2012; De Costa, 2016). Researchers must constantly be aware of their biases, power dynamics at play, and the ethical implications of their interactions with the participants to ensure that the stories are represented authentically and ethically (Guillemin & Gillam, 2004). In addition, researchers must let go of their "unquestioned privilege" (De Costa, 2016, p. xiv) and honor the participants' voices, however ambivalent they may be. The question of whose voice is being heard in the research output is complex, as the agenda of the researcher and that of the participants may differ (Okada, 2017). For example, my agenda in my illness narrative projects was to analyze *how* the participants negotiate, construe, and communicate their experiences through narrative (Okada, 2011, 2014). Although the participants claimed to have understood my purpose as an applied linguist, their purpose was to be heard — in other words, their focus was on the *what*. They saw the participation as an opportunity for their illnesses and disabilities to be known and understood through the research output. Giving the participants the authority as storytellers and honoring their voices while fulfilling the researcher's agenda is a challenging ethical imperative that narrative researchers must consider.

In sum, the nature of ethics in narrative inquiry is dynamic and context-sensitive. Researchers need not only to adhere to the broader macroethical principles, but also maintain sensitivity to the microethical, situational (and potentially unexpected or hidden) consequences and challenges (Guillemin & Gillam, 2004;

Kubanyiova, 2008). To effectively navigate the complex ethical landscape of narrative inquiry, researchers must always be reflexive, adaptable, and thoughtful.

Conclusion

I am deeply committed to the pleasures of narrative inquiry in Applied Linguistics; however, I realize it is not for everyone. I am unlikely to convince skeptics of its potential contributions to the field. But for those who have stories to tell, who learn from listening to and documenting the stories of others, and who find sensible ways to analyze and interpret narratives, no other research approach can provide a multilingual, multicultural field like Applied Linguistics with so much *life* — with so many ways to connect to others who differ from ourselves. Perhaps the main peril is that of not being aware of and transparent about the perils themselves. This peril applies to all research, of course; narrative inquiry is not unique in this regard.

Debates about the purposes of narrative inquiry may continue in Applied Linguistics and other social science fields. In an era that increasingly demands political accountability and scientific certainty, narrative inquirers need to be armed with persuasive responses to many vexing questions (Barone, 2007). Who can do research with multilingual, multicultural people? Does the inevitable co-participation of researchers invalidate what we can say about others? If we are not concerned with truth and certainty (as post-positivist Phillips, 1994, 1997, urges we should be) but with meaningfulness, how do we demonstrate meaningfulness in narrative work? As with other forms of qualitative inquiry, how do we assess the goodness of narrative research (Polkinghorne, 2007)? Finally, should our narratives merely describe, or should they protest injustices and contribute to social change (Atkinson & Delamont, 2006; Barone, 2009) as in work by the critical applied linguists (Pennycook, 2022)?

I appeal to readers to ponder such questions before leaping into the pleasures of a narrative research project. Above all, it is crucial to be transparent about the details of our research approaches and underlying assumptions in narrative inquiry, as in all inquiry in Applied Linguistics and beyond.

Acknowledgements

This chapter is partially based on an early collaborative project with my mentor and friend, Christine Pearson Casanave. I thank her for the many discussions we have had on narrative inquiry and good stories — our shared passion.

References

American Association for Applied Linguistics. (2019). *Promotion and tenure guidelines.* Retrieved on 8 October 2024 https://www.aaal.org/promotion-and-tenure-guidelines#Refereed%20book%20chapters

Atkinson, P. (1997). Narrative turn or blind alley? *Qualitative Health Research, 7*(3), 325–344.

Atkinson, P., & Delamont, S. (2006). Rescuing narrative from qualitative research. *Narrative Inquiry, 16*(1), 164–172.

Bailey, K.M. (1980). An introspective analysis of an individual's language learning experience. In R. Scarcella & S. Krashen (Eds.), *Research in second language acquisition: Selected papers of the Los Angeles second language research forum* (pp. 58–65). Newbury House.

Bamberg, M. (2013). Narrative discourse. In C.A. Chapelle (Ed.), *The encyclopedia of applied linguistics* (pp. 1–7) Blackwell.

Barkhuizen, G. (Ed.). (2011). Narrative research in TESOL [Special issue]. *TESOL Quarterly, 45*(3).

Barkhuizen, G. (2013). *Narrative research in applied linguistics.* Cambridge University Press.

Barkhuizen, G. (2014). Narrative research in language teaching and learning. *Language Teaching, 47*(4), 450–466.

Barkhuizen, G. (Ed.). (2017). *Reflections on language teacher identity research.* Routledge.

Barkhuizen, G. (2019). Core dimensions of narrative inquiry. In J. McKinley & H. Rose (Eds.), *The Routledge handbook of research methods in applied linguistics* (pp. 188–198). Routledge.

Barkhuizen, G. (2022). Ten tricky questions about narrative inquiry in language teaching and learning research: And what the answers mean for qualitative and quantitative research. *LEARN Journal: Language Education and Acquisition Research Network, 15*(2), 1–19.

Barkhuizen, G., Benson, P., & Chik, A. (2013). *Narrative inquiry in language teaching and learning research.* Routledge.

Barone, T. (2007). A return to the gold standard? Questioning the future of narrative construction as educational research. *Qualitative Inquiry, 13*(4), 454–470.

Barone, T. (2009). Comments on Coulter and Smith: Narrative researchers as witnesses of injustice and agents of social change? *Educational Researcher, 38*(8), 591–597.

Barone, T.E. (1992). A narrative enhanced professionalism: Educational researchers and popular storybooks about school people. *Educational Researcher, 21*(8), 15–24.

Bell, J.S. (2002). Narrative inquiry: More than just telling stories. *TESOL Quarterly, 36*(2), 207–213.

Bell, J.S. (2011). Reporting and publishing narrative inquiry in TESOL: Challenges and rewards. *TESOL Quarterly, 45*(3), 583.

Benson, P. (2014). Narrative inquiry in applied linguistics research. *Annual Review of Applied Linguistics, 34*, 154–170.

Benson, P. (2018). Narrative analysis. In A. Phakiti, P. De Costa, L. Plonsky, & S. Starfield (Eds.), *The Palgrave handbook of applied linguistics research methodology* (pp. 595–613). Palgrave Macmillan.

Benson, P., Barkhuizen, G., Bodycott, P., & Brown, J. (Eds.). (2013). *Second language identity in narratives of study abroad.* Palgrave Macmillan.

Birbili, M. (2000). Translating from one language to another. *Social Research Update, 31.* Retrieved on 8 October 2024 on http://sru.soc.surrey.ac.uk/SRU31.html

Block, D. (2006). *Multilingual identities in a global city: London stories.* Palgrave MacMillan.

Block, D. (2003). *The social turn in second language acquisition.* Georgetown University Press.

Bochner, A. (2002). Criteria against ourselves. In N. K. Denzin & Y. S. Lincoln (Eds.), *The qualitative inquiry reader* (pp. 257–265). Sage.

Bochner, A. P., Ellis, C., & Tillmann-Healy, L. (1998). Mucking around and looking for truth. In B. M. Montgomery & L. A. Baxter (Eds.), *Dialectical approaches to studying personal relationships* (pp. 41–42). Lawrence Erlbaum Associates.

Bold, C. (2012). *Using narrative in research.* Sage.

Bouchard, J. (2021). *Complexity, emergence, and causality in applied linguistics.* Palgrave Macmillan.

Bourdieu, P. (1986). The forms of capital. In J. G. Richardson (Ed.), *Handbook of theory and research for the sociology of education* (pp. 241–258). Greenwood Press.

Cameron, D., Frazer, E., Harvey, P., Rampton, B., & Richardson, K. (1992). *Researching language: Issues of power and method.* Routledge.

Canagarajah, A. S. (1993). Critical ethnography of a Sri Lankan classroom: Ambiguities in student opposition to reproduction through ESOL. *TESOL Quarterly, 27*(4), 601–626.

Canagarajah, A. S. (1996). From critical research practice to critical research reporting. *TESOL Quarterly, 30*(2), 321–330.

Casanave, C. P., & Li, X. (Eds.). (2008). *Learning the literacy practices of graduate school: Insiders' reflections on academic enculturation.* University of Michigan Press.

Catford, J. C. (1998). Language learning and applied linguistics: A historical sketch. *Language Learning, 48*(4), 465–496.

Clandinin, D. J. (Ed.). (2007). *Handbook of narrative inquiry: Mapping a methodology.* Sage.

Clandinin, D. J., & Connelly, F. M. (2000). *Narrative inquiry: Experience and story in qualitative research.* Jossey-Bass.

Consoli, S., & Barkhuizen, G. (Eds.) (2021). Pushing the edge in narrative inquiry [Special issue]. *System, 102.*

Davis, K. A. (2013). Ethnographic approaches to second language acquisition research. In C. A. Chapelle (Ed.), *The encyclopedia of applied linguistics* (pp. 1–8). Blackwell.

De Costa, P. I. (Ed.). (2016). *Ethics in applied linguistics research: Language researcher narratives.* Routledge.

De Costa, P. I., Randez, R. A., Her, L., & Green-Eneix, C. A. (2021). Navigating ethical challenges in second language narrative inquiry research. *System, 102,* 102599.

De Fina, A. (2009). Narratives in interview: The case of accounts for an interactional approach to narrative genres. *Narrative Inquiry, 19*(2), 233–258.

De Fina, A., & Georgakopoulou, A. (2012). *Analyzing narrative: Discourse and sociolinguistic perspectives.* Cambridge University Press.

De Fina, A., & Georgakopoulou, A. (2020). Rethinking narrative: Tellers, tales and identities in contemporary worlds. In A. Georgakopoulou & A. De Fina (Eds.), *The Cambridge handbook of discourse studies* (pp. 91–114). Cambridge University Press.

Denzin, N. (2000). Foreword: Narrative's moment. In M. Andrews, S. D. Sclater, C. Squire, & A. Treacher (Eds.), *Lines of narrative: Psychosocial perspectives* (pp. xi–xiii). Routledge.

Dyer, J., & Keller-Cohen, D. (2000). The discursive construction of professional self through narratives of personal experience. *Discourse Studies, 2*(3), 283–304.

Ellis, C., & Bochner, A. (2000). Autoethnography, personal narrative, reflexivity: Researcher as subject. In N. K. Denzin & Y. S. Lincoln (Eds.), *Handbook of qualitative research* (2nd ed., pp. 733–768). Sage.

Finlay, L. (2006). 'Rigour', 'ethical integrity' or 'artistry'? Reflexively reviewing criteria for evaluating qualitative research. *The British Journal of Occupational Therapy, 69*(7), 319–326.

Finlay, L. (2008). Reflecting on 'reflective practice'. *Practice-based Professional Learning Paper 52.* The Open University.

Firth, A., & Wagner, J. (1997). On discourse, communication, and (some) fundamental concepts in SLA research. *The Modern Language Journal, 81*(3), 285–300.

Frank, A. W. (2000). The standpoint of storyteller. *Qualitative Health Research, 10*(3), 354–365.

Freeman, M. (2004). Data are everywhere: Narrative criticism in the literature of experience. In C. Daiute & C. Lightfoot (Eds.), *Narrative analysis: Studying the development of individuals in society* (pp. 63–81). Sage.

Goffman, E. (1959). *The presentation of self in everyday life.* Doubleday.

Gubrium, J. F., & Holstein, J. A. (1998). Narrative practice and the coherence of personal stories. *Sociological Quarterly, 39*(1), 163–187.

Guillemin, M., & Gillam, L. (2004). Ethics, reflexivity, and "ethically important moments" in research. *Qualitative Inquiry, 10*(2), 261–280.

Habibie, P., & Burgess, S. (Eds.) (2021). *Scholarly publication trajectories of early-career scholars: Insider perspectives.* Springer.

Hammersley, M. (2003). Conversation analysis and discourse analysis: Methods or paradigms? *Discourse & Society, 14*(6), 751–781.

Hendry, P. M. (2007). The future of narrative. *Qualitative Inquiry, 13*(4), 487–498.

Holstein, J. A., & Gubrium, J. F. (Eds.). (2012). *Varieties of narrative analysis.* Sage.

Johnson, K. E., & Golombek, P. R. (Eds.). (2002). *Teachers' narrative inquiry as professional development.* Cambridge University Press.

Journal of Narrative and Life History. (n.d.). Retrieved on 8 October 2024 from https://benjamins.com/catalog/jnlh

Kalaja, P., & Melo-Pfeifer, S. (Eds.). (2019). *Visualising multilingual lives: More than words.* Multilingual Matters.

Kanno, Y. (2003). *Negotiating bilingual and bicultural identities: Japanese returnees betwixt two worlds.* Lawrence Erlbaum Associates.

Kouritzin, S. G. (2000a). Bringing life to research: Life history research and ESL. *TESL Canada Journal, 17*(2), 1–35.

Kouritzin, S. G. (2000b). A mother's tongue. *TESOL Quarterly, 34*(2), 311–324.

Kramp, M. K. (2004). Exploring life and experience through narrative inquiry. In K. deMarrais & S. D. Lapan (Eds.), *Foundations for research: Methods of inquiry in education and the social sciences* (pp. 103–121). Routledge.

Kramsch, C. (2015). Applied linguistics: A theory of the practice. *Applied Linguistics, 36*(4), 454–465.

Kubanyiova, M. (2008). Rethinking research ethics in contemporary applied linguistics: The tension between macroethical and microethical perspectives in situated research. *The Modern Language Journal*, 92(4), 503–518.

Lantolf, J. P., & Pavlenko, A. (2001). (S)econd (L)anguage (A)ctivity theory: Understanding second language learners as people. In M. P. Breen (Ed.), *Learner contributions to language learning: New directions in research* (pp. 141–158). Routledge.

Lazaraton, A. (1995). Qualitative research in applied linguistics: A progress report. *TESOL Quarterly*, 29(3), 455–472.

Mishler, E. G. (1986). *Research interviewing: Context and narrative*. Cambridge University Press.

Mishler, E. G. (2006). Narrative and identity: The double arrow of time. In A. De Fina, D. Schiffrin, & M. Bamberg (Eds.), *Discourse and identity* (pp. 30–47). Cambridge University Press.

Murray, G. (2009). Narrative inquiry. In J. Heigham & R. A. Croker (Eds.), *Qualitative research in applied linguistics* (pp. 45–65). Palgrave Macmillan.

Norton, B. (2000). *Identity and language learning: Gender, ethnicity, and educational change.* Longman.

Norton, B. (2001). Non-participation, imagined communities and the language classroom. In M. P. Breen (Ed.), *Learner contributions to language learning: New directions in research* (pp. 159–171). Longman.

Norton Peirce, B. (1995). Social identity, investment, and language learning. *TESOL Quarterly*, 29(1), 9–29.

Ochs, E., & Capps, L. (2001). *Living narrative: Creating lives in everyday storytelling*. Harvard University Press.

Okada, H. (2011). Negotiating the invisible: Two women making sense of chronic illness through narrative. In P. McPherron & V. Ramanathan (Eds.), *Language, body, and health* (pp. 143–167). Mouton de Gruyter.

Okada, H. (2014, March 22–25). *"And then there was a battle": Constructing disability identity through narratives of struggles* [Conference presentation]. American Association for Applied Linguistics Conference, Portland, OR, United States.

Okada, H. (2017). Researching people with illnesses and disabilities: Ethical dimensions. In J. McKinley & H. Rose (Eds.), *Doing research in applied linguistics: Realities, dilemmas, solutions* (pp. 124–133). Routledge.

Okada, H. (2019, March 9–12). Perils of narrative inquiry: When unexpected distressing stories unfold. In M. T. Prior (Organizer), *Addressing trauma, resilience, and well-being in applied linguistics research: Implications for training and practice* [Colloquium]. American Association for Applied Linguistics Conference, Atlanta, GA, United States.

Pavlenko, A. (2001). Second language learning by adults: Testimonies of bilingual writers. *Issues in Applied Linguistics*, 9(1), 3–19.

Pavlenko, A. (2002). Narrative study: Whose story is it, anyway? *TESOL Quarterly*, 36(2), 213–218.

Pavlenko, A. (2003). The privilege of writing as an immigrant woman. In C. P. Casanave & S. Vandrick, S. (Eds.), *Writing for scholarly publication: Behind the scenes in language education* (pp. 177–193). Lawrence Erlbaum Associates.

doi Pavlenko, A. (2007). Autobiographic narratives as data in applied linguistics. *Applied Linguistics, 28*(2), 163–188.

doi Pennycook, A. (2022). Critical applied linguistics in the 2020s. *Critical Inquiry in Language Studies, 19*(1), 1–21.

doi Phillips, D. C. (1994). Telling it straight: Issues in assessing narrative research. *Educational Psychologist, 29*(1), 13–21.

doi Phillips, D. C. (1997). Telling the truth about stories. *Teaching and Teacher Education, 13*(1), 101–109.

doi Pinnegar, S., & Daynes, J. G. (2007). Locating narrative inquiry historically. In D. J. Clandinin (Ed.), *Handbook of narrative inquiry: Mapping a methodology* (pp. 3–34). Sage.

Polkinghorne, D. E. (1988). *Narrative knowing and the human sciences.* State University of New York Press.

Polkinghorne, D. E. (1995). Narrative configuration in qualitative analysis. In J. A. Hatch & R. Wisniewski (Eds.), *Life history and narrative* (pp. 5–23). Falmer.

doi Polkinghorne, D. E. (2007). Validity issues in narrative research. *Qualitative Inquiry, 13*(4), 471–486.

Prior, M. T. (2016). *Emotions and discourse in L2 narrative research.* Multilingual Matters.

doi Prior, M. T. (2019). Elephants in the room: An "affective turn," or just feeling our way? *The Modern Language Journal, 103*(2), 516–527.

Richardson, L., & St. Pierre, E. A. (2018). Writing: A method of inquiry In N. K. Denzin & Y. S. Lincoln (Eds.), *The Sage handbook of qualitative research* (5th ed., pp. 818–838). Sage.

Ricoeur, P. (1988). *Time and narrative* (Vol. 3). University of Chicago Press.

Riessman, C. K. (2008). *Narrative methods for the human sciences.* Sage.

doi Riessman, C. K., & Speedy, J. (2007). Narrative inquiry in the psychotherapy professions. In D. J. Clandinin (Ed.), *Handbook of narrative inquiry: Mapping a methodology* (pp. 426–456). Sage.

doi Riley, T., & Hawe, P. (2004). Researching practice: The methodological case for narrative inquiry. *Health Education Research, 20*(2), 226–236.

Schmidt, R. W., & Frota, S. (1986). Developing basic conversational ability in a second language: A case study of an adult learner of Portuguese. In R. R. Day (Ed.), *Talking to learn: Conversation in second language acquisition* (pp. 237–326). Newbury House.

Schumann, F. M., & Schumann, J. H. (1977). Diary of a language learner: An introspective study of second language learning. In H. D. Brown, R. H. Crymes, & C. A. Yorio (Eds.), *On TESOL '77: Teaching and learning English as a second language: Trends in research and practice* (pp. 241–249). TESOL.

Shoaib, A., & Dörnyei, Z. (2005). Affect in lifelong learning: Exploring L2 motivation as a dynamic process. In P. Benson & D. Nunan (Eds.), *Learners' stories: Difference and diversity in language learning* (pp. 22–41). Cambridge University Press.

doi Smith, H. J., Chen, J., & Liu, X. (2008). Language and rigour in qualitative research: Problems and principles in analyzing data collected in Mandarin. *BMC Medical Research Methodology, 8*(1), 44.

doi Temple, B. (1997). Watch your tongue: Issues in translation and cross-cultural research. *Sociology, 31*(3), 607–18.

doi Temple, B., & Young, A. (2004). Qualitative research and translation dilemmas. *Qualitative Research, 4*(2), 161–178.

PART III

Reflective and reflexive studies

CHAPTER 10

An autoethnography of migration, language, and power dynamics

Ellie Nik
University of New South Wales

This chapter explores the influence of power structures and social imaginaries on my language choices as a migrant residing in Australia and using English as a foreign language. The methodology adopted in this chapter is critical autoethnography. It critically examines the phenomenon of English linguistic imperialism. Through the sharing of personal narratives, the chapter highlights instances where I have observed power imbalances in my everyday interactions as a migrant in Australia, prompting me to switch to English in the presence of others. By delving into these experiences, this research sheds light on the complex dynamics of language use and the implications of power differentials within a multicultural context. This chapter contributes to enhancing the understanding of sociolinguistic challenges confronted by migrants and the influence of dominant language ideologies on their linguistic practices. By providing insights that foster increased awareness and empathy, it offers a pathway towards promoting a more inclusive and equitable language environment within multicultural societies.

> I face it every day,
> Starting with my morning greetings,
> Which one should I say?
> Good morning or *Sobh bekheir*[1] or *Saharun Xeyr Ölsun*?[2]
> This just happens at home.
> When I step out, it is even more complicated.
> The language that felt safe once,
> My mother tongue,
> The language I said my first words in,
> The familiar sounds, senses, and tastes,
> Are fading.
> And how much I dread it!

---

1. This is good morning in Farsi, written using English letters.
2. This is good morning in Azeri, written using English letters.

https://doi.org/10.1075/rmal.8.10nik

This chapter invites critical thought on how power structures and social imaginaries influence my language choices as a migrant in Australia and a speaker of English as a foreign language.

This chapter belongs to this book as it discusses a very important tool in everyday life, which is language, sharing the intricacies and the dynamics of its use in various contexts among different users with real-life examples. As Darvin (2017) notes, "language is at once a means to unite and to divide, to empower and to disempower, to express compassion and to sow hatred" (p. 289). Moreover, a reflective and reflexive approach is utilised, namely critical autoethnography, to include the dominant narratives as well as the writer's perceptions, which is fertile ground for better relatability for the readers. This work further follows Grabe (2012) and his fifth emphasis on Applied Linguistics research, which deals with,

> multilingualism and bilingual interaction in … community, and work and in professional settings … Because most people in the world are to some extent bilingual, and because this bilingualism is associated with the need to negotiate life situations with other cultural and language groups. (p. 39)

Research approach

Life narratives, evocative stories, and dialogues within social contexts demonstrate how language is utilised to navigate the unequal power relations between different speakers of English, with varying proficiency levels. The qualitative nature of the methods used enables a nuanced exploration of language's role in navigating power relations. These methods capture diverse perspectives of the people in the margins and contextualise language within social dynamics, illuminating how power intersects with factors like proficiency levels and social identities. The rich data collected through these approaches offers comprehensive insights into language-mediated power dynamics, enhancing our understanding of how individuals negotiate, contest, and reinforce unequal power relations in English-speaking contexts.

Critical autoethnography (CAE) is adopted as the methodology in this chapter. In CAE, the term "critical" denotes an ongoing, dynamic process that connects theory and personal narrative, emphasising their interdependence; it underscores that theory is a language for thinking about and acting on experiences and cultural dynamics, promoting a deeper understanding and potential for change (Holman Jones, 2016). In this chapter, the "critical" part of CAE interrogates the power relations (Reed-Danahay, 2017) and the hegemony of the English language that influences language choice on a daily basis. In other words, it critiques

English linguistic imperialism (Phillipson, 1992). The "auto" part of autoethnography delineates my personal experiences as a migrant in Australia. Sharing these experiences can elucidate similar experiences that other migrants may have encountered. The "ethno" part of autoethnography is the writings: the stories describing the context and the cultures where these events occurred. According to Jones and Harris (2019), "stories animate and become the change we seek in the world" (pp. 1–2). And, following Ellis and Bochner (2006), I want my autoethnographic account "to elicit caring and empathy" (p. 431). Putting the political, personal, and cultural together, autoethnography as a research approach can help us envision a better future (Adams et al., 2022) where all speakers of different languages (particularly the ones whose first language is not English) can converse comfortably in their language of choice as well as in varieties of English, without fear of judgement or discrimination. While I understand that this perspective may appear idealistic, the act of sharing stories, along with the utilisation of innovative methodologies such as critical autoethnography in Applied Linguistics, serves as an initial step towards fostering awareness and advocating for incremental changes.

Daycare Story, 30 March 2021

It is day 3. I drop Eleanora at daycare. She just clings to me and does not want to let go. I try to soothe her and am having a conversation with her room teacher at the same time.

Ellie: "When she takes a nap during the day, she usually wakes up in 20 or so minutes but if you cuddle her and give her a dummy, she may continue to sleep".

Teacher: "Oh, I did not know she had a dummy in her bag. You know we are a new centre, and everyone is learning". (She chuckles)

Eleanora is still clinging to me. I am not sure whether to soothe her in my mother tongue, Azeri, or in English. I have always talked to her in Azeri. But I feel uneasy to use it in her teacher's presence. I am not sure if it is the feeling of "shame", "being polite", or "not being enough".

Finally, I speak in English.

Ellie (to Eleanora): "It's okay, Mummy. You are going to learn new things. You are going to make new friends. Mummy loves you".

She knows the last sentence. She looks at me with her big brown eyes, tears in them, holding onto her water bottle. I hug her. My heart is racing but I need to keep calm. My mood will affect her mood. So, I need to play it cool.

The teacher returns to the class to give us a bit more time. Now I speak to her in Azeri: the familiar language to her. She understands most of it and smiles for a second, but she is still unsettled because she already knows she is going to stay here. I walk her to the babies' classroom door. The teacher takes her while she cries and stretches her arms for me. I know I need to leave, not to make it harder for her.

My heart is racing even faster. I can hear its "boom, boom" in my ears. I rush out of the door. I hold my tears with much effort. I know I need to calm down, so I take a deep breath. I need to go home and do the courses I have enrolled in. I might need to change direction. There might be a career detour. I am not sure.

Throughout my life, I have personally experienced the hegemony of the English language since I learnt my ABCs in secondary school. I have perceived it as a 'superior' language and dedicated considerable effort over the past 23 years to improve my proficiency in it, inadvertently exemplifying the phenomenon of linguistic imperialism. Logically, I should take pride in my multilingualism as a form of cultural capital (Bourdieu, 1986, 2002). However, it always depends on who I am talking to, where I am, how good their English is compared to my English, and what other languages they can speak. Or as Darvin (2017) puts it,

> in any situation where two interlocutors are face to face, the language they choose to communicate with one another, the contexts in which they are able to speak and be listened to, and the conditions that shape their legitimacy as speakers are all circumscribed by power.   (p. 289)

Theoretical lens

To enhance the contextualisation and comprehension of the stories I share, it is essential to briefly discuss two theoretical concepts that serve as critical lenses: linguistic imperialism and social imaginaries.

Linguistic imperialism

In this chapter, I focus on English linguistic imperialism because English is the linguistic currency of the world at the moment, as well as being the national language of Australia, where the stories occurred. English linguistic imperialism is a subcategory of linguicism. Linguicism — which was coined by Tove Skutnabb-Kangas in the 1980s — is defined as "ideologies, structures, and practices which are used to legitimate, effectuate, and reproduce an unequal division of power and resources" (Phillipson, 1992, p. 47). Linguicism studies deal with topics related to language and education; they probe the legitimisation of linguistic hierarchies as well as the role of language in constructing disproportionate power relations (Phillipson, 1997). According to Phillipson (1992), "the dominance of English is asserted and maintained by the establishment and continuous reconstitution of structural and cultural inequalities between English and other languages" (p. 47). What is important to highlight here is the "othering" (Holliday, 2006) that the English language fosters in today's world, and the opportunities it promises if one has the competency to communicate using this language. It is worth noting that it is not the language itself which exerts hegemonic control, but the power associated with the language which equips it with the dividing force or, as Bourdieu and Wacquant (1992) put it, "authority comes to language from outside" (p. 147).

In the context of the stories used in this chapter, English is the gatekeeping language and its users as a first language usually hold the power in communications, or so is the case in my social imaginary. In other words, I perceive people who speak English as a first language as 'smarter' or more 'powerful' in my encounters. This perception is something that has been internalised in me through the power of the English language in the current political climate as well as the stereotypes reverberating superiority of English speakers as a first language. I am not alone in yielding my power to the English language and its speakers. For instance, in one study in Canada, participants rated non-English-speaking doctors as less competent when comparing them with their English-speaking counterparts (Baquiran & Nicoladis, 2020). Australia, the context where these stories occur, advocates itself as a multilingual country; however, the reality is this multilingualism is through a monolingual mindset (Adoniou, 2018). While individuals may opt to use their native language, it is necessary to engage in daily activities in English.

Social imaginaries

Different researchers have contributed to the notion of imaginaries (Appadurai, 1996; Rizvi, 2007, 2011; Taylor, 2002, 2004). "An imaginary is a set of beliefs or 'stories' about a particular phenomenon that people in a society adhere to and which function to support particular ideologies" (Jones & Hafner, 2021, p. 136). Taylor (2004) defines social imaginaries as:

> the ways in which people imagine their social existence, how they fit together with others, how things go on between them and their fellows, the expectations that are normally met, and the deeper normative notions and images that underlie these expectations.   (p. 23)

However, social imaginaries are not fixed. As Rizvi (2011) puts it, "It is through the collective sense of imagination that a society is created, given coherence and identity, but is also subjected to social change, both mundane and radical" (p. 229). Hence, the imaginaries of a society or an individual may evolve over time. The modern era is characterised by influential factors such as the internet, media, and television, which can shape people's perceptions and imaginaries. Following Taylor (2004), I opt for the word imaginaries here as all humans can relate to this concept, and we all rely on our perceptions of ourselves and of others to make sense of and to be understood in social encounters. In contexts where shared perceptions are limited and power struggles exist, insecurities can be heightened as a result of intersecting elements such as languages used, varying English competencies, and their influence on people's perceptions of each other.

Name change dilemma

One form of discrimination that migrants face is to do with their names, if the names sound or look so different from the "good old Harry". Research demonstrates that many resumes are simply dismissed because the names on the top of them are categorised as "other" (Adamovic, 2022). The abstract letters holding hands on paper and constructing a person's name can become a source of uncertainty and a target for discrimination when one crosses borders. Unlike language choice in various contexts, individuals do not have agency in choosing their birth name or last name. Multiple factors, including geographic location, parental aspirations, community languages, and numerous other variables, can influence the name assigned to an individual at birth.

On my arrival in Sydney, I realised it was difficult for many people to pronounce my name (i.e., Elham) so in my encounters I would say, "My name is Elham, but you can call me Ellie". And honestly, I did not like the way some people pronounced my name; they either added or subtracted something (e.g., Elkham, Elam!). This strategy worked until I started applying for jobs after the completion of my PhD. I applied for so many jobs with no response. And after reading about the possibility of discrimination due to one's name, I decided to change both my first and last names. As Wang (2020) beautifully puts it, I was "feeling the pressure to change my name to fit in, to find a job, to have my resume read (to hope it was read)" (p. 164). And I surrendered.

I perceive my name change as a form of assimilation, adopting an English-sounding name to assimilate into the society I consider my 'home' and an attempt to be less "othered" by the people I encounter. Here, I have succumbed to linguistic imperialism.

Late September 2020, a conversation with Sarah[3]

Sarah: "I have been thinking about changing my name for a while. My first name is just fine. [Australian] people can pronounce it. But my last name, especially the second part. No way. It is just too long. I am tired of spelling it on the phone!"

Ellie: "I hear you. It must be frustrating".

Sarah: "Hmm, it is. You know what? I just want to shorten it. But what about my two publications? They are already under my previous name. What if I decide to stay in academia? What will happen then? Do you think I can ask the journal editors to change my name since the papers are not published yet? Or do you think I can write both my names on papers from now on?"

I pause for a moment before responding. I have thought about this question 1,000 times before, and I know name-changing is frowned upon in academia, but my name-change has already happened. I have already decided.

Ellie: "I am not sure really. You can write to the editors if you like. At the end of the day, it is your choice".

Sarah: "Hey Ellie, how do you feel about your name change?"
    Oh, I dreaded this question and here it is!

Ellie (clearing my throat): "Well, everyone was calling me Ellie before changing my name and I was tired of saying, 'My name is Elham, but you can call me Ellie'. And for my last name, I wanted a sense of unity with the new family I have created here in Australia. It took me three years to finally decide and do it. Though the last name I chose is the same as my husband's and my daughter's, I do not see it in conflict with my feminist views. It is just a constructed last name for our family to function in Australia with more ease (My husband had already shortened his last name before we married). So, in a way, it was a practical decision".

Ellie (to myself): "There, I said it. Phew!"

I have few publications under my former name and this book chapter is one of the first formal publications under my new name. It is almost two years since I changed my name and I am still not sure how I feel about it. On low days, I keep asking myself, "What if I did not have to migrate? What if my parents had chosen a more Western-sounding name for me in the first place?" I have no answers to such questions. But honestly, they keep coming to my mind. This exemplifies how my life is overshadowed by my imaginaries and the dominance of English linguistic imperialism.

---

3. This conversation was in Farsi and here is a translation of it.

In my case, while I received interviews after changing my name, as a researcher, I acknowledge that I cannot attribute my name change directly to being invited to interviews, as there could have been other factors at play.

With my name change I wanted to fit in, to say I belonged to this society; something like, "Look! I am one of you now". But the question is, "has that really happened?"

Playground story, January 2022

It is the weekend again and we need to think of some form of entertainment for Eleanora. After some discussion, we decide to go to a kids' café at a nearby shopping centre. I go in with her and my husband goes to buy some clothes for work. It is our first time at this place, so we have a look around and find the place for the kids under five. Eleanora is excited to go in and play. She tries the soft stairs and the slide. The piano on the ground catches my attention, mainly because it can be played using the feet instead of fingers. I play the notes: C, D, and E by jumping on each key.

At this moment, another kid comes to this section. She has fair skin and blonde hair. She seems to be as old as Eleanora: about two years old. I look at her and smile, but I am not sure if she can see it as I am wearing a mask. The kid's dad helps her to get on a slow merry-go-round. Eleanora wants to follow her and play with her. As she is about to jump on board, I help her and tell her (in Azeri) that she needs to wait for Mummy to get on the machine. The kid looks at me puzzled. As her father helps her to get off the merry-go-round, Eleanora wants to follow her again. This time on the slide. I decide to speak in English. "Wait for the baby, please," I say. I shifted my language intentionally so that the kid would feel at ease and in the hope that she would think we belonged to the playground as well! I had heard the father speaking in English, in an Australian accent. The kid and the father's "symbolic power" as English speakers and Australians made me shift my language.

In deciding what language to speak in different contexts, I weigh "the relative costs and rewards of speaking one language rather than another" (Wei, 2008, p. 8) and choose the one that equalises the power relations present in the situation I am in. And usually, I need to shift to English even when I am only speaking with my family members, but there are other people around who can hear us. I always feel the pressure not to be labelled as "other". Here, both the hegemonic power of the English language and my imaginaries of how I might be othered by the language I choose to speak are at play.

A few minutes later, the kid and her father went to a different section, and I immediately shifted to Azeri. This is not the only time I have shifted from Azeri to English at the playground; it happens all the time: while picking Eleanora up from daycare or dropping her off, at the shopping centre, and the list goes on. It is significant to note that the inclusion of these stories does not mean that I see myself as a victim or in a defeated position. There are moments when I feel I hold the power.

Though my confidence may vary while speaking to "native" English speakers, it is not the same when the coin is flipped and I am amongst a group whose first languages are not English. Thanks to my parents who enrolled me in private English classes since secondary school, as well as my dedication to learning this language — to the point where I have been teaching it for many years — I consider myself a "proficient" English user. This belief has been strengthened by comments from my PhD supervisors, previous teachers, my students, and the people in my community. It is worth noting that my confidence as an English speaker fluctuates based on my daily encounters. It is augmented by positive comments, and it diminishes when I feel like I have made a mistake or when I rate my linguistic capability as lower while conversing with an interlocutor who has the privilege of speaking English as their first language. One of my mental mantras (read: mental judgement) is, "Look how beautifully they[4] stated those sentences. Just if I could do the same".

End of term cathering in the café, June 2021

I am from a geographical place called Iran, and I am from a minority group in Iran called Azeris or Azerbaijanis (Northwest of Iran). So, I identify as an Azeri-Iranian.

Interestingly, I have become more attached to my Azeri identity than my Iranian identity since my immigration to Australia, mainly because of the negative reputation the so called Islamic Republic has in the Western world. Also, countries — developing or developed — are tagged with social classes and there are hierarchies among them (Kelly, 2012). Iran is not considered a country with symbolic capital; at least not in the Western world.

Feeling closer to my Azeri roots after crossing borders, when I heard about an opportunity to learn Azeri dance from a professional Azerbaijani dancer, I jumped at it. The dance group usually had an end of term gathering to plan for the upcoming term. All the students were originally from Iran and could speak Farsi, but the teacher only spoke Azerbaijani and Russian, so the conversations were in English.

---

4. "They" refers to people having English as their first language.

Leila:[5] "I am thinking about becoming a vegetarian. Does any of you have any experience?"

Tahereh: "I am not sure about that, but I was a pescatarian for three months. You might not believe it, but I lost weight, had more energy, and felt just great".

Leila: "Hmm, interesting. What do you think Ellie?"

Ellie: "Actually, I am a flexitarian [I smile], which means I eat everything and use meat on special occasions. It is good for me and for the environment as well".

The teacher (with a big smile on her face): "Ellie, I love the way you speak English. I just want to listen to you the whole day. Believe me".

I blush, say a quick thank you, and we continue the conversation. I am not new to these comments and still love hearing them each time I hear one. Thus, I possess linguistic, cultural, and symbolic capitals in scenarios where I am amongst people who belong to the Iranian community. An extreme example is when we were guests at our friend's house, and they had an Australian guest. He was the only one having English as the first language and everyone else had English as a foreign language. Before his arrival, the host approached me and said, "Ellie, you are our hope in making conversations with our Australian guest as your English is better than everyone else's!"

As illustrated by the stories thus far, in all communications where English language is used as a means of exchange, power is exerted as well. Depending on the interlocutors' English linguistic prowess and their perceptions of other interlocutors' English proficiencies in the conversation, the power seesaw fluctuates.

On occasions, I intentionally attempt at exerting some power — by resorting to my linguistic toolkit — when I feel there is a power imbalance in the room.

La vie est belle, May 2021

It is a week since I started a new job as an employment consultant. Everything is new to me, and I feel so overwhelmed. My manager tells me I need to go to a different branch to shadow some colleagues to accelerate my learning. When I arrive there in the morning, a young girl in the reception greets me and shows me where I can sit while I am at this office. I put my stuff on the table, turn on the computer, type in my newly acquired username and password, and resume the courses I need to do before doing the practical side of the job. A few minutes later,

---

5. These are all pseudonyms.

the colleague I am here to shadow arrives. I introduce myself and tell her why I am here. She has a strong Aussie accent.

Margaret: "So, when did you start working at this company?"

Ellie: "Just a week ago".

Margaret: "Oh, so you are so new. Have you done this type of work before?"

Ellie: "Not really. I want to try a different field and see how I go".

Margaret: "Hmm, I see. I can't help but notice you have an accent. Where is that from? I can't quite tell".

Ellie: "I am originally from Iran. I came to Australia a few years ago".

Margaret: "Oh, interesting. Let's get to work then. I will show you some important documents you can refer to and we can also see some clients together. Feel free to ask questions at any time".

We go through the documents, and I help with some clients. I struggle to find the sections I need to refer to on the computer and do not understand some of the words they refer to. By noon, I have a throbbing headache, so I take a break to have lunch and rest a bit. I see a small blackboard with some chalk on the table where I am having my lunch. I just pick it up and write "La vie est belle" on it. It grabs the receptionist girl's attention. She approaches and asks, "Oh, what have you written on this?" pointing at the blackboard.

Ellie: "La vie est belle. It means life is beautiful in French".

Receptionist: "Oh, nice. You speak French?"

Ellie: "Just a bit".

Receptionist: "Good on you. I can only speak English".

Ellie: "Isn't that all you need in this world, for the time being?"
    She smiles and goes back to her work.

To me, writing that phrase on that board was a demonstration of symbolic capital, exerting my linguistic power, and stating that I have linguistic access to a language that is as important as English. This is the case, at least, in my imaginary. French, having previously been the *lingua franca* of the world, has the symbolic capital to compete on more equal grounds with English than the first languages I speak (i.e., Azeri and Farsi). So, the demonstration of my linguistic capital using the French medium was my intentional way of moving my side of the power seesaw in that context, to resist English linguistic imperialism. Honestly, it felt comforting to me at the time.

The shift of power in language choice, July 2022

Up until now, I have discussed how I shift between languages in different contexts. Now that my daughter is growing up — she is almost two and a half — she leans more towards English as it is the main language her educators use at daycare. Her second choice would be Farsi. It is mainly because I mostly speak in Farsi with my husband who has a limited command of Azeri. Eleanora might shift to Azeri if I speak to her (I mostly speak to her in Azeri) or if she needs something from me. She already knows I respond better when she makes a request in Azeri. Hence, she is the one shifting between languages.

Grapes are one of her favourite fruits. The other day, I brought some grapes in a bowl for her and said, "*üzüm yiyisan maman?*",[6] and she replied, "Mummy, these are grapes!". I then explained to her that these are the same words in two different languages (i.e., *üzüm*=grapes).

I think this slight power shift in language choice is only the beginning, and I must wait for more interesting encounters and power plays of the languages as my daughter grows up and her language abilities improve. To me, this vignette is another example of resisting English linguistic imperialism by exerting my power in using my mother tongue with my daughter in a safe space called home.

Affordances and limitations

Critical autoethnography was selected as the methodology for this chapter for several reasons. In this section, I elaborate on the applied and theoretical assets and challenges with the use of this methodology relevant to Applied Linguistics. Firstly, autoethnography gives voice to the voiceless and shares stories of the people in the margins that otherwise might go unheard. As a person in the minority in Australia who speaks and attempts to teach a minority language to her daughter in an English-dominant environment, I felt the necessity to share these autobiographical accounts to criticise the hegemonic power of the English language in the Australian society and to demonstrate the pressure bi/multi-lingual parents/carers might endure passing on their linguistic and cultural heritage to the next generations. This is illustrated through the daycare and kids café vignettes, where I felt pressured to switch to English when speaking to my daughter in public.

Secondly, as language learning and teaching are emotionally loaded, autoethnography has the potential to transmit those intricacies to the reader by using evocative stories and dialogues in an interactive way. This way, the readers can

---

6. Do you want grapes, Mummy?

reflect on their own lives and empathise with the narrator (Méndez, 2013). Emotions are an integral part of each experience. My autoethnographic accounts have particularly attempted to capture emotions by sharing my personal experiences across a variety of contexts and demonstrating how power relations were experienced. The emotional aspect is particularly evident in the daycare story, where I had to navigate the feelings of separation from my child, invest in her independence by sending her to daycare, and confront my own insecurities while navigating my career in a new country. This chapter can specifically be relevant to other minority language users who live in English-dominant geographies.

A notable advantage of creating autoethnographic texts is the opportunity it provides for the writer to be reflective, and this reflection can be extended to the reader as well. For instance, pondering on my experiences when I immediately shift to English in others' presence, demonstrated in the playground and daycare stories, as well as my name change, I see them as "pre-emptive obedience" as Seidlhofer (2012) notes. That is to say, I surrender to the native speaker's norms and conventions. I believe it happens because of the insecurity I feel regarding the intersections of my linguistic and national identities. As a result, it leads to my exertion of power using linguistic forms that I perceive hold more power (e.g., the French language as depicted in the *La vie est belle* vignette). This type of reflecting on experiences to understand ourselves and how the world around us operates can also be extended to readers of autoethnography. They could recall instances where they felt the need to surrender linguistically, culturally or socially. This could meet one of the autoethnography's purposes: to "elicit caring and empathy" (Ellis & Bochner, 2006, p. 431).

However, this methodology has its own limitations. One limitation is that the narratives are presented solely from my perspective. For instance, in the daycare, playground, and café gathering stories, I am uncertain how other individuals involved perceived the linguistic dynamics or felt when hearing a language other than English spoken in their presence. This results in a one-sided account of my experiences.

Additionally, my social imaginaries — preconceived notions of how to act in specific situations — have influenced my interpretation of events and the consequent language shifts. This subjectivity is inherent in autoethnographic research.

Another limitation is the fallibility of memory. Although I have recounted these events in detail, it is well-known that memory is inherently flawed. Therefore, my accounts represent a semblance of reality rather than an objective truth. Furthermore, the temporal distance from the events at the time of narration introduces variability. Each time I revisit these incidents, my interpretations evolve based on my current emotional state, career stage, and my daughter's growth. This ongoing reinterpretation should be taken into consideration when sharing auto-biographical accounts.

For example, as I finalise this chapter in June 2024, reflecting on the daycare and playground stories, I feel more confident speaking in my mother tongue in public, influenced by my greater sense of settlement and my daughter's maturity. This shift underscores the dynamic nature of my interpretations and highlights another limitation of using autoethnography as a research methodology.

Ethical considerations

As already noted in chapters 2 and 6, there are important ethical considerations when using autoethnography as a methodology. Of the ethical considerations when doing autoethnography and writing autoethnographic accounts is when the evocative stories shared involve loved ones, friends, and colleagues. It is not possible to get consent from everyone included in the vignettes. A solution for this dilemma is to keep in mind that autoethnography is an ethical practice in itself, as Ellis (2007) notes the author needs to be ethical and honest about the people involved and the events that occurred. Honesty and ethical integrity have been followed in this chapter as well. I have recollected the stories as accurately as I could and have used pseudonyms to adhere to the research's ethical practices.

I acknowledge that all the stories I have shared here are interpreted through my own lens and influenced by my social imaginaries, my upbringing, and my understanding of power relations regarding the English language, which I perceive as the language of power. I also recognise that other individuals present in the accounts included in this chapter may have had different interpretations of the events and the language shifts I made. Acknowledging these differences is an important ethical consideration when writing autoethnographic accounts.

Again, it is imperative to emphasise that memory is flawed and that the vignettes are verisimilitudes of reality (Grant, 2010).

Final reflection

In this chapter, I have shared stories about how I perceived power imbalances in my daily encounters as a migrant in Australia. When writing this chapter, I am mostly uncomfortable using my first language in public and usually shift to English as soon as other people are present. On the one hand, as a parent raising a child in Australia, I feel the responsibility to preserve my mother tongue and dread it will go extinct within a few generations (Lo Bianco & Slaughter, 2009).

On the other hand, as a human, I want to be accepted and have a sense of belonging to the society I now call 'home'.

Moreover, the stories highlight the unequal power relations among speakers of English in different contexts. Thus, this chapter is an invitation for all speakers of English to reflect on how they position themselves in various contexts where English speakers with varying proficiencies are present, and how this positioning might affect people's confidence in speaking English or using other languages. I believe treating each situation and each encounter with more curiosity and empathy is the way forward.

This work further recognises the integral role of language in colonial processes and its implications for gaining a deeper understanding of the challenges migrants face during their settlement in a new place.

This chapter adopted critical autoethnography as its methodology to illustrate how this innovative research approach can illuminate how migrants' everyday language choices are influenced. This is only one aspect of the migrant experience; there is much more to consider. This chapter invites the application of critical autoethnography in Applied Linguistics further to explore the role of language in daily life. It encourages using this methodology to reflect on daily activities, choices, and fears and to challenge hegemonic and colonial powers. Moreover, it promotes self-awareness and acceptance of the languages we speak and our choices, while respecting others' language and life choices.

References

Adamovic, M. (2022). When ethnic discrimination in recruitment is likely to occur and how to reduce it: Applying a contingency perspective to review resume studies. *Human Resource Management Review*, 32(2), 100832.

Adams, T. E., Holman Jones, S., & Ellie, C. (2022). Introduction: Making sense and taking action: Creating a caring community of autoethnographers. In T. E. Adams, S. Holman Jones, & C. Ellie (Eds.), *Handbook of autoethnography* (2nd ed., pp. 1–19). Routledge.

Adoniou, M. (2018). Monolingualism in multicultural Australia: Paradoxes and challenges. In Y.-K. Cha, S.-H. Ham, & M. Lee (Eds.), *Routledge international handbook of multicultural education research in Asia Pacific* (pp. 272–285). Routledge.

Appadurai, A. (1996). *Modernity at large: Cultural dimensions of globalization* (Vol. 1). University of Minnesota Press.

Baquiran, C. L. C., & Nicoladis, E. (2020). A doctor's foreign accent affects perceptions of competence. *Health Communication*, 35(6), 726–730.

Bourdieu, P. (1986). The forms of capital. In J. Richardson (Ed.), *Handbook of theory and research for the sociology of education* (pp. 241–258). Greenwood.

Bourdieu, P. (2002). The forms of capital (R. Nice, Trans.). In N. W. Biggart (Ed.), *Readings in economic sociology*. Blackwell.

Bourdieu, P., & Wacquant, L. J. (1992). *An invitation to reflexive sociology.* The University of Chicago Press.

doi Darvin, R. (2017). Social class and the inequality of English speakers in a globalized world. *Journal of English as a Lingua Franca, 6*(2), 287–311.

doi Ellis, C. (2007). Telling secrets, revealing lives: Relational ethics in research with intimate others. *Qualitative Inquiry, 13*(1), 3–29.

doi Ellis, C. S., & Bochner, A. P. (2006). Analyzing analytic autoethnography: An autopsy. *Journal of Contemporary Ethnography, 35*(4), 429–449.

Grabe, W. (2012). Applied linguistics: A twenty-first-century discipline. In R. B. Kaplan (Ed.), *The Oxford handbook of applied linguistics* (2nd ed., pp. 34–44). Oxford University Press.

doi Grant, A. (2010). Writing the reflexive self: An autoethnography of alcoholism and the impact of psychotherapy culture. *Journal of Psychiatric and Mental Health Nursing, 17*(7), 577–582.

doi Holliday, A. (2006). Native-speakerism. *ELT Journal, 60*(4), 385–387.

doi Holman Jones, S. (2016). Living bodies of thought: The "critical" in critical autoethnography. *Qualitative Inquiry, 22*(4), 228–237.

doi Jones, R. H., & Hafner, C. A. (2021). *Understanding digital literacies: A practical introduction.* Taylor and Francis.

Jones, S. H., & Harris, A. M. (2019). *Queering autoethnography.* Routledge.

doi Kelly, P. F. (2012). Migration, Transnationalism, and the spaces of class identity. *Philippine Studies: Historical and Ethnographic Viewpoints, 60*(2), 153–185.

Lo Bianco, J., & Slaughter, Y. (2009). *Second languages and Australian schooling.* ACER Press.

doi Méndez, M. (2013). Autoethnography as a research method: Advantages, limitations and criticisms. *Colombian Applied Linguistics Journal, 15*(2), 279–287.

Phillipson, R. (1992). *Linguistic imperialism.* Oxford University Press.

doi Phillipson, R. (1997). Realities and myths of linguistic imperialism. *Journal of Multilingual and Multicultural Development, 18*(3), 238–248.

doi Reed-Danahay, D. (2017). Bourdieu and critical autoethnography: Implications for research, writing, and teaching. *International Journal of Multicultural Education, 19*(1), 144–154.

doi Rizvi, F. (2007). Lifelong learning: Beyond neo-liberal imaginary. In D. N. Aspin (Ed.), *Philosophical perspectives on lifelong learning* (pp. 114–130). Springer.

doi Rizvi, F. (2011). Beyond the social imaginary of 'clash of civilizations'? *Educational Philosophy and Theory, 43*(3), 225–235.

doi Seidlhofer, B. (2012). Anglophone-centric attitudes and the globalization of English. *Journal of English as a Lingua Franca, 1*(2), 393–407.

doi Taylor, C. (2002). Modern social imaginaries. *Public Culture, 14*(1), 91–124.

doi Taylor, C. (2004). What is a "social imaginary"? In G. Dilip Parameshwar, K. Jane, L. Benjamin, & W. Michael (Eds.), *Modern social imaginaries* (pp. 23–30). Duke University Press.

doi Wang, Y. I. (2020). De-Chinese and re-Chinese: Negotiating identity. In P. Stanley (Ed.), *Critical autoethnography and intercultural learning: emerging voices* (pp. 162–173). Routledge.

doi Wei, L. (2008). Research perspectives on bilingualism and multilingualism. In L. Wei & M. G. Moyer (Eds.), *The Blackwell guide to research methods in bilingualism and multilingualism* (pp. 3–17). Blackwell.

CHAPTER 11

Duoethnographic inquiry into translingualism and language teacher identity
Challenges and opportunities

Zhe (Zoey) Zheng & Luke Lawrence
Heriot-Watt University | Nihon University

Recent investigations into multilingualism and translanguaging by language teachers have highlighted the importance of individual identity and social context in determining the scope or ability to carry out translingual practices and enact preferred identities (Nagashima & Lawrence, 2020). In this chapter we take up the call issued by Lee and Canagarajah (2019) to examine the ways in which "contradicting ideologies about language and language teaching and their experience of power, privilege, marginalization or other lived experiences and identities interplay in enacting translingual dispositions" (p. 361). We do this by adopting a two-stage duoethnographic approach to explore the experiences of two multilingual migrant English teachers; one a "non-native speaker" teaching in the "native" English environment of the UK, and the other a "native speaker" teaching in the "non-native" environment of Japan. The study reveals that monolingualism and native-speakerism in the local communities have heavily influenced our willingness to claim a bilingual identity, preventing us from adopting a translingual disposition. It also puts constraints on our autonomy in professional identity negotiation and results in us de-emphasising or concealing our national origins. However, our stories also show that teachers' small acts of resistance can afford them the possibility to challenge existing ideologies.

Introduction

Recently, against a backdrop of increased mixing and exchange of populations, resources and cultures, the traditional static framework of bounded languages is

https://doi.org/10.1075/rmal.8.11zhe

no longer adequate to capture the fluid and dynamic language practice of migratory peoples. To address this issue, scholarship in multilingualism has undergone a paradigm shift known as the "multilingual turn" (May, 2014). Engaging with the multilingual turn, scholars challenge the traditional monolingual bias against multilingualism and reconceptualize the relationship between different languages as fluid and interconnected within a single repertoire. This repertoire is drawn upon by bilinguals/multilinguals as a sense-making resource. Bilingual speakers, therefore, are no longer viewed as "two monolinguals in one person" (Grosjean, 1989, p.3) but as individuals who are able to "shuttle between languages, treating the diverse languages that form their repertoire as an integrated system" (Canagarajah, 2011, p.401). Their practice of traversing languages to make sense of the world is known as "translanguaging" (Garcia, 2009).

Embracing this new epistemological stance, scholars distinguish between the terms "bilingual teacher" and "translingual teacher". The concept of a "translingual teacher" highlights the capacity of bilingual/multilingual teachers to integrate their various linguistic identities (Zheng, 2017) and acknowledges the transforming impact of language learning experience on their linguistic repertoire, as well as the pre-existing linguistic and professional identity (Motha et al., 2012). Being bilingual/multilingual does not automatically confer a teacher's translingual identity (Zheng, 2017); instead, it requires active effort on the part of teachers to move away from the monolingual ideology and adopt a "translingual disposition" (Lee & Canagarajah, 2019). The scope or ability to engage in translingual practices and enact preferred identities is found to be impacted by individual identity and social context (Nagashima & Lawrence, 2022). While recent research (e.g., Motha et al., 2012; Zheng, 2017) has shown how teachers can strategically tap into their translingual identity as pedagogy, limited attention has been paid to the challenges teachers confront during this process.

In this chapter, we respond to the call made by Lee and Canagarajah (2019) to examine how "contradicting ideologies about language and language teaching and their experience of power, privilege, marginalization or other lived experiences and identities interplay in enacting translingual dispositions" (p.361). By adopting a two-stage duoethnographic approach involving personal narratives and dialogic engagement, we identify three themes in this chapter: exclusive and inclusive ideologies, professional identity and autonomy, and hidden identities. The analysis reveals how monolingualism and native-speakerism, along with their manifestation in the local communities, have an impact on our willingness to claim a bilingual identity, provide limited space for identity negotiation, and result in our choices in hiding parts of our identities.

Conceptual lens

Native speakerism

Native-speakerism is a pervasive ideology that posits that the native-speaker English teacher represents the ideal teacher of the language, and that communicative pedagogical methodologies associated with the West are superior to non-Western styles of teaching and learning (Holliday, 2006; Lowe, 2020; Phillipson, 1992). By implication therefore, non-native speaker English teachers that practice alternative methodologies to the Western-approved variety are seen as deficient and less than desirable. In this era of neoliberal hegemony in which capital interests dictate language learning policy and hiring decisions (O'Regan, 2021), this native-speakerist ideology can have far-reaching real-world consequences for non-native speaker English teachers and their professional identities. For example, participants in Nagashima and Lawrence's (2021) study of non-native speaker (they were all also non-Japanese), female teachers working in the Japanese context, were asked to hide their true nationalities and speak in American accents in order to satisfy the perceived demands of parents and stakeholders.

In recent years, scholars have attempted to broaden the notion of native-speakerism to include various kinds of discrimination and marginalization faced by native speaker English teachers (Houghton & Rivers, 2013). This iteration of native-speakerism focuses on the pressure felt by native-speaker teachers in EFL contexts to conform to the stereotype of a monocultural, monolingual entity and perform the role of "professional foreigner" (Houghton & Rivers, 2013; Nuske, 2014). This desire for native speaker teachers to perform the role of "pure foreigner", again, created and promoted by the dictates of the perceived demands of the market, can have similar repercussions in terms of identity performance. This is especially true for long-term immigrants who have embraced the culture and language of the host society. Although this alternative definition of native-speakerist ideology has been rightly criticized for failing to address the systemic inequalities that native-speakerism represents (see Lowe, 2020), the points raised are nevertheless valid for a large number of teachers in the field.

The native-speakerist concept outlined above acts as one part of the theoretical lens for our data analysis, with the other aspect drawing on Bakhtin's dialogism.

Dialogism

The notion of Dialogism, proposed by Bakhtin (1981), is instrumental in helping us comprehend the development of our identities as teachers and the tension between our teacher identities and the broader context. According to Bakhtin, the world is constructed through a dialogue among different discourses, including the interaction between internally persuasive discourse and authoritative discourse. These dialogues take place both within individuals and in their interactions with the external world, and the interaction between these discourses is filled with tensions.

Our beliefs and sense of self are closely associated with our personal identity, where the internally persuasive discourse resides. Internally persuasive discourse can be described as "what each person thinks for him- or herself, what ultimately is persuasive to the individual" (Freedman & Ball, 2004, p. 8). However, because internally persuasive discourse could be "denied all privilege, backed by no authority at all, and is frequently not even acknowledged in society" (Bakhtin, 1981, p. 342), we might encounter barriers when trying to integrate our beliefs and personal identity with the culturally accepted professional identity in a particular context.

In contrast, authoritative discourse is congruent with the socially stereotyped professional identity as it represents the voice of authority and tradition, and is typically considered unquestionable. The harmonious integration of both discourses is deemed essential for teachers to develop their identity (Beijaard et al., 2004; Pennington & Richards, 2016). The tensions between these two discourses could potentially lead to an identity crisis, but they can also provide opportunities for teachers to revise their self-perceptions and reconstruct their identities. It is through the negotiation and struggle of these two discourses that individuals develop their identity (Assaf, 2005). Consequently, identity, is a fluid and ongoing process, with new experiences influencing our ideas and beliefs, and ultimately shaping who we are as teachers.

In this chapter, we draw on Bakhtin's notion of internally persuasive discourse and authoritative discourse to interpret the interaction between our personal and professional identities. In doing so, we associate our identity formation and negotiation with the wider social context, including the classroom at the micro level, the institution at the meso level and the societal context at the macro level, to understand the opportunities and challenges to enacting our preferred teacher identities.

Methodology

Two-Stage duoethnographic research process

As a methodology, duoethnography is still emerging in the fields of Applied Linguistics and English Language Teaching (ELT) (see Lawrence & Lowe, 2020 for an overview), but has so far been utilised to explore gender, race and sexuality (Lawrence & Nagashima, 2020), professional development (Smart & Cook, 2020), pedagogical practice (Lowe & Lawrence, 2020) as well as native-speaker and non-native speaker identity (Hooper et al., 2020) and translanguaging practice as it pertains to teacher identity (Nagashima & Lawrence, 2021). In these studies, duoethnography has proved to be a flexible and accessible methodology that fits well with the broad intellectual demands of a complex field such as Applied Linguistics, as well as the more classroom-based orientation of ELT research. In this study, we built on these previous studies in Applied Linguistics and introduced a two-stage process for data collection.

The two-stage process that we followed for this project began with the writing of personal narratives that documented our personal and professional journeys with language and identity (Stage 1). We each wrote a single extended narrative, based on rough guidelines that we set out before writing to share whatever we felt was relevant to our careers in relation to translingual practice. The narratives as presented below are the full versions of the original documents after undergoing several rounds of editing to eliminate superfluous statements. After sharing our narratives with one another we then used these as a springboard to delve deeper into points of interest raised (Stage 2) through a duoethnographic spoken dialogue. Due to the difference in our own personal backgrounds and current teaching circumstances, we felt that duoethnography, a key tenet of which is juxtaposition of story and experience (Sawyer & Norris, 2013), would be the perfect fit for our investigation into identity and translingualism. Duoethnography empowers us to actively engage in reflective conversations about our life experiences. For instance, it helps us become more conscious of our deliberate concealment of our identity in front of students, a response to the pervasive monolingualism and native-speakerism in our contexts.

In order to allow the reader, who we see as the third co-participant in the research (Sawyer & Norris, 2013), inside the research process, we first present the Stage 1 data without comment and invite the reader to join us on the research journey. This is followed by the Stage 2 data, presented as reconstructed dialogues and broken down into three themes. The themes were decided by mutual agreement after we each examined the dialogue transcripts separately, and then came together to share our idea and interpretations.

In this chapter, our own identities and *currere* (life histories) (Pinar, 1974) constitute the "research site in relation to lived cultural worlds" (Sawyer & Norris, 2013, p. 16). In order to keep the topic of plurilingual identity at the center of the chapter, rather than set out our positionings explicitly by providing biographies, we will allow our identities to emerge out of the data. Again, we hope that this approach will allow the reader to experience the data in the same way that we did. It should be noted, however, that at the beginning of the project we had little knowledge of each other's background and history. The impetus of the project was a shared interest in multilingualism/translanguaging and identity and a desire to explore issues related to this.

In terms of ethics, any co-authored research project has the potential for issues of power imbalances between researchers to emerge (Lawrence & Nagashima, 2020). However, the intimate nature of duoethnographic research can often serve to mitigate these imbalances as both researcher-participants are required to reveal personal stories and deep-rooted experiences. In this research project, although there is no difference in our occupational status, Luke represented an older, male, more experienced researcher (especially with regard to experience with the duoethnographic method), from a Western research tradition who was writing in his first language. On the other hand, Zoey is a younger, female, Asian researcher, working in her second language, taking part in her first duoethnography. Due to his previous experiences (see Lawrence & Nagashima, 2020), Luke was acutely aware of this potential power imbalance and although it is true that he took the lead in terms of the practical aspects of how the duoethnography was conducted and proposed the first conceptual lens of native-speakerism, the second theoretical framework (Bakhtin's dialogism) was put forward by Zoey and the interpretation of data was done jointly.

Stage 1 — Personal narratives

Zoey

Growing up in a small town in Guangdong, China, I speak Teochew Dialect, Mandarin and Cantonese. However, I never considered myself "bilingual/multilingual" until I learned and became fluent in English. Even then, English had been only a subject for me and rarely related to a "new identity" until I began living in a more international environment.

Since 2014, I have worked as a teacher in English education in three different universities in China and the UK. The department I worked at in my first job offered two compulsory English courses: oral English class and "comprehensive English" class. The first one was taught by international teachers and often considered "fun" while the latter one was delivered by Chinese teachers and often viewed as "boring/ serious" by the students. I felt this arrangement gave me little power to negotiate my identity. This was probably why I felt excited when I found out there would be no segregation between Chinese and international teachers in my second job. In this position, I felt valued and was growing fast as a teacher by communicating with colleagues from all over the world. I was motivated to show my students that I can be as competent and fun as other international teachers. Teaching the same course with other international teachers did bring some sense of insecurity but it never played a big part in my teaching career until I started to work in the UK, teaching Chinese students Msc (Masters of Sciences) TESOL course and pre-sessional English course. Having a good knowledge about Chinese students' expectations, I believe students are likely to feel disappointed when they know their teacher is Chinese after travelling to the other side of the world to experience something "different" and an "authentic" English speaking environment. My feeling was complicated: I was proud of my identity as I believe it shows the students who are future English teachers the possibility of achieving this position as a non-native English-speaking teacher; I was also worried about showing this identity too soon as it could damage my teacher authority. Therefore, I strategically chose not to explicitly reveal my Chinese identity until I believed I had established my competent teacher image.

Luke

I was born and grew up in the South East of England in a completely monolingual environment. When I moved to Japan in 2002, my colonialist/native-speakerist mindset was so strong that it didn't even occur to me to try to learn the language before I came. For my first five years in Japan, I was teaching at an eikaiwa (English conversation) school. Eikaiwa are notorious for propagating an English-only, native-speakerist agenda. This agenda suited my monolingual, native speaker identity very well and even though I'd started attending Japanese classes and was trying to learn the local language, I did little to resist being ascribed a monolingual identity even when I was not quite monolingual anymore.

Later, I started teaching as a Team Teacher, working alongside Japanese English teachers in public secondary schools. There wasn't much translanguaging as such in the classes, but there was a huge amount of codeswitching and "parallel monolingualism" (Heller, 1999) enacted by the Japanese teachers and the students, but notably not from me. Again, I was expected to present as a monolingual foreigner and for the most part I was still (kind of) happy to do so.

I'm currently working at a private university, teaching mostly compulsory classes to undergraduates. There is no official policy at my institution regarding language use in the classroom, but there seems to be an understanding that as a "native speaker" teacher I am expected to present myself as such, which inevitably involves performing my role monolingually. I do quite a bit of "passive translanguaging" in that I often listen to the students talking or asking a question in Japanese, but I always reply in English. When I'm at home with my family I feel like I have a very strong multilingual identity. However, this does not translate across to my language teacher identity. I don't know whether this is from fear, embarrassment at my relatively low level of Japanese ability, an automatic reaction to play the part I am expected to, or maybe it's just the only way that I know.

Stage 2 — duoethnographic dialogues

Theme 1 — exclusive and inclusive ideologies

The discussion presented in this section demonstrates how intertwining issues, including proficiency levels and ideology, embedded in our second language's communities influence our willingness to claim a bilingual identity.

Luke: *I've read a lot of the literature on translingualism and I'm aware that the modern idea of being bilingual is that you don't have to be perfectly proficient in both languages at all. But something in my brain kind of, I don't know, I just don't recognise myself as that kind of person.*

Zoey: *Where do you think that comes from?*

Luke: *I don't know. Maybe I'm completely wrong, but I've got a feeling that it's because Japanese is a closed language, if you know what I mean. Japanese is only spoken in Japan. The gatekeeping of who is allowed to call themselves bilingual seems more demanding in Japan. It seems to me that maybe Japanese culture is more closed and it's not open to people becoming a member. On the other hand, I see a lot of people whose second language or second culture is English or, you know, UK-based culture, and they seem more ready to call themselves bicultural and bilingual.*

Zoey: *It sounds more related to culture instead of proficiency. They are closely related I guess.*

Luke: *Yeah, maybe you are right, but I think it's related to language as well.*

Zoey: *It is harder to become a member of that society if you don't have that certain level of proficiency.*

Luke: *But, the strange thing is that there is a lower expectation. People don't expect you to have that higher level of proficiency, which maybe they expect you to have in the UK. So, maybe you are right, it could be more about culture. I don't know, I'm just really hesitant to label myself like that.*

Zoey: *Do you think it is related to the society where you are in?*

Luke: *Yeah, definitely. I think that I'm not seen as fully part of Japanese society, which maybe makes me hesitant to identify as bicultural myself. For example, in class the other day, some students were talking about a musician they liked. When I asked them who they were talking about, they were like "ah, it's OK, it's a Japanese artist, maybe you don't know them". They were saying it like because I'm not Japanese, that I wouldn't know them. They don't see me as part of "their" culture. But then I wondered why I was so keen for them to tell me the name as if I was kind of too eager to prove that I do know Japanese culture and that I am a part of it. That's pretty sad. So, how about you? When did you become comfortable calling yourself bilingual or bicultural?*

Zoey: *I can't remember at what point, but it was definitely after I chose English as my major as I immersed myself in the English-speaking environment 24/7, which helped me to improve my English. Then at some point, I started to feel that my English is enough for me to do some daily communication. I think I felt comfortable calling myself bilingual then. I also asked my students this question in their presentations. They said they were bilingual, but not balanced ones.*

Luke: *I think part of my discomfort and hesitancy stems from the lack of acceptance of multilingual or translingual use, especially from my students, which I suppose is tied up with my identity as a "native-speaker" teacher.*

Zoey: *OK. What? Uhm. Can you give me an example, like how is it not accepted?*

Luke: *Well, if I use a Japanese word or phrase in my lessons, just using one word is enough for the class to erupt into laughter.*

Zoey: *OK. So most of the time, students found it funny? I guess in China, it is kind of similar. I remember my international colleague told me "I speak some very simple Chinese and people are like, oh wow, your Chinese is so good!"*

Luke: *Yeah yeah, that's the big stereotype over here as well. But, you know, there's nothing funny about using the word, it's just because it's me, a visible foreigner, that says it. That is why they are laughing. I used to play up to it and used it as part of my skill as a language teacher to improve the rapport. But I realized that I was perpetuating this idea that foreign people are monolingual and can't speak Japanese, and if they do, it's a funny novelty. I kind of realized that I was doing that and I tried to stop it.*

The dialogue shows our different orientations towards bilingual identity. Zoey is comfortable calling herself bilingual while Luke is less inclined to adopt this label. Our willingness to identify as bilinguals indicates the extent to which we embrace the new identity that emerged with the acquisition of a second language, shedding light on our dispositions towards language diversity.

For Zoey, she felt ready to consider herself bilingual when her English allowed her to engage in basic daily communication. Language competence also plays a role in Luke's reluctance to view himself as bilingual. However, the willingness to use the label of bilingual goes beyond the linguistic aspect. Luke observes that individuals whose second language is English appear to be more willing to embrace the term "bilingual". This readiness is also reflected in Zoey's students, who regarded themselves as bilingual despite their imbalanced language competence. As English is widely spoken in the world, becoming a member of the English-speaking community could be less demanding than being recognized as a member in a more exclusive society, such as Japan. Luke's experience of being positioned as a monolingual, monoculture foreigner by his students can be seen as a direct reflection of native-speakerist ideology that hinders him from being integrated into Japanese society and claiming his bilingual identity. Although situated in different contexts, Zoey's description of her colleagues' experience in China echoes the monolingual foreigner stereotype held by the exclusive community members, suggesting a strong native-speakerist outlook that categorizes teachers into binary roles.

As Zheng (2017) notes, labelling ourselves as "bilingual" does not guarantee a translingual disposition. However, hesitancy to embrace a bilingual identity as a first step may lead to a separation of the new identity and the pre-existing one, which prevents us from "engag[ing] with language difference and social diversity", and thus hindering us from adopting a translingual disposition (Lee & Canagarajah, 2019, p.354). Bakhtin's notions of internally persuasive discourse and authoritative discourse enable us to understand the reasons behind our different approaches to adopting the bilingual label. Zoey's internal persuasive discourse and the outside authoritative discourse were aligned as she identified as bilingual and was accepted as such. However, for Luke the authoritative discourse of the exclusive Japanese context served as a controlling mechanism for his own internally persuasive discourse, resulting in a reluctance to embrace a bilingual identity.

Theme 2 — professional identity and autonomy

In this second dialogue, we discuss the constraints on personal autonomy in our professional lives. These were found to be deeply affected by context and wider societal stereotypes and expectations.

Luke: *You mentioned in the narrative that in your first job, there was a segregation between native speaker teachers and the local teachers. How did you feel about that?*

Zoey: *I think this segregation only perpetuated the stereotype. It made me feel powerless. I don't think I had the power to negotiate my identity.*

Luke: *Why? Why do you feel that you didn't have the power?*

Zoey: *Uhm, because when I structured my class, I had to think about the final assessment. I've got to go through certain course materials to reach a certain target. A fun class sometimes requires a lot more practice time, which I didn't have. So, I was pretty restricted in a sense. It's not that I didn't try. I made an attempt to change things. I tried to bring a fun class to my students, but it didn't work out.*

Luke: *Why not?*

Zoey: *I think it was in the middle of the semester so probably not the best time to try because students had got used to the teacher-centred class. I tried to do an information gap activity with my students. A very small number of students cooperated, which was very disappointing. I don't think my students expected this from me. They expected me to lecture them and teach them what they need for the exam, just like what they experienced in high schools with their Chinese teachers. Also, it was a huge class. I've got 50, 60 students and these kind of small group activities, fun activities, work better with a smaller number of students. I was trying to bring what I learnt in my Master's degree to my class. But there is a disconnection between what you learn in school and what you can do in your context because my context was totally different.*

Luke: *Right*

Zoey: *Actually, even to have that realisation that I need to do something, to bring what I learned to my class took me a while. As a novice teacher, it is very easy to get influenced by how other people teach in your context and totally forget what you learn in your degree. And those experienced Chinese teachers, they have accepted the stereotype and have been doing things in a certain way for years and years. It's just so difficult to change how students expect the class would run, especially when everyone else is teaching in a certain way which enhances this stereotype. You need a context that gives you certain freedom to create a fun class. I didn't have that.*

Luke: *It is interesting to see your description of segregation in the narrative and listen to your opinion on it because this is exactly the same in Japan. To be honest, it's also not a very rewarding existence to always teach in a "fun" way as a foreign teacher. It is not very fulfilling. I think students also have a stereotype about foreign teachers. Like, my students often seem surprised when I mention my research. I think they don't see the foreign teachers as being academics. They are just seen as English teachers.*

Zoey: *This reminds me of one of my students' comments in the UK. It was the start of a new module and they were discussing their new teachers in a group chat which I was in. A student said, "Unfortunately, I've got a Chinese teacher. She has a strong accent. She must be very good at research.".*

Luke: *Interesting. I don't know, I think some of the students don't even see me as a teacher. I think they see me as a foreign person who happens to be teaching.*

Zoey: *OK. Do they see you as an opportunity to practice their English?*

Luke: *Yeah, which is fine, that's my job! But I think they do see me as this monolingual, monocultural object. For example, when I worked as a Team Teacher the Japanese teacher would often translate everything I said for the students. Again, this is OK, but it implied that I needed an interpreter as I wasn't able to say the same things in Japanese myself. Obviously I often could, I just wasn't allowed to. I think this perpetuated the monolingual stereotype. Similarly, there were often activities included where the students explained some aspects of Japanese culture to the teacher. We kind of had to pretend that we didn't know. As you can imagine, this felt pretty demeaning.*

Zoey: *How do you feel about that? 'Cause as a language learner, you probably want to use the language more often?*

Luke: *It seems ridiculous to restrict your skill set and to pretend that you don't have this particular knowledge. I mean, even putting aside the identity part, it seems silly not to utilize that skill set. Although, I guess at that stage I didn't really know enough Japanese for it to be a bigger part of my identity, so I didn't really care about that side of it, but it just seemed a bit ridiculous.*

This dialogue again provided evidence of native-speakerist categorisation and revealed striking similarities of feeling a lack of professional autonomy towards how we negotiated our teacher identities in the classroom, but from very different viewpoints. In Zoey's case, native-speakerism was manifested when her efforts to adopt a more "fun" persona and incorporate the communicative language teaching (CLT) methodologies that she had learnt on her Master's course were stymied. This resistance came directly from the students themselves as her failed experiment with an information gap activity illustrates. It also came from the systemic adherence to segregated teaching styles that reflected native-speakerist thinking and were part of commonly understood social behaviours in the institutional and social framework of a Chinese university.

In contrast, Luke's struggle to assert agency in his professional teacher capacity involved attempts to escape a less serious and "fun" persona. Context-bound native-speakerist stereotypes around the role of foreign teachers in Japan led to students seeing his role as an unacademic one. This could be directly compared to Zoey's example of the Chinese teacher in the UK who was seen as more academic due to her pronounced accent, which would presumably disqualify her from teaching more communicative classes (at least in the eyes of the students). In addition, the role of "professional foreigner" (Heimlich, 2013) assigned to Luke meant that the stereotype of foreign teachers as monolingual and monocultural served to suppress the Japanese language and culture part of his emerging translingual identity. In both of our examples, the tension between Bakhtin's (1981) internally persuasive discourse and authoritative discourse can clearly be seen, with the authoritative discourse wielding the greater influence.

Theme 3 — hidden identities

In this final theme, the discussion turns to the aspects of our identities that we attempt to keep hidden from our students:

Zoey: *After you picked up Japanese, you said you did little to resist being ascribed a monolingual identity, even though at that time you were learning a new language. Why?*

Luke: *I guess I still very much had a native-speakerist mindset. I felt that the Japanese language was not relevant to what I was doing as a teacher. Being a native speaker was such a big part of the job and it didn't seem to make sense to kind of burst that bubble by, you know, introducing complications. And that was one of the things that made me kind of good at that job. You know, it was having that kind of purity of foreign identity. So, why would I jeopardize that? You know, that was my job.*

Zoey: *I know, performing a foreign identity is so desirable in the English teaching world, right? Working in the UK, I always worry that my students would feel disappointed when they know that their teacher is Chinese because they've travelled all the way here to experience something different, an "authentic" English-speaking environment but instead they've got someone from their home country.*

Luke: *Yeah, I wanted to ask you about that. Did you see any evidence that students actually did feel like that? Can you think of any specific incidents?*

Zoey: *I actually attended one of my students' interview in his dissertation project, which was about native-speakerism. In the interview, I told him my sense of insecurity when first walking into the class as a Chinese teacher. He told me that "when you first walked in, we did have the feeling of uncertainty". But later they talked to other students who were in the native speaker teachers' classes and realised: "Okay, Zoey is not bad. I'm glad that I am in her class". And I also thought about it myself, how would I feel as a Chinese student at their age, travelling all the way to experience some foreign culture? I would probably be disappointed as well. When I was a student, I was eager to have some interaction with international students and native-speaker teachers. Although not anymore. But I understand how they might feel.*

Luke: *Yeah, yeah, I mean, I totally understand that. You said in your written narrative that you are worried that showing or over-emphasising the Chinese side of your identity too soon would damage your teacher authority? In what way?*

Zoey: *I think that would have an impact on both sides. If I came in and said: I'm a Chinese teacher. For me, I would probably feel more insecure. For students, their stereotype about Chinese teachers would play a role and even before you deliver the class, they might already have a certain expectation. I think this would be difficult to change. And I'm not saying that I won't be able to change it, but it will require more effort to some extent.*

Luke: *OK, but at the start of a course, it's pretty common for teachers to introduce themselves. Are you saying that you don't do that?*

Zoey: *I did, but it wasn't about nationality. Actually, for me, this issue is not even about being a native speaker or non-native speaker teacher. It's about that I don't want to be seen as a Chinese teacher. I don't mind if you see me as someone from Japan, Singapore or Malaysia. But I just don't feel comfortable being known as a Chinese teacher. Because if I told them that I'm a Japanese teacher, they wouldn't have this kind of assumption about who you are and what kind of class you would teach.*

Luke: *Okay, and to bring it back to multilingualism, does that also mean that you don't use Chinese in the class?*

Zoey: *I don't. But when there are chances, I do speak a little bit of Chinese, not much.*

Luke: *But surely there must be hundreds of chances every lesson.*

Zoey: *Yeah, I know. But when I'm speaking in front of the whole class of students, I don't usually use Chinese. Particularly at the start as I don't feel comfortable enough, right? But slowly, I'm starting to feel more comfortable with my identity and when there is a difficult concept which a related Chinese word can sum up well, I would use them in my class. But it is very rare. I think apart from my sense of insecurity, I am aware that it is a British university and students come to the class with a certain expectation. They would expect their teacher to speak English in class and for parity reasons, it also makes sense for me to speak English. For students' language use, I hold a relatively loose language policy but again, students are in a British university and some of them, particularly as future English teachers, see the overseas study experience as an opportunity to practice English. Although they are in the UK and seem to have a lot of opportunities to do so. But it is not the case, at least not in my context.*

Luke: *When you were saying about how you don't necessarily say you're from China when you are introducing yourself, it made me realise that I've stopped doing that as well. I kind of deliberately don't introduce where I'm from, unless I'm asked directly, of course.*

Zoey: *OK, so what's the reason behind yours?*

Luke: *I think mine is the same reason as yours. I think I don't want them to have that stereotype. Also, I think I don't want to make the nationality or native-speaker part of my identity a big part of it. I don't want it to be important to them. I just want to identify myself as a teacher, not a native speaker teacher. I used to do it all the time. I used to have a whole lesson on introductions. They would introduce themselves, and I'd introduce myself and they'd ask questions and stuff, and it was like a big part of the course. I suppose it's just in the last two years that I've completely stopped doing it. I still ask the students to introduce themselves to each other, I just don't include myself anymore.*

In this final dialogue, issues related to native-speakerism are shown to affect our teacher identities in the form of de-emphasizing, and at times concealing our national origins. For Zoey, the mainstream definition of native-speakerism that marginalizes non-native teachers can be seen to play a part in this. For Luke, it is the expanded definition of native-speakerism as propagated by Houghton and Rivers (2013) that may go some way towards helping to explain his identity performance decisions in the classroom.

In Luke's case, his recent decision to stop introducing himself directly to students at the start of a course, not only shows his desire to de-emphasise his nationality, but also to present himself as a teacher first and as a native English-speaking person second. As well as hiding this element of himself, he also revealed that he hides the Japanese language and culture aspect of his identity from his students too, resulting in a double-hidden identity. By this act of double concealment, it may be seen that Luke is perpetuating the native-speakerist ideology of the monolingual, monocultural foreigner on one hand, whilst simultaneously attempting to mitigate it on the other.

For Zoey, her position as a Chinese teacher of English teaching in the UK to classes of Chinese students led to her hiding her nationality from her students in order to avoid their preconceived notions of her pedagogical style. By this action, she is not attempting to pass as a native-speaker teacher, it is specifically her background as a Chinese national that she is intentionally concealing. This complicates the approach that places the self-othering caused by native-speakerist ideology as the usual factor in identity issues for non-native speaker English teachers.

Zoey's decision not to reveal her common nationality with her students indicates her internally persuasive discourse of herself as a competent teacher, who refuses to accept the authoritative discourse prevalent among the students, challenging the stereotypes imposed on Chinese teachers.

Conclusion

Language teachers' translingual dispositions could allow them to perform success-ful translingual practice, acknowledge students' linguistic repertoire and influence their classroom experience (Lee & Canagarajah, 2019). However, to enact such dis-positions, language teachers may confront a series of challenges. Our research reveals how contexts play a role in this process at three interconnected levels. Mono-lingual ideology and native-speakerism at the macro level shape and are reflected in institutional frameworks and students' expectations of teacher identity at the meso and micro levels. Both Zoey and Luke were positioned by their students, institu-tions and the wider social context to some extent, which restricted recognition of their bilingual identities and left little autonomy in identity negotiation.

This powerful contextual influence results in moments when we are subject to the authoritative discourse, which perpetuates monolingual ideology. For instance, Luke's decision to hide his Japanese speaker's identity could further "serve to reinforce patterns of inequality" (Motha et al., 2012, p. 18). However, our internal persuasive discourse also leads us to strategically conceal our national origins, which goes some way towards challenging the authoritative discourse. The way we presented ourselves is an effort to alter the 'image-text' (Simon, 1995) that our students constructed of us, which has the potential to challenge stu-dents' stereotypes and be utilised as a teaching pedagogy (see Morgan, 2004). In other words, the tension between the two discourses provides an opportunity for teachers to reflect on and renegotiate their teacher identity, paving the way for the adoption of a translingual disposition, regardless of individual background or teaching context.

References

Assaf, L. C. (2005). Exploring identities in a reading specialization program. *Journal of Literacy Research, 37*(2), 201–236.

Bakhtin, M. M. (1981). Discourse in the novel. In M. Holquist (Ed.), *The dialogic imagination: Four essays (269–422).* University of Texas Press.

Beijaard, D., Meijer, P., & Verloop, N. (2004). Reconsidering research on teachers' professional identity. *Teaching and Teacher Education, 20,* 107–128.

Canagarajah, A. S. (2011). Codemeshing in academic writing: Identifying teachable strategies of translanguaging. *Modern Language Journal, 95,* 401–417.

Freedman, S. W. & Ball, A. F. (2004). Ideological becoming: Bakhtinian concepts to guide the study of language, literacy, and learning. In A. F. Ball & S. W. Freedman (Eds.), *Bakhtinian perspectives on language, literacy, and learning* (pp. 3–33). Cambridge University Press.

Garcia, O. (2009). Education, multilingualism and translanguaging in the 21st century. In A. Mohanty, M. Panda, R. Phillipson, & T. Skutnabb-Kangas (Eds.). *Multilingual education for social justice: Globalising the local* (pp.140–158). Orient Blackswan.

Grosjean, F. (1989). Neurolinguists, beware! The bilingual is not two monolinguals in one person. *Brain and Language*, 36(1), 3–15.

Heimlich, E. (2013). The meaning of Japan's role of professional foreigner. In S.A. Houghton & D.J. Rivers (Eds.) *Native-speakerism in Japan: Intergroup dynamics in foreign language education* (pp.169–179). Multilingual Matters.

Heller, M. (1999). *Linguistic minorities and modernity: A sociolinguistic ethnography.* Longman.

Holliday, A. (2006). Native-speakerism. *ELT Journal*, 60(4), 385–387.

Hooper, D., Oka, M., & Yamazawa, A. (2020). Not all eikaiwas (or instructors) are created equal: A trioethnography of 'native speaker' and 'non-native speaker' perspectives on English conversation schools in Japan. In R.J. Lowe & L. Lawrence (Eds.), *Duoethnography in English language teaching: Research, reflection and classroom application* (pp. 29–49). Multilingual Matters.

Houghton, S.A., & Rivers, D.J. (2013). Introduction: Redefining native-speakerism. In S.A. Houghton & D.J. Rivers (Eds.), *Native-speakerism in Japan: Intergroup dynamics in foreign language education* (pp.1–16). Multilingual Matters.

Lawrence, L., & Lowe, R.J. (2020). An introduction to duoethnography. In R.J. Lowe & L. Lawrence (Eds.), *Duoethnography in English language teaching: Research, reflection and classroom application* (pp.1–26). Multilingual Matters.

Lawrence, L. & Nagashima, Y. (2020). The intersectionality of gender, sexuality, race, and native-speakerness: Investigating teacher identity through duoethnography. *Journal of Language, Identity & Education*, 19(1), 42–55.

Lee, E., & Canagarajah, S. (2019). Beyond native and nonnative: Translingual dispositions for more inclusive teacher identity in language and literacy education. *Identity & Education*, 18(6), 352–363.

Lowe, R.J. (2020). *Uncovering ideology in English language teaching: Identifying the 'native speaker' frame.* Springer.

Lowe, R.J., & Lawrence, L. (2020). Duoethnography in the language class. In R.J. Lowe & L. Lawrence (Eds.), *Duoethnography in English language teaching: Research, reflection and classroom application* (pp.155–170). Multilingual Matters.

May, S. (2014). Introducing the "multilingual turn". In S. May (Ed.), *The multilingual turn. implications for SLA, TESOL and bilingual education.* Routledge.

Morgan, B. (2004). Teacher identity as pedagogy: Towards a field-internal conceptualisation in bilingual and second language education. *International Journal of Bilingual Education and Bilingualism*, 7, 172–188.

Motha, S., Jain, R. & Tecle, T. (2012). Translinguistic identity as pedagogy: Implications for teacher education. *International Journal of Innovation in English Language Teaching & Research*, 1(1), 13–28.

Nagashima, Y., & Lawrence, L. (2021). Intersectional identities: Voices from the margins of ELT in Japan. In J. Kroo, & K. Satoh (Eds.), *Linguistic tactics and strategies of marginalization in Japanese* (pp. 87–111). Palgrave Macmillan.

Nagashima, Y., & Lawrence, L. (2022). To translanguage or not to translanguage: Ideology, practice, and intersectional identities. *Applied Linguistics Review*, 13(5), 735–754.

Nuske, K. (2014). It is very hard for teachers to make changes to policies that have become so solidified: Teacher resistance at corporate eikaiwa franchises in Japan. *The Asian EFL Journal*, 16(2), 283–312.

O'Regan, J. P. (2021). *Global English and political economy*. Routledge.

Pennington, M. C., & Richards, J. (2016). Teacher identity in language teaching: Integrating personal, contextual and professional factors. *RELC Journal*, 47(1), 5–23.

Phillipson, R. (1992). *Linguistic imperialism*. Oxford University Press.

Pinar, W. (1974). Currere: Toward reconceptualization. In J. Jelinek (Ed.), *Basic problems in modern education* (pp. 147–171). Arizona State University.

Sawyer, R. D., & Norris, J. (2013). *Duoethnography*. Oxford University Press.

Simon, R. I. (1995). Face to face with alterity: Postmodern Jewish identity and the eros of pedagogy. In J. Gallop (Ed.), *Pedagogy: The question of impersonation* (pp. 90–105). University of Indiana Press.

Smart, B., & Cook, C. (2020). Professional development through duoethnography: Reflecting on dialogues between an experienced and novice teacher. In R. J. Lowe & L. Lawrence (Eds.), *Duoethnography in English language teaching: Research, reflection and classroom application* (pp. 91–111). Multilingual Matters.

Zheng, X. (2017). Translingual Identity as Pedagogy: International teaching assistants of English in college composition classrooms. *The Modern Language Journal*, 101, 29–44.

CHAPTER 12

Past, present, and future

Examining the process of using *currere* to develop critical pedagogy for language educators

Jing Tan & Xiali Chang
Miami University | Indiana University Bloomington

Exploring how to teach languages effectively in educational research is an ongoing process. In order to contribute to language education research, this chapter introduces and demonstrates how to apply the research approach of *Currere* (Pinar, 1994) in developing critical pedagogy for language educators by deconstructing the past, co-constructing the present, and reconstructing the future. *Currere* provides a methodological framework for the researchers to follow when they examine their teaching pedagogy, and serves as a counter-narrative for traditional language teaching methods through a transformative lens. This collaborative research project has four main parts based on the methodological framework: the regressive step of the past language learning and teaching experiences; the progressive step of the future goals for social justice and educational democracy; the analytical step of how our past, present, and future reshape our teaching practices and critical pedagogy; and the synthetical step of reconstructing Applied Linguistics and language education research (Pinar, 1994). Through this research, we advocate for the *Currere* approach and argue that the transtemporal and trans-conceptual steps within *Currere* can bring an inner critical perspective for researchers and educators in the field of Applied Linguistics and language education to advance their teaching pedagogy and related research.

Introduction

Critical pedagogy asks, "how and why knowledge gets constructed the way it does" and "how our everyday commonsense understandings-our social constructions or 'subjectivities'-get produced and lived out" (McLaren, 2017, p.58). It is essential for educators to examine their knowledge on an everyday basis so that they can critically understand the nature of their knowledge and reconstruct it

https://doi.org/10.1075/rmal.8.12tan

through disrupting assumptions and biases with reflections and learning. According to Cook (2003), "Language is at the heart of human life" (p. 3). This study focuses on the issues of language and education using stories and reflections to examine the relationship between language education and critical pedagogy for teacher educators by applying the research approach of *Currere* (Pinar, 1994). This approach engages researchers' lived experiences in "an embodied deconstruction of the past to reconstruct the future through wide-awake study in the present" (Sawyer, 2017, p. 90).

Pinar (1994) asked "what has been and what is now the nature of my educational experience?" (p. 20). The researchers of this study, Jing and Xiali, reflect and share how their language acquisition experiences have been enlightening and directing their critical pedagogy as teacher educators in practice while reflecting on how they engage their own resistance to educational stereotypes and assumptions. The authors of this chapter are both educators in the U.S. higher education institutions and they conducted this research collaboratively to examine their expert blind spots (Nathan & Petrosino, 2003) and develop their critical pedagogy by reflecting on their educational background and teaching practices critically applying the research approach of *Currere*.

Using *Currere* for this collaborative research project provides a methodological framework for the researchers to follow (1) when they reflect on their teaching philosophy and practices critically, which means thinking with complexity and analyzing within their historical, cultural, and ideological contexts (Sensoy & DiAngelo, 2017, p. 23); (2) when they develop their critical pedagogy through examining their expert blind spot, which refers to the concern "that expertise in a subject area may make educators blind to the learning processes and instructional needs of novice students and that educators with such expertise often are entirely unaware of having such a blind spot" (Nathan & Petrosino, 2003, p. 906); and (3) when they collaborate with others in research because a collaborative *Currere* project "allows teachers to understand their lives via a community that values self-understanding, but acts towards a future that is collective" (Kanu & Glor, 2006, p. 112). Such collaboration requires researchers to detach from their own experiences to be able to examine these reflexive narratives, dialogue with other educators, and theorize them for possible change. Only when we understand why we learn the way we do and why we teach the way we do as educators, can we develop our critical pedagogy by deconstructing our past, co-constructing our present, and reconstructing our future.

We argue that using *Currere* in Applied Linguistics and language education research can help educators reflect on their past, rethink their future, analyze and react to their present, and develop their critical pedagogy at individual and collective levels. However, when educators reflect on the past, they do not have to share everything with others. The reflective and reflexive process should create a safe, comfortable, and meaningful environment for educators to research and grow. It is also intertwined with theory and practice, such as using theory to guide our reflection and using reflection to reconceptualize theory. Critical pedagogy also leads educators to become active and responsible agents of positive social changes and school transformation.

This study has significant meanings for Applied Linguistics and language education research because of its analysis of language, pedagogy, power, and education. It can serve as a counter-narrative for traditional language teaching methods and empower authentic and marginalized voices in language development and teacher education. As an example study, it presents how to use *Currere* and its scholarly significance in Applied Linguistics related research. For example, *Currere* can help language educators critically reflect on the curriculum and teaching methods/pedagogy by "encountering the failures and re-imagining a better way forward" (Tan, 2020, p. 26). In addition, challenges and ethical issues with the use of *Currere* are also being discussed. Although this approach can "explore the complex relation between the temporal and conceptual" and disclose the relation "to the Self and its evolution and education" (Pinar, 1994, p. 19), it requires multidimensional and critical thinking, pedagogy, and reflections in daily practices for educators to utilize.

In addition, *Currere* adds a transformative lens to Applied Linguistics and language education, a perspective which recognizes that "realities are constructed and shaped by social, political, cultural, economic, and racial/ethnic values, and indicates that power and privilege are important determinants of which reality will be privileged in a research context" (Mertens, 2007, p. 212). As language educators, this methodology can help us to apply a holistic view when teaching languages based on the school environment, student population, and other sociocultural elements through meaningful language contextualization and culturally relevant practices (Ladson-Billings, 1995). Therefore, it is an effective methodological framework to apply in Applied Linguistics and language education, especially in the research area related to language learning process and language teacher education.

Currere

This study applies *Currere* as its main research approach to guide the critical reflections. There are four steps of *Currere*: regressive, progressive, analytical, and synthetical (Pinar, 1994). In the regressive step, "one returns to the past, to capture it as it was" (Pinar, 1994, p. 21). Progressive envisions future possibilities in education. The analytical step is about "juxtapose[ing] the three [dimensions]: past, present, future. What are their complex, multidimensional interrelations? How is the present in the past, the past in the future, and the present in both?" (Pinar, 1994, p. 26). The synthetical step refers to, in our own voices, "what is the meaning of the present?" (Pinar, 1994, p. 26) "*Currere* returns educational experience to the person who lived it, so that the experience can be examined for latent and manifest meaning " (Kanu & Glor, 2006, p. 105) and implications of such research approach can guide educators to reflect on and interpret their teaching practices as active social justice agents.

When collecting and analyzing data, this research uses a collaborative approach to gather dialogues, discussions, and reflections, which is borrowed from duoethnography, (Sawyer & Norris, 2013). Pinar (1975) mentioned that *Currere* in duoethnography means a person's life as a curriculum and it views the perspectives of the self and other as the research site (as cited in Le et al., 2021). Duoethnographers employ their personal experiences to deepen the understanding of the subject or the field being explored, emphasizing that "the journey is mutual and reciprocal" (Norris & Sawyer, 2012, p. 3).

When the two authors met at the *Currere* Exchange Conference, they found themselves drawn together due to their shared interests and learning experienced in both China and the U.S. The initial conversations sparked a realization that their experiences could bring a richer and in-depth conversation and scholarship to their research agenda about education. Recognizing this potential synergy, they decided to start this collaborative *Currere* project. As a result, they established regular meetings to deeply discuss, reflect, critique, and refine their ideas. Over time, this process of collaborative *Currere* allowed them to blend their unique insights, leading to a more comprehensive and critical understanding of the topics at hand.

The following part of this chapter exemplifies how to apply *Currere* as a research approach in this collaborative research project. We use the four steps described above to structure our chapter based on the methodological framework: the regressive step of the past language learning and teaching experiences; the progressive step of the future goals for social justice and educational democracy; the analytical step of how our past, present, and future reshape our teaching practices and critical pedagogy; and the synthetical step of reconstructing Applied Linguistics and language education research (Pinar, 1994). Through the lens of *Currere*, language education contextualizes critical pedagogy for teacher educators.

Collaborative *Currere* project

Jing struggled with learning English at her high school and fell in love with the English language later in college. Her own language learning experiences have been guiding her teaching practices. She has taught both English and Chinese in China and the U.S. Now, Jing is teaching Sociocultural Studies in Education at a predominantly white institution in the U.S. She uses *Currere* as a teacher educator to reflect on her daily teaching practices and deconstruct and reconstruct her teaching pedagogy.

Xiali has not followed a traditional path in her profession but worked as a practitioner in China for more than a decade. She taught English as a second language in China, ranging from undergraduate to K–12. Besides teaching, she also held the position as a teacher educator and gained valuable experiences by recruiting, training and assessing English teachers at both public and private institutions. Now, she is a doctoral student in Curriculum Studies and Teacher Education program in the U.S. By following the four steps of the *Currere* research approach (Pinar, 1994), she explores her unique journey as a teacher educator.

Regressive: Past language learning and teaching experiences

Jing

To return and observe the past (Pinar, 1994), I share my past language learning and teaching experiences. There are two types of educators for me: the ones that have an exam-oriented teaching style and stay with their old method of teaching forever, and the ones that focus on authentic communication (Netten & Germain, 2012) in daily life and are always willing to try new methods of teaching. When I started learning English in middle school, the first English teacher I had was exam-oriented. All she did was to ask us to memorize the spelling and grammar rules. The Chinese language is quite different from English. For example, it uses characters that represent words, and English uses letters that build words. As a result, I faced difficulty in my English language learning due to the linguistic differences between the two languages.

Then I had the teachers who contextualized the language learning process for me by using authentic texts and providing opportunities for language practices through conversations, such as showing us English in movies and encouraging us to have conversations with native English speakers in college. I started watching English movies and made friends with some Fulbright students from the U.S. With the language context, I gradually understood English as a new language and improved my English proficiency.

When I was in college, I taught English to high school Chinese students. Due to the Chinese college entrance examination, my job was to help the students get higher scores on their exams. I was exam-oriented because that's the high school students' needs in China. Later when I was teaching English at Wright State University to international students, my teaching pedagogy transformed from exam-oriented to authentic communication (Netten & Germain, 2012) because the students' needs were to prepare for their academic programs in U.S. higher education.

Xiali

Everyone is influenced and shaped by the times they live in, and in return, we understand a person to understand his/her world. Our personal experiences and choices are inevitably intertwined with the historical period we are living through. Born in the 1980s, I witnessed China's rapid development and experienced its educational reforms during the past decades, such as the increase of enrollment in higher education in 1999, the curriculum reforms in 2000 which drove attention to STEM and English education, and quality education in the meantime. In addition to the societal context, my father, an engineer, learned English through listening to his favorite folk music. As a young girl, I often went with him to a section of the railroad track near our home on Sunday mornings. Sometimes, he read English aloud while I played nearby. I don't know whether I was influenced by the social context of that time or by my father. Regardless, I chose English language and literature as my undergraduate major. When I graduated from university, I began to teach English as a second language in China.

As a teacher of English as a second language, I experienced several stages in my pedagogical development: (1) Traditional exam-based teaching. In this stage, neoliberalism, Exam-oriented culture, and globalization go hand in hand shaping my understanding of education and teaching. My understanding of teaching and learning was narrow, and I believed that the purpose of teaching was to improve students' scores. The most common English language class is like this: teachers use past test papers as teaching materials, and they use mostly L1 (Chinese) to teach English grammar and test points in the examination domain. The most common pedagogy is test-teach-test which involves lots of teachers' talking and the students are passive recipients. After explaining the test points, students are asked to practice these questions again and again to make sure they are familiar with the test format.

(2) An emerging teacher educator. This stage of my growth in pedagogical competencies was related to a critical experience in a CELTA (Cambridge Certificate in English Language Teaching to Adult) program that prepared me as a teacher educator. In 2016, I was selected to participate in a one-month teacher

education program in Bangkok. In this program, I was exposed to an excellent example of a coherent teacher education program under the framework of constructivism. Our tutors made the tacit knowledge of teaching explicit through carefully designed activities, modeling, discussions, assignments, reflection activities, and class observation tasks. This teacher education program broadened my horizons and helped me connect my experiences with theories and inspired me to work as a teacher educator.

(3) Experience as a teacher educator. I designed an induction program based on the CELTA model to make novice teacher education more coherent and systematic in my department. I tried to combine student-centered teaching with high-stake testing in this induction program. In this stage, I learned to be a teacher educator by trial and error.

Jing and Xiali

This part of the conversation unfolded the background of the researchers, as language learners and educators, in order to understand why we teach the way we do. We go back to the past to understand our present. Both of our early teaching philosophies and practices were highly impacted by the societal environments, national educational policies, and family backgrounds. Through professional development and educational experiences, we developed critical pedagogy and learned the importance of student centered teaching methods.

Progressive: Educational democracy and social justice

Jing

When I "imagine a future" (Pinar, 1994, p. 25), I think of democracy and liberation. According to Dewey, "democracy is a commitment to the idea that by working, thinking, speaking, and learning together, we can continually grow as a society and meet whatever challenges the future might bring" (as cited in Quantz, 2015, p. 8). No matter the class, ethnicity, gender, the color of the skin, etc., students are provided with "the kind of education needed by everyone in a democratic society in order to provide the knowledge, skills, values, and dispositions necessary to fulfill their roles as citizens in a democratic society" (Quantz, 2015, p. 7). No discrimination. No marginalization. No social hierarchy. The students feel safe and comfortable in classrooms. They can be who they are and discover what their potentials are freely in educational spaces. They are being supported, loved, and cared for by the community.

Educators develop critical pedagogy and practice their reflexive and reflective skills to think, assess, analyze, and react to educational context for positive changes.

Within the global environment, all of the educators collaboratively work towards a peaceful and hopeful future for the next generations. No exam-oriented teaching. No assumptions in teaching. No privileges in teaching. Teachers build a trustful relationship with the students first and grow with them together. The curriculum not only can help students discover who they are, but also educates them to be a life-long learner and critical thinker, which is practical for training students' problem-solving skills in daily life.

Xiali

Important lessons I learned from COVID are in such a changing world, your established world could collapse at any moment. Teaching is more complex than it was in the past. As such, teacher candidates may not solve all the social problems through teaching, but teacher education programs should prepare them to know that the issues "[affecting] our lives outside of school will influence students inside their school" (Zeichner & Liston, 2014, p. xii).

When I envision the field of teacher education, I don't see a clear picture now, but I want to adopt a poststructural perspective to help me imagine what a future could look like, since it requires everyone to free themselves from positioning inside of a category and move beyond formalities (Morris, 2016b). As a doctoral student and teacher educator, I think we should think and "break through the wall" (Morris, 2016b) when we are not restrained by any duties or positions yet. Therefore, I think I will keep searching in this field and moving forward on this path. No matter where I am, I will constantly remind myself of my role as a teacher educator, and ask myself the important questions: what is the role of the teacher in social justice? What are the duties and responsibilities of the teacher educators in the process? How can teacher education programs incorporate social justice into curricula? How can we connect teaching with the ultimate goal of education? As my advisor Professor Barton said, "everyone in education wants to improve practice, but with even the best ideas, we're probably only going to do that in small and/or indirect ways, and that should be good enough." I know we can't change the world on our own, but we can advance the field in our own way.

Jing and Xiali

As educators, most people have their own utopia. Our common goal is to transform the existing educational environment and contribute to the advancement of the field. We all want the best for our students. We all want social justice and democracy in education. We all want to be better educators.

Analytical: Connecting the dots

Jing

To describe and respond to my "biographic present," I use Pinar's (1994) "three photographs" — "What are they; what is their individuality? What fundamental biographic theme(s) do they express? Why are they as they are?" (pp. 25–26). My presents include teaching Sociocultural Foundation in Education in college and learning as a Ph.D. student studying educational leadership at Miami University. My teaching pedagogy centers on self-reflections, students' feedback, peer support, and institutional power. I am not only an instructor, a researcher, a graduate student, but also a daughter, a wife, and a sister. I am a native Chinese speaker, a fluent English speaker, and know a little bit of German.

My past language learning experiences have impacted my identities and teaching philosophy as a language educator. Through my reflexive and reflective practices in language acquisition, my identities developed from an English learner to an Asian; English as a second language; female graduate student; and instructor of Sociocultural Foundations of Education. My teaching philosophy is student-centered, relationship-first, and context-based. I am not and will not be an exam-oriented educator. I am and will be an innovative educator and always try new methods of teaching based on the students' needs. My present is made of my past and will make my future. Therefore, it is important to reflect on the past, think and react in the present, and build a better future with the lessons I have learned.

Xiali

Back in 2019, I was at the turning point of my career. Being a teacher educator for three years, I craved expanding my knowledge based on the theoretical level and further exploring in teacher education, so I decided to pursue my doctoral program in the U.S.

Before I joined this Ph.D. program in teacher education, my understanding of education was narrow, and I believed that the goal of education was to help students improve their test scores. My doctoral program emphasizes social justice, multicultural education, and democratic citizenship education. Almost every professor would put much emphasis on these topics. Systematic learning through coursework, self-reflection activities, and assignments in this doctoral program expanded my understanding of education and teaching. These activities inspire me to explore more important questions in education in a more critical and reflective way: what is the *best method of teaching*? or is there a method of teaching that fits all? Are the Western practices always more advanced and progressive? How can we include diversity, equity, and social justice in our teaching? Whose voices are missing? These reflective activities enabled me to critically reflect upon my past experiences and encourage me to explore more in this direction. I began to look at the issues I used to take for granted, such as the marginalized groups, the minority groups, etc. I also initiated my own research project on teacher education for social justice and equity. All these practices require me to discuss the values, responsibilities, and standards of the existing institutional system and help me focus on more important issues than test scores. My learning experience in the U.S. helped me understand how a teacher educator is educated. Teaching experiences don't develop a teacher educator. Only "purposeful study and inquiry into one's teaching shapes one's understanding of the nature of a pedagogy of teacher education" (Loughran, 2013, p. 29).

Jing and Xiali

Through our holistic review and analysis, we expanded our understanding of teaching and learning. We began to explore teaching ethics, theory, and practice on a deeper level. As educators, every step counts. Our past, present, and future can shape who we are and guide our unique paths.

Synthetical: Reconstructing applied linguistics and language education research

Jing

When I think about "the meaning of the present" (Pinar, 1994, p. 26), I realized that I teach based on the students' needs and the educational environment. When I was teaching high school English in China, the students needed a higher test score; so, I was exam-oriented. When I was teaching English at a U.S. higher education institution, the students needed authentic communication (Netten & Germain, 2012); so, I focused on language use in daily life.

Then I think who decides the students' needs and the educational environment? Test scores are important for Chinese high school students because of the College entrance examination. Communication is important for international students because they need to survive in the U.S. academic environment. The policy makers at the federal level decide what language is the official language for schools and how to assess students' learning nationally. McDonnell and Elmore (1987) stated that "Policies work by bringing the resources of government-money, rules, and authority-into the service of political objectives; and by using those resources to influence the actions of individuals and institutions" (p. 133).

However, states, school districts, communities, school leaders, parents, even students can make changes when they implement the policies if they advocate and are being heard by the dominant power. Ravitch (2011) argued that:

> Those who make policy are most successful when they must advance their ideas
> through a gauntlet of checks and balances, explaining their plans, submitting
> them to a process of public review, and attempting to persuade others to support
> them. If the policymaker cannot persuade others, then his plans will not be
> implemented. That's democracy.   (pp. 10–11)

The question is whether the policy makers would hear the public's voices and
value the feedback they get.

At last I ask myself who has the power to decide how to teach? The policy
makers, the principals, the teachers, or the students? How do we resist the institutional power and the existing educational system? We need strategies, knowledge, and support. We need to have a voice. Power sharing should be a part of
the practice for developing critical pedagogy. Learning and teaching a language
should not be about surviving an educational system, but about thriving in social
contexts. When we deconstruct and reconstruct who we are and how to teach during the reflective and reflexive process, critical pedagogy plays a significant role in
cultural and knowledge production and reproduction.

Xiali

Autobiographical curriculum theorizing is an important approach to teacher education and teachers' professional development. It is essential for teachers to constantly go back to themselves to examine their assumptions and practices since
the "meaning of the present" (Pinar, 1994, p. 26) is based on how you view your
identity through positioning, becoming, and doing (Liao & Maddamsetti, 2019).
Positioning refers to how we deal with multiple relationships with others: the relationship with our students, with our colleagues, and within the institutions in
which we are situated (McAnulty & Cuenca, 2014; McNeil, 2011). However, when
we are in a culture/context, these relationships are invisible. In this sense, we need
to step out to see how these contextual factors shape your identity development,
beliefs, values, and pedagogy. When I reflected on my learning and teaching experience, I realized every critical stage of my identity development emerged when I
stepped out of my comfort zone to embrace new experiences. These new experiences, in return, facilitated me to examine my previous experiences.

Becoming sees the teacher's identity as an ongoing, fluid process. In this developing process, "imagined identity (i.e., a teacher educator's envisioning of what particular type of teacher educator one wants to become) makes up an important part
of one's identity" (Liao & Maddamsetti, 2019, p. 3). As some researchers pointed out,
these imagined identities could be our own teachers, professors, experienced colleagues, or experts in our field. They will guide our practices and help us approach
an "idealized self-image" (Liao & Maddamsetti, 2019, p. 3). Although you may not

be clear about that image, these imagined identities will lead you to the right path. That's why we need to constantly look forward and envision the future.

Doing could be understood as our present practices. Through ongoing teaching practices, I see myself shifting my emphasis from content knowledge to students' learning, and shifting my belief of meritocracy to social justice and education equity. In this process, we need to "[coordinate] multiple duties imposed by the contexts" (Liao & Maddamsetti, 2019, p. 3) and recognize teachers as active agents in transforming ourselves and our communities through critical reflection on our practices.

Positioning, becoming, and doing enable us to view the richness of our own cultural and personal experiences as assets. Although I didn't follow the traditional path in academia, I am still glad that I'm here and starting my new stage in life. Returning to campus after so many years of working experience in China, I know my journey just started and every step counts.

Jing and Xiali

Freire (1998) argued that teaching is not about transferring knowledge or contents, but to create the possibilities for the production or construction of knowledge. It's our shared responsibility to empower teachers as social agents to seek for educational democracy in theory and practice. As educators, we are privileged and should share our power in our classrooms. We also need to resist institutional power and the exam-oriented educational system, and advocate for positive changes in curriculum.

Currere as an approach in applied linguistics and language education research

Why use currere

Currere guided us, as researchers, to reflect on our past language learning experiences and current teaching experiences. The four steps of *Currere* helped us to organize our reflection process and connect all the past, current, and future knowledge together. Language learning and teaching issues, as an essential part of the Applied Linguistics, were addressed throughout this project. *Currere* was first developed by Pinar and Grumet focusing on issues of "subjectivity, identity, agency, transformation, and so forth" (Deng, 2018). Morris (2016a) argued that curriculum studies are always subjective and perspectival since "discourse is situated, partial and incomplete" (p. 6). Therefore, scholars need to connect their subjective engagement with what we study since our interpretation is inevitably linked to ourselves (Morris, 2016a). Through learning different perspectival and subjective knowledge, we learn the whole range of meanings in the field. As Morris (2016a) pointed out, every scholar must contribute a new way to interpret the issues in a creative way to advance the field. The research approach of *Currere* (Pinar, 1994) offers teacher educators an alternative way to theorize their personal knowledge in their field.

Currere research approach helps us view the role of teachers as active practitioners instead of technicians. If teachers are trained to be technicians to deliver the curriculum, then spoon-feeding teaching would be adopted and prioritized in teacher education programs. If teachers are educated as active practitioners, then teacher educators need to prepare them in a more critical and reflective approach. To prepare students for the pluralistic society, teacher candidates must be informed citizens first. Teacher education programs have been focusing on teacher preparations through practical and external training, such as assignments, coursework, and topics chosen for reflection. *Currere*, on the other hand, can serve as an internal tool to enhance teacher candidates' inner cognition and development by guiding them to review their teaching pedagogy within a holistic societal environment. It also helps teacher education programs transform their traditional content-based knowledge teaching training to a more democratic, social justice centered education.

Currere bridges practice and theory. It not only helps educators to reflect on their past educational experiences, but also helps them to examine their teaching philosophy and assumptions. Serving as a self-reflection tool, it enables teacher candidates to elicit their personal theories. According to Zeichner and Liston (1987), the reason many teacher education programs have little effect on teacher candidates is because of their experiences before entering the teacher education program. Teacher candidates' personal theories- their set of beliefs, values, and assumptions, understandings are heavily influenced by their memories as a student, and the external environment, such as the discourses, national policies, and socio-economic factors. In addition, by surfacing students' personal theories, teacher candidates would be aware of their own experiences and practices and would be able to compare their personal theories with those of others'. Juxtaposing their personal experiences with alternative theories, student teachers would expand and clarify their personal theories through the challenges of comparing and contrasting so that they would overcome the limitations and biases of their practices. Personal theories would serve as a link to help teacher candidates bridge the gap between theory and practice.

Ethical considerations when using currere

With the development of the past decades, *Currere* has been recognized as a legitimate research field, but it also has its own ethical issues. For example, *Currere* scholars and other self-study researchers are still confronted with the issues over "multiple identities as researchers; tensions among and between collaborators; and the vulnerability of a public-facing methodology" (Cuenca, 2020, p. 465). When applying *Currere* in this research project, both of the authors were vulnerable when they shared their educational backgrounds and teaching practices. It was challenging to critically reflect with another person. However, we overcame this barrier because we both built not only a critical, but also respectful relationship during the reflection process so that we could share enough information with each other to develop our critical pedagogy. We also understand that we don't have to share everything with each other because education is an ongoing and lifelong process. If we don't have enough time, space, or courage to unpack some of the issues, we will eventually work on them as long as we keep practicing *Currere* in our learning and teaching. Some theorists have criticized the idea of collective biography as entailing the possibility for risk to the individuals involved in the process (for example, the risk of self-exposure). However, as educators "not growing is costlier still" (Kanu & Glor, 2006, p. 112).

Through this research, we clarify three common misunderstandings of using *Currere* in language education research to address the ethical issues in the field. Misunderstanding #1: researchers don't need theories to support their studies while using *Currere*. Our past educational experiences can help us reflect and learn, but theories are essential for meaningful reflective and reflexive practices. Theory and practice are closely connected with each other during research in education. According to Freire (1998), "Critical reflection on practice is a requirement of the relationship between theory and practice" (p. 30). When we reflect on the past and make meanings of our present, we need to use theories to guide our research-based reflections and practices. In addition, our past and present practices can help researchers rethink and reconceptualize theories for educational reimagination and advancement.

Misunderstanding #2: researchers need to share everything. *Currere* as a self-examining research approach for teachers and teacher educators is inevitably associated with identity, race, gender, sexual orientation, etc. In every step of *Currere*, teachers and teacher educators might need to expose values, thoughts, and beliefs so that these implicit practices and processes are made explicit. In this sense, researchers may feel the vulnerability created by the "discomfort of presenting a vulnerable self to the public" (Cuenca, 2020, p. 474), the lament you have when you revisit your previous experiences (Cuenca, 2020), and making the results of your research go public. However, *Currere* as a self-examining research approach doesn't mean you need to share everything about your life. It is more about how you make sense of your actions, how you reconsider your role, not only as a researcher but as a witness of your own experiences. *Currere* is also about the recognition of power. It facilitates us to examine how our identity is shaped and reshaped by existing social, political, and economic factors of the existing social order.

Misunderstanding #3: researchers need to reflect on their educational experiences individually. Through this critical and collaborative research, we argue that *Currere* can bring researchers together to collaboratively reflect, learn, and grow. This research approach can be applied in both individual and collective settings. It provides researchers space to not only examine their own teaching pedagogy, but also critically help each other to discover hidden assumptions and become a better researcher and educator.

Currere as a research approach to prepare active social justice agents

Currere requires teacher educators to rethink teachers' roles and practices. Gore and Zeichner (1991) argued that teacher educators need to understand that student teachers have the least formal power in the educational arena, and they may not change the social problems through student teaching, however, it is necessary to include the critical dimension in the teacher education program. Gore and Zeichner (1991) believe that:

> We should be aiming for the creation of a learning environment in our programs which, through the issues that it draws students' attention to, reflects a commitment to certain fundamental values (e.g., social justice and fidelity to persons). We should be aiming for an impact on individual students that involves the loss of innocence about the inequalities and injustices in society (Goodlad, 1990) and that helps individual students see themselves as part of a community of people working for a closer alignment between schooling and education for everyone's children.   (p. 124)

It is teacher educators' responsibility to prepare teacher candidates to pay attention to the moral and ethical issues of their everyday teaching (Gore & Zeichner, 1991) using critical reflexive and reflective approaches, such as *Currere*. Student candidates can practice their critical pedagogy by asking meaningful questions, such as what's the purpose of my teaching? How can I teach more effectively? Would my class activities and teaching perpetuate inequalities? How can I help students who have different needs? These questions require "deliberate intervention" (Gore & Zeichner, 1991, p. 125) and power-sharing in teacher education programs.

Conclusion

Through this research, we advocate for the *Currere* research approach and argue that the transtemporal and trans-conceptual steps within *Currere* can bring an inner critical perspective for researchers and educators in the field of Applied Linguistics and language education to advance their teaching pedagogy and related research. *Currere* has transformative potential in language education. In many countries, language education has a narrow curriculum that only focuses on a target language. For example, English education in China puts much emphasis on grammatical knowledge and overlooks the purpose of language education as a social means of identity development and interactive communication, rendering teachers curriculum technicians and students passive recipients of English language. In this sense, *Currere* challenges language educators to examine their own assumptions and learn from multiple perspectives/voices by practicing critical pedagogy in their teaching. This process brings transformation to teachers' practices. When educators have a critical understanding of their experiences, they can help their students do the same.

References

Cook, G. (2003). *Applied linguistics*. Oxford University Press.

Cuenca, A. (2020). Ethics of self-study research as a legitimate methodological tradition. In J. J. Loughran, M. L. Hamilton, V. K. LaBoskey, & T. L. Russell (Eds.), *International handbook of self-study of teaching and teacher education practices* (pp. 461–482). Springer.

Deng, Z. (2018). Contemporary curriculum theorizing: Crisis and resolution. *Journal of Curriculum Studies, 50*(6), 691–710.

Freire, P. (1998). *Pedagogy of freedom: Ethics, democracy, and civic courage*. Rowman & Littlefield.

Goodlad, J. (1990). The occupation of teaching in schools. In J. Goodlad, R.. R. Soder. & K. Sirotnik (Eds.), *The moral dimensions of teaching*. Jossey Bass.

Gore, J. M., & Zeichner, K. M. (1991). Action research and reflective teaching in preservice teacher education: A case study from the United States. *Teaching and Teacher Education, 7*(2), 119–136.

Kanu, Y., & Glor, M. (2006). 'Currere' to the rescue? Teachers as 'amateur intellectuals' in a knowledge society. *Journal of the Canadian Association for Curriculum Studies, 4*(2).

Ladson-Billings, G. (1995). Toward a theory of culturally relevant pedagogy. *American Educational Research Journal, 32*(3), 465–491.

Le, G. N. H., Tran, V., & Le, T. T. (2021). Combining photography and duoethnography for creating a trioethnography approach to reflect upon educational issues amidst the COVID-19 global pandemic. *International Journal of Qualitative Methods, 20*, 1–12.

doi Liao, W., & Maddamsetti, J. (2019). Transnationality and teacher educator identity development: A collaborative autoethnographic study. *Action in Teacher Education, 41*(4), 287–306.

doi Loughran, J. (2013). *Developing a pedagogy of teacher education: Understanding teaching & learning about teaching.* Routledge.

doi McAnulty, J., & Cuenca, A. (2014). Embracing institutional authority: The emerging identity of a novice teacher educator. *Studying Teacher Education, 10*(1), 36–52.

doi McDonnell, L. M., & Elmore, R. F. (1987). Getting the job done: Alternative policy instruments. *Educational Evaluation and Policy Analysis, 9*(2), 133–152.

McLaren, P. (2017). Critical pedagogy: A look at the major concepts. In A. Darder, R. D. Torres, & M. Baltodano (Eds.), *The critical pedagogy reader* (3rd ed., pp. 56–78). Routledge.

doi McNeil, B. (2011). Charting a way forward: Intersections of race and space in establishing identity as an African-Canadian teacher educator. *Studying Teacher Education, 7*(2), 133–143.

doi Mertens, D. M. (2007). Transformative paradigm: Mixed methods and social justice. *Journal of Mixed Methods Research, 1*(3), 212–225.

Morris, M. (2016a). *Curriculum studies guidebooks: Concepts and theoretical frameworks.* Peter Lang.

Morris, M. (2016b). *Curriculum studies guidebooks: Concepts and theoretical frameworks.* Peter Lang.

doi Nathan, M. J., & Petrosino, A. (2003). Expert blind spot among preservice teachers. *American Educational Research Journal, 40*(4), 905–928.

doi Netten, J., & Germain, C. (2012). A new paradigm for the learning of a second or foreign language: The neurolinguistic approach. *Neuroeducation, 1*(1), 85–114.

Norris, J., & Sawyer, R. (2012). Toward a dialogic method. In J. Norris, R. Sawyer, & D. Lund (Eds.), *Duoethnography: Dialogic methods for social, health, and educational research* (pp. 9–40). Left Coast Press.

Pinar, W. F. (1975). Toward reconceptualization. In W. F. Pinar (Ed.), *Curriculum theorizing: The reconceptualists* (pp. 396–414). McCutchan.

Pinar, W. F. (1994). *Autobiography, politics, and sexuality: Essays in curriculum theory 1972–1992.* Peter Lang.

Quantz, R. A. (2015). *Sociocultural studies in education: Critical thinking for democracy.* Paradigm Publishers.

Ravitch, D. (2011). *The death and life of the great American school system: How testing and choice are undermining education.* Basic Books.

Sawyer, R. D., & Norris, J. (2013). *Duoethnography.* Oxford University Press.

Sawyer, R. D. (2017). Tracing dimensions of aesthetic *currere*: Critical transactions between person, place, and art. *Currere Exchange Journal, 1*(1), 89–100.

Sensoy, Ö. & DiAngelo, R. (2017). *Is everyone really equal? An introduction to key concepts in social justice education* (2nd ed.). Teachers College Press.

Tan, J. (2020). Bilingual education ascertains global citizenship. *Currere Exchange Journal, 4*(2), 23–27.

doi Zeichner, K., & Liston, D. (1987). Teaching student teachers to reflect. *Harvard Educational Review, 57*(1), 23–49.

Zeichner, K. M., & Liston, D. P. (2014). *Reflective teaching: An introduction.* Routledge.

CHAPTER 13

When children don't learn to read

A narrative inquiry and an intervention study

Sandra Jack-Malik & Janet L. Kuhnke
Cape Breton University

Children who learn to read fluently are more likely to experience academic success. Many youngsters however fail to meet literacy, learning outcomes. This chapter describes a study involving children in grade three, labelled as struggling readers. Using narrative inquiry as the research methodology, we worked in partnership with the principal and classroom teacher to co-design a study including a structured literacy intervention. Narrative inquiry methodology was utilized because it supports the collection of rich data (stories). Using the narrative inquiry framework of commonplaces: temporality, sociality and place, the research was designed, lived out, analyzed, and reported. The methodology also provided a framework for dealing with ethical challenges encountered. Our goal was to come alongside children, families and teachers through time to deepen understandings of how they experienced learning to read and reading remediation. We were interested in understanding efforts to shift away from struggling reader identity stories. Included is an overall narrative of the study and participant and researcher stories. Furthermore, researcher and participant artwork and artifacts are embedded because they provide nuances beyond words on the page. We attended a First Nation's in-community school, two mornings per week over five-months. Our plan had been to conduct the research over a two-year period, following the children from grade three to four. The plan, however, was interrupted by the global pandemic and related restrictions on school access.

Introduction

"The most fundamental responsibility of schools is teaching students to read. Because reading affects all other academic achievement and is associated with social, emotional, economic, and physical health [...]" (Moats, 2020, p. 4). Many children, however, are not learning to read. Using stories abut lived experiences, this narrative intervention study focuses on a group of children living in a First

https://doi.org/10.1075/rmal.8.13jac

Nation community, identified as struggling readers. Using narrative inquiry, a relational, multimodal, qualitative research methodology, we worked in partnership with the school principal and classroom teacher to co-design a study including a structured literacy intervention. We had two intentions. First, to deepen understandings of the instructional and relational components that best support children labelled as struggling readers as they worked to develop grade appropriate literacy skills. Next, as relationships with the children and teacher developed through time, we aimed to deepen understandings of how their life making experiences were being shaped by the struggling reader label, the intervention and efforts to shift and live out stories as competent readers.

Therefore, we include an overall narrative of the study as well as researcher and participant narratives in efforts to share understandings grounded in relational knowing. Furthermore, researcher and participant artwork and artifacts are embedded because they provide affective, sensory and emotional understandings beyond words on the page. Our plan had been to conduct the research over a two-year period, following the children from grade three to four. This was our intention because it takes time to remediate reading and writing (Moats, 2010) and to shift identities. The plan, however, was interrupted by the global COVID pandemic and related restrictions on school access.

The importance of this work

This work is important because it has the potential to steer reading researchers away from solely collecting and disseminating literacy data as aggregated, decontextualized skill development or lack thereof. Rich and diverse field texts provide a glimpse into the complex efforts of L'nu children, labelled as struggling readers as they worked to shift their identity stories towards competent readers. Furthermore, the study is important because it demonstrates how narrative inquiry allowed for culturally sensitive documentation of lives and stories, while also providing a framework for imagining and supporting participants to live out educative stories while resisting discourses of failure and othering. If we are to understand and capitalize on what is involved in the development of a literate identity, by children identified as struggling readers we must first inquire into their lived experiences. Finally, this work is important because yearly, provincial literacy scores are proving to be stubbornly resistant to improvement. It is important therefore to conduct research that deepens understanding of why groups of children are not learning to read, while making culturally sensitive recommendations for change.

Researcher positioning and research puzzles

Sandra is a former classroom teacher, school administrator and an experienced literacy tutor; Janet is a community-based nurse, researcher, and educator. We worked at the same university and often collaborated on research projects and ongoing reflexive practices.[1] Through discussions, we came to appreciate a shared passion for the importance of learning to read. Through time and as we collaborated, we shifted our positioning to co-learners and co-creators (Hollingsworth, 1994). We learned from our research, relationships practices, readings, and dangerous conversations (LeFevre & Sawyer, 2012). We also came to experience research as transactional (Fecho & Meacham, 2007); teaching and learning opportunities exist for us and participants. Furthermore, we understood the quality of the research relationships we negotiate influences the quality of the understandings, knowledge and insights gained[2] (Clandinin, 2013). We focused on coming alongside each other and participants as a reflection of ontological commitments, including attending to "the lives, the experiences, of those with whom we live in relation. Our commitments are not first and foremost to the inquiry puzzle but to the lives of the people involved" (Clandinin et al., 2015, p. 23). We never questioned the importance of research focused on deepening understandings of the experiences of children struggling to read because we appreciated and routinely observed the lack of opportunities that often exist for youngsters who struggle to read.

Concepts and theories that framed the study

Dewey (1938a) provided the theoretical framework for the study: "things and events belonging to the world, physical and social, are transformed through the human context they enter, while the live creature is changed and developed through its intercourse with things previously lived" (pp. 246–247). This understanding allowed us to hope the children, teachers, families and ourselves would experience change related to study experiences. For the children, we imagined literacy development resulting in them becoming fluent readers while self-identifying as such. We also imagined that the school, as a system, and individual teachers would support and

---

1. Etherington (2004) states reflective practice is an opportunity to review how we research, teach and engage patients; this is an opportunity to gain insight and understanding.

2. Alongside: our ontological commitments shape how we live in the world…and come alongside participants. These commitments, include attending to "the lives, the experiences, of those with whom we live in relation. Our commitments…are to the lives of the people involved" (Clandinin et al., 2015, p. 23).

encourage the children to shift their literacy identity stories and join the lived experiences of their formally more competent classroom peers. This would require teachers to shift their stories of the children away from struggling reader identity stories. We also wondered how families would experience and support their youngsters throughout the study.

Finally, we wondered how our stories as researchers would shift because of our involvement with the study. Dewey's theory of experience (1938a) helped us to conceptualize the connections between narratives and education because it provided a framework to understand through the lens of narrative inquiry. The criteria, continuity, interaction, and situation led to deeper understandings of experience, which allowed us to understand how educational stories are valued, positioned, shaped and lived out through time. Moreover, the work of Clandinin et al. (2006) helped us understand stories, experiences and narrative understandings of identities. They wrote: "stories to live by are multiple, fluid and shifting, continuously composed and recomposed in the moment to-moment living alongside children, families, administrators, and others, both on and off the school landscape" (p. 9). Fluid and shifting identity stories allowed us to consider participants within various contexts. Moreover, Carr (1986) helped us to understand how participants worked to ensure their stories were coherent:

> Coherence seems to be a need imposed on us whether we seek it or not. Things need to make sense. We feel the lack of sense when it goes missing. The unity of self, not as an underlying identity but as a life that hangs together, is not a pre-given condition but an achievement. Some of us succeed, it seems, better than others. None of us succeed totally. We keep at it. What we are doing is telling and retelling, to ourselves and to others, the story or what we are about and what we are. (p. 97)

As well, Enriquez et al. (2016) allowed us to wonder how participants were "shaped by different histories, valued differentially, and open to re-signification across contexts" (p. 9).

Another theoretical notion that guided the research was culturally relevant pedagogies (CRP). "Culturally relevant pedagogy is a theoretical model that focuses on multiple aspects of student achievement and supports students to uphold their cultural identities...[it] calls for students to develop critical perspectives that challenge societal inequalities" (California Department of Education, 2022, par. 1). Ladson-Billings (1995) noted three criteria that culturally relevant teaching includes: "an ability to develop students academically, a willingness to nurture and support cultural competence, and the development of a sociopolitical or critical consciousness" (p. 483). Leaning into this work, Brown-Jeffy and Cooper (2011) developed a conceptual framework of CRP teaching behaviors which includes five themes: identity and achievement, equity and excellence, developmental appropriateness, whole child teaching, and student-teacher relationships. This research attends to two themes, identity and achievement and student-teacher relationships. The authors noted "in order for teachers to be culturally attuned to the identities of their students, they should be aware of their own identities, as well as how those identities may be divergent from the identities of their students" (p. 4). Moreover, "students need to know teachers care and teachers should recognize and respect their students for who they are as individuals and as members of a cultural group" (p. 6). These notions informed us as we planned, delivered and reflected on the tutoring and the children's and teacher's responses to it.

An example of how culturally relevant pedagogies informed the research

During a research conversation we discussed tutoring activities. We began with decodable readers that did not include illustrations, nor culturally relevant narratives. The children were excited to be able to read the stories; however, they had no relatable schema. Tanaka (2016) reminded us of the importance of providing a variety of learning activities and choices for learners. At Janet's tutoring table we introduced culturally relevant picture books. This was purposeful because we wanted the children to see themselves and their lived experiences reflected in the stories. We selected books written and or illustrated by Indigenous authors and illustrators. The children also played games and made artwork related to emotional regulation. They shared stories and increasingly they asked questions. Some of their questions informed us as we planned the next visit. The children worked hard, and they laughed. None of the children were accustomed to the intensity of one-on-one tutoring. It took each child time to build up emotional and cognitive endurance and we observed the culturally relevant picture books scaffolded their efforts to attend. They quickly came to see they were improving and this in turn helped with attendance and endurance (*Field notes*, November & December 2019).

Methodology

We used narrative inquiry, a relational, qualitative research methodology (Clandinin, 2013) because it is a promising fit for research focused on understanding families, teachers and children living in-community (Clandinin et al., 2006; Lessard et al., 2015; Tanaka, 2016). The methodology includes a framework to inquire into, understand and account for the shaping influences of sociocultural systems: institutional, historical, and cultural narratives (Lewis et al., 2007) on literacy development and efforts to shift readers' identity stories. Narrative inquiry allowed the researchers to inquire into and understand their own shaping influences on the research (Knight, 2009). Furthermore, the methodology accounts for participants' stories[iv] of experience as part of their efforts to shift their identities. The rich and diverse field texts[v] created throughout the research allow the reader a glimpse into the children's complex efforts to be known as readers. Guided by the narrative inquiry commonplaces: temporality,[3] sociality[4] and place,[5] we inquired into stories and experiences of seven children, identified by the school resource team as struggling readers, their families and their classroom teacher. The commonplaces provided a conceptual and interpretive framework for the inquiry.

Our goal was to listen to stories and to share experiences for the purpose of understanding the influences on identity making of failing to meet learning outcomes. Also, we wanted to deepen understanding of the impacts of a specific reading intervention on the children's efforts to be known as readers. Experience was the focus of the inquiry; expressed narratively through stories. "This is important because we understand teaching children to read is critical: "no other skill shapes the trajectory of a person's life more than the ability to read. Bridging the literacy gap is achievable, urgent, and the most effective tool for improving ... lives" (Frontier College, 2022, par. 2). Al Dahhan and colleagues (2016) also noted "children with reading difficulties are less likely to graduate from high school and are at a greater risk for future unemployment, underemployment, and incarceration" (p. 2). Shaywitz and Shaywitz, (2005, 2008) found that children who complete grade three without becoming skilled readers most often will continue to struggle because their reading weaknesses are not remediated. Moreover, through time this group tends to demonstrate social behaviors that are not a best fit for school-based learning (Metsala et al., 2017; Miles & Stipek, 2006). "While some students seem to figure out how the print system works through incidental exposure, most do not" (Moats, 2020, p. 6).

Attending to stories is central to a narrative inquiry methodology. Connelly and Clandinin (1999) used the term, stories to live by: "narrative constructions that take shape as life unfolds and that may, as narrative constructions are wont to do, solidify into a fixed entity... or they may continue to grow and change" (p. 95). Connelly and Clandinin (2006) used four terms to describe stories and to "structure the process of self-narration". Lived stories are those we live. Told stories are

---

3. Temporality: "Events under study are in temporal transition" (Connelly & Clandinin, 2006, p. 479), that is, events and people always have a past, present, and a future.

4. Sociality: "... feelings, hopes, desires, aesthetic reactions, and moral dispositions" (Connelly & Clandinin, 2006, p. 480) of the inquirer and study participants. By social conditions they draw attention to the existential conditions, the environment, surrounding factors and forces, people and otherwise, that form each individual's context.

5. Place: "the specific concrete, physical and topological boundaries of place or sequence of places where the inquiry and events take place" (Connelly & Clandinin, 2006, p. 480).

those we tell. Retold stories are those used "to interpret lives as told in different ways, to imagine different possibilities" (p. 478). To relive stories is "to live out the new person" (p. 478). In this study we carefully selected the stories to inquire into and describe because we understand "what happens in schools is an identity shaping process; lives are written and rewritten, storied and restoried" (Clandinin et al., 2006, p. 15). Clandinin's (2013) "concept of stories to live by [is] a narrative term for identity" (p. 37). Inquiring into stories allowed us to wonder what lay beneath the dominant narrative of literacy as the acquisition of skills. The inquiry allowed us to consider the children's stories as part of their efforts to live out lives as fluent readers. Furthermore, because we thought narratively with stories, we understood the children were composing stories of who they were and who they might become. We came to understand the children's stories were shaped by, and shaped, the narratives in which they were embedded (Huber et al., 2013). Naming stories as life-making provided a lens from which to view efforts to shift identity stories from within the nested, temporal stories of their lives.

The research begins

During our twice-weekly, 35-minute drive to the community school we engaged in research conversations. We reflected on the tutoring and our experiences within the classroom and school. As a result of these conversations, we read related literature and subsequently made changes to the tutoring, to how we encouraged a child, and to our word choices. We became increasingly aware of how we were shaping the tutoring spaces. We discussed who we were when tutoring, who we were in the classroom and who we might become.

One morning as we entered the classroom, Charlotte yelled, *"Take me first!"* When we asked her why she wanted to be first, she commented, "every day during silent reading I sit and look at the pictures. I choose books that look easy and skip over words I don't know. I'm kinda a good reader[6] but I want to be great" (*Field note*, November 2019).

Charlotte and some of her classroom peers, identified as struggling readers previously experienced multiple literacy interventions including: All Kids Early (Nova Scotia Government, 2022), junior kindergarten, (half day), senior kindergarten, (full day), Leveled Literacy Intervention (Nova Scotia Government, 2017),

---

6. "Reading is a matter of studying reality that is alive, reality that we are living inside of, reality as history being made and also making us. We can also see how it is impossible to read texts without reading the context of the text, without establishing the relationships between the discourse and the reality which shapes the discourse" (Freire, 1985, p. 18–19).

Resource Center small group pullout, the Lindamood phoneme sequencing program for reading, spelling, and speech (Lindamood & Lindamood, 2011), and Seeing Stars (Lindamood & Bell, 2022). Moreover, some of the children had been retained[7] because they had not met previous grade level outcomes. When the teacher shared the most recent reading achievement data, we noted none of the participants' reading levels were higher than grade one level. During related research conversations we reflected on our previous experiences working in-community with First Nations members. These conversations helped us remember that relying solely on pedagogical approaches, tracking systems, required texts and mandatory testing could limit the effectiveness of the intervention. We knew the importance of focusing on relationships, creating spaces, opportunities, and time for the children to share their knowledge. We began to learn their individual interaction and communication styles and adjusted accordingly, "discern[ing] the possibilities and limitations of ... [our] teaching and students' learning" (Hollingsworth, 1994, p.24). We avoided standard rules of classroom behavior and attended to the specific needs of the child sitting across from us. The more we relaxed in the tutoring spaces, focusing on relationships with individual learners the more willing and likely they were to persist with the activities. The children began to describe how their reading was improving. They described picking harder books and being able to accurately read more words. They increasingly shared jokes and we laughed.

How the relational shaped the tutoring spaces

As time passed and as research conversations with the teacher and children occurred, tutoring was adapted to reflect changing needs, improvement and to account for the teacher's insightful observations. As experiences were shared, trust grew. Stories, feelings, hopes, worries and positionings were also shared. We continued to read related literature in efforts to link and understand what we were experiencing and learning. We continued to make and reflect on field notes in efforts to deepen understanding.

One day at recess the teacher shared. She explained how happy she was to see the children improving and that they were more willing to engage and persist with learning activities. This thrilled us. She also told us if the children did not reach a predetermined Fountas and Pinnell (2019) reading level by June, they would be

---

7. "The term "retention" in regards to school means repeating an academic year of school. Retention in school is also called grade retention, being held back, or repeating a grade. Grade retention is the opposite of social promotion, in which children continue with their age peers regardless of academic performance" (*Encyclopedia of Childern's Health*, 2022, par. 1).

retained (Encyclopedia of Children's Health, 2022). For some participants, this would be the second time they were not promoted to the next grade. Progress was being made; however, there was still a long way to go to reach grade level reading outcomes. We talked about this at length; thinking about the children failing to progress resulted in complex stress for each of us (*Field Notes*, November 2019, February 2020).

Our relationships with the children and the teacher were blossoming. We cared about them. We did not want the children to be retained. An urgency entered our research conversations: how could we speed up the reading remediation? We wondered if we might attend three mornings per week, stay all day the two days we were there, anything to avoid retention. We brought urgency to the tutoring tables and to our relationships. We acknowledged we were experiencing tensions[8] (Jack-Malik & Kuhnke, 2020). The methodology provided a framework for us to think through the tension in educative ways. As a result, we adapted our plans. When a child was absent, we saw this as an opportunity to extend the tutoring time for children who were present. We frequently reminded ourselves to focus on the relational, enjoying the child who sat across the table. We could not control comments written in June report cards; however, we could fully attend to each individual child.

Specific examples of how a focus on the relational supported the research

An example of how we carried the importance of relational knowing with us into the classroom is demonstrated through our relationship with Ronnie (see Figure 2). He was reluctant to tutor. He would answer questions with single words and respond to all prompts; however, he would not initiate conversation. Sandra observed he was quickly understanding the code. He tentatively began to apply his developing phoneme knowledge when reading text. When working with Janet "he regularly asked if he could make cards and take them home" (*Field note*, February 2020). He came to understand text (words, illustrations) carried meaning and he wanted to share this with his family. Janet observed his comfort when making cards. In these moments he would initiate discussions about his family and slowly he began to ask about Janet's family. The relational component of the methodology allowed for and supported these tentative and then increasingly complex conversations. The methodology also supported the notion that each researcher positioned herself in different ways. Janet's personality and the outcomes planned

---

8. Tensions that "live between people...are a way of creating a between space, a space which can exist in educative ways" (Clandinin et al., 2010, p. 82).

for the tutoring at her table had plenty of space for the children to think and create with various mediums, listen and respond. When she showed the children pictures of her dogs and old glass bottles she had collected, they were thrilled. The children gave their trust first to Janet and this trust was slowly extended to Sandra. We saw this as Ronnie increased his engagement with Sandra. His answers were thicker, and he began to ask questions. Furthermore, it led to Ronnie making small, insightful jokes and then tentatively looking to see if we laughed. If he saw us laughing, he would share a tiny smile. This led to increased engagement and a readiness to tutor. We also observed, as did the teacher, that increasingly he was looking, waiting for his turn and finally, asking for his turn to tutor.

Charlotte, was quick to laugh, and funny. She read[9] relational spaces, picking up on social cues and responding with humour. She came to school every day. When she made a mistake, she referred to herself as dumb. When she did so, we would pause and gently ask why she thought she was dumb. We wondered what stories she told herself about why she was not achieving grade level outcomes. We thoughtfully planned our response to Charlotte's self-deprecating comments. We wanted to be respectful of Charlotte and we wanted her to understand the power of words. We wanted her to experience our comments as a traction story (Jack-Malik, 2012) and not as a reprimand. As the tutoring continued, Charlotte referred to herself as dumb less often. When she did, we paused in silence, waiting for her to speak.

She began telling us she was becoming a reader; she could read more words. We understood she was trying on a reader's identity (Gee, 1996). She was articulate, wrote us notes; loved to draw and play the feelings game. She sometimes required redirection. She was easily drawn into conflict with classmates; her emotions could be large. As her reading improved, she became increasingly vocal about her tutoring time; she wanted to tutor. We understood this as part of her efforts to shift away (Dewey, 1938b) from the struggling reader label that clung to her since repeating grade one. Greene (1995) reminded us, "[to] be yourself is to be in process of creating a self, an identity" (p. 20). Greene (1995) also helped us understand the process Charlotte was engaged in:

> to speak of a dialectic is to speak of forces in contest: the factors that hold us in place, that stand in the way of our growing, and the factors that provoke us to act on our desires, to break through the obstacles, and to become different, to be.
>
> (p. 112)

---

9. "Reading can be seen as the ability to make meaning of that which can be read. As such, gestures, moods, sounds, art, weather conditions and the like can be read, in that we can interpret meanings from them" (Fecho & Meacham, 2007, p. 167).

As Charlotte interacted (Dewey, 1938b), with provincial and Mi'kmaw Kina'mat-newey,[10] and teachers (classroom & resource room) (Dewey, 1938b), we observed she was struggling desperately to be known as a reader; however, her lived experiences shaped her efforts. Dewey wrote: "every experience both takes up something from those which have gone before and modifies in some way the quality of those which come after" (p. 35). Thinking about this we wondered what it would take for Charlotte to be known as a reader and who she might become if she was a reader. Below is a pastel drawing on canvas that Charlotte created and presented to Sandra. She wanted Sandra to know the tutoring made her happy (see Figure 1) and she wanted as much tutoring as we offered.

Figure 1. Charlotte shares her joy (pastel crayons and paper)

Our developing field texts

Our field texts included transcripts of research conversations, report cards, assessment data, notebooks utilized by each child, drawings and art created by the children and Janet, photographs taken by Sandra, and our research journals. The

---

10. Mi'kmaw Kina'matnewey is "the collective voice for Mi'kmaq education" (2021, para. 5).

creation and inquiry into these field texts allowed us to slow down the experiences we had at school and focus on individual moments, gaining deeper understanding of ourselves, the children and the tutoring. We wondered how and when a moment began and where it might lead to (Clandinin et al., 2006). When Janet created the sketch (see Figure 2) of a child reading sitting next to an adult, we began to discuss the links between youngsters who struggle to read and possible future links to health and wellness (DeWalt & Hink, 2009; Shahid et al., 2022).

Figure 2. Child reading with an adult (pencil and paper)

In response to the mounting tensions, (related to possible retention) we were experiencing, Janet created squish art (Moon, 2010) (see Figure 3). She described tensions between the hope she experienced watching the children slowing improving and the fact the children would not pass into grade four if they did not reach grade level reading outcomes. For some children this would be the second time they were retained. We discussed how hard the children were working, how desperately they wanted to read. There was a chasm between who the children were struggling to become as readers and the ever-present June deadline. Knowing reading remediation takes time, we sometimes felt hopeless in our ability to ensure each child passed and yet the children did not falter in their efforts to improve. Once they experienced improvement, they wanted more; they wanted to be readers!

Our research conversations also included discussions related to the children's future educational paths. We discussed high school and wondered how the children would cope if they continued as struggling readers. Sandra took this photograph (see Figure 4) and we discussed post-secondary doors, would they be open